Dave,
I believe you w...

Kyle,
This may help you with the election. If not this time, in the future.

Bob Snedden

HEALING OUR WORLD

THE OTHER PIECE OF THE PUZZLE

Revised Edition

Dr. Mary J. Ruwart

SunStar Press

****

Kalamazoo, Michigan

Published by SunStar Press
P.O. Box 342
Kalamazoo, Michigan 49005-0342

Library of Congress Cataloging-in-Publication Data

Ruwart, Mary J.
  Healing our world: the other piece of the puzzle / Mary J.
Ruwart. —Rev. ed.
    p.   cm.
  Includes bibliographic references and index.
  ISBN 0-9632336-2-9 : $14.95
      1. United States—Politics and government—1989-   2. United
States—Economic policy—1981- 3. United States—Social
policy—1980- 4. United States—Moral conditions.   I. Title.
E881.R88   1993
300.973—dc20   92-35338
                                                         CIP

To my mother,

Jean Mary Choiniere Ruwart,

who in living taught me how to love others

and in dying taught me the importance of loving myself.

ACKNOWLEDGEMENTS

A book such as this one takes only years to write, but its preparation takes decades. Along the way, some very special people marked the milestones in that journey. This book would not be complete without acknowledging their contributions.

My first introduction to political awareness came from Walt Disney's programs on our nation's founding. My parents, who brought me up in loving, in learning, and in awareness, nurtured my early research into the full meaning of the American Revolution. In college, Gary Fairfax introduced me to the enlightening writings of Ayn Rand. Years later, Sheryl Loux expanded my political consciousness further by exposing me, in great detail, to the application of libertarian principles and by encouraging me to run for local office.

When Roger Gary suggested that I run for the 1984 presidential nomination of the Libertarian Party, I discovered yet another dimension of political life: the common perception that principles and practicality, ends and means, are disassociated. All of these pieces of the puzzle fell into place through interactions with R. Francis White who unwittingly inspired me to put pen to paper. Without the experiences that these people brought into my life, this book might never have been written.

Throughout the years of writing, my sister, Martie Ruwart, shared the vision from which this book was created. She encouraged me, inspired me, and expertly critiqued my drafts. Without her in my life, I'm not sure I would have persevered. My father shouldered more than his share of our rehabilitation business, giving me time to work on the manuscript. In addition to my sister and father, Sheryl, Roger, and Gary read over my drafts, giving me helpful suggestions. Other valuable comments came from Julie Bortnik, Dick Brown, Mac Calhoun, Lynette Dumble, Carol Hoeve, Janet Howard, Andre Marrou, Pat Peterson, Bob Rush, Clark Smith, Michael Smith, Karen Ruwart Swindell, Jerry van Natta, Connie Vinci, Luanne Willbanks, and Jarret Wollstein. Their input helped me to address each issue thoroughly.

I am also grateful for the excellent assistance of my editor, Barbara Hart, and her staff at Publications Professionals; Brian Betzold, my cartoonist; David Howard, who designed the cover; and Ed and Judy Petzold of PCCResources for preparing the computer-drawn figures and the text formatting. They all provided me with talent beyond my own.

Many other people gave me support, encouragement, and suggestions when they learned about this book. To them, I also extend my heartfelt thanks. Let me remind everyone who participated in this undertaking, in however small a way, of the importance of each contribution. No one writes a book like this one alone—but then, we are never really alone!

FOREWORD

HEALING OUR WORLD is a rare book that challenges numerous aspects of conventional wisdom that we accept as axiomatically true. For example, a major dimension of this book is its linkage between our spiritual perspective and our economic well-being. At first, these two might seem like strange bedfellows, but Dr. Ruwart leads readers with her gentle touch to a world in which the interdependence of the hard sciences, social sciences, and spirituality become clear. Hard facts presented in a sensitive, readable style focus attention on the urgent need for our policy makers to be more careful about the "evidence" upon which many of their policies are based.

HEALING OUR WORLD gently and provocatively challenges its readers to recognize the coercive nature of the government intervention we often consider as inevitable and even desirable. Seldom do we question the morality of government-initiated aggression in prescribing day-to-day regulations and taxes. Dr. Ruwart's book is a refreshing and unusual approach that refocuses public attention on the danger of sanctioning collective action that would be repugnant to us if practiced individually. Herein, Dr. Ruwart claims, is the key to the "easy way out" to a win-win world of abundance and harmony. HEALING OUR WORLD paints a clear and compelling picture of a vision within our grasp, thereby empowering and inspiring every person working for a better world.

—Frances Kendall and Leon Louw

Nobel Peace Prize nominees, 1989, 1991, 1992

The history of the world is none other than the progress of the consciousness of freedom.

—George Hegel, 1821

TABLE OF CONTENTS

>   War and poverty are caused, not by "selfish others," but
>   by our own reactions to them. If we wish to change the
>   world, we must first change ourselves.

PART I. GIVE US THIS DAY OUR DAILY BREAD: BACK TO BASICS

>   We are well aware that if we commit certain actions
>   against our neighbors, fighting and impoverishment will
>   result. Somehow we think these same actions create
>   peace and plenty if applied to our community, state,
>   nation, and world.

>   Wealth is created when we use existing resources in new
>   ways. Since creativity is virtually limitless, wealth is too.

PART II. FORGIVE US OUR TRESPASSES: HOW WE CREATE POVERTY IN A WORLD OF PLENTY!

>   When we use aggression to increase the wealth of disad-
>   vantaged workers, we succeed only in making them
>   poorer.

>   "Only in America" could penniless immigrants become
>   affluent by starting their own businesses. Today, our
>   aggression keeps the disadvantaged from following in
>   their footsteps.

>   Licensing of health care services gives us the illusion that
>   we are protected against selfish others who would defraud
>   us. Instead, our aggression boomerangs back to us,
>   costing us our wealth, our health, and our very lives.

In the following pages I offer nothing more than simple facts, plain arguments and common sense; and have no other preliminaries to settle with the reader, other than that he will divest himself of prejudice and prepossession, and suffer his reason and his feelings to determine for themselves; that he will put on, or rather that he will not put off, the true character of a man, and generously enlarge his views beyond the present day.

—Thomas Paine

INTRODUCTION

THE IMPOSSIBLE DREAM?

War and poverty are caused, not by "selfish others," but by our own reactions to them. If we wish to change the world, we must first change ourselves.

Humankind is poised on the brink of an evolutionary leap. In the last few decades, we have become increasingly aware of the source of our inner peace and enrichment. Depending on our personal background, we express this great discovery differently. The practical, down–to–earth individuals among us "take responsibility for our lives" as described in Wayne W. Dyer's YOUR ERRONEOUS ZONES. Those of us with a metaphysical outlook "create our own reality" as Shirley MacLaine did in OUT ON A LIMB. The spiritual among us know that "the kingdom of God is within" and follow THE ROAD LESS TRAVELED (M. Scott Peck). Sometimes we simply "find ourselves" through the power of love as Richard Bach did in THE BRIDGE ACROSS FOREVER. Ultimately, our inner harmony and abundance depend on how we react to our outer world.

The creation of peace and plenty in our outer world, however, frequently seems hopelessly beyond our control. In the past century, we've supported widespread social reform. Nevertheless, people are still starving in a world capable of feeding all. In our own country, homelessness and poverty are on the rise. Violence is no longer limited to overseas wars: our streets, even our schools, are no longer safe. The environment that nurtures us is ravaged and raped.

When we acknowledge how our reactions contribute to our inner state, we gain control. Our helplessness dissolves when we stop blaming others for feelings we create. In our outer world, the same rules apply. Today, as

The essential psychological requirement of a free society is the willingness on the part of the individual to accept responsibility for his life.

—Edith Packer
clinical psychologist

...collectively held unconscious beliefs shape the world's institutions, and are at the root of institutionalized oppression and inequity ....By deliberately changing the internal image of reality, people can change the world.
—Willis Harman
PATHS TO PEACE

...whatsoever a man soweth, that shall he also reap.
—THE HOLY BIBLE
Galatians 6:7

a society, as a nation, as a collective consciousness, "we" once again feel helpless, blaming selfish others for the world's woes. Our nation's laws, reflecting a composite of our individual beliefs, attempt to control selfish others—at gunpoint, if necessary. Striving for a better world by focusing on others instead of ourselves totally misses the mark. When others resist the choices we have made for them, conflicts escalate and voraciously consume resources. A warring world is a poor one.

Attempting to control others, even for their own good, has other undesirable effects. People who are able to create intimacy in their personal relationships know that you can't hurry love. Trying to control or manipulate those close to us creates resentment and anger. Attempting to control others in our city, state, nation, and world is just as destructive to the universal love we want the world to manifest. Forcing people to be more "unselfish" creates animosity instead of good will. Trying to control selfish others is a cure worse than the disease.

We reap as we sow. In trying to control others, we find ourselves controlled. We point fingers at the dictators, the Communists, the politicians, and the international cartels. We are blithely unaware that our desire to control selfish others creates and sustains them. Like a stone thrown in a quiet pond, our desire to control our neighbors ripples outward, affecting the political course of our community, state, nation, and world. Yet we know not what we do. We attempt to bend our neighbors to our will, sincere in our belief that we are benevolently protecting the world from their folly and short-sightedness. We seek control to create peace and prosperity, not realizing that this is the very means by which war and poverty are propagated. In fighting for our dream without awareness, we become the instruments of its destruction.

If we could only see the pattern! In seeking to control others, we behave as we once did as children, exchanging our dime for five pennies, all the while believing that we were enriching ourselves. When a concerned adult tried to enlighten us, we first refused to believe the truth. Once awareness dawned, we could no longer be fooled, nor was laborious deliberation necessary for every transaction. Once we understood how to count money, we automatically knew if we benefited from such a trade.

Similarly, when the fact and folly of controlling others first come to our attention, we're surprised and full of denial. I certainly was! When we care about the state of our world, however, we don't stop there. I trust you are concerned enough to persevere and to consider seriously the shift in consciousness this book proposes.

Once we have the courage to accept responsibility for our part of the problem, we automatically become part of the solution, independent of what others do. We honor their non-aggressive choices (even if they are selfish) and stop trying to control them. In doing so, we dismantle their most effective means of controlling *us*.

Others only ignite the flames of war and poverty. We feed the flames or starve them. Not understanding their nature, we've fanned the sparks instead of smothering them. Not understanding *our* contribution to the raging inferno, we despair that a world full of selfish others could ever experience universal harmony and abundance.

Nothing could be further from the truth! Widespread peace and plenty can be created within our lifetime. When we understand how to stop fueling the flames of war and poverty, we can manifest our dream.

We are each one of us responsible for every war because of the aggressiveness of our own lives....And only when we realize...that you and I are responsible...for all the misery throughout the entire world, because we have contributed to it in our daily lives...only then will we act.
—J. Krishnamurti
FREEDOM FROM THE KNOWN

The truth will set you free—but first it will make you damn mad...
—M. Scott Peck
author of THE ROAD LESS TRAVELED

We are not liberated until we liberate others. So long as we need to control other people, however benign our motives, we are captive to that need. In giving them freedom, we free ourselves.
—Marilyn Ferguson
THE AQUARIAN CONSPIRACY

PART I

GIVE US THIS DAY
OUR DAILY BREAD

Back to Basics

CHAPTER 1

THE GOLDEN RULE

We are well aware that if we commit certain actions against our neighbors, fighting and impoverishment will result. Somehow we think these same actions create peace and plenty if applied to our community, state, nation, and world.

THE PRINCIPLE OF NON-AGGRESSION

As children relating to others, we learned a great deal about creating peace and prosperity. Most of us can remember Mom or Dad prying us apart from a playmate after we came to blows. "Who started it?" often determined who received the most severe punishment. Even at a tender age, we could see that if no one hit first, no fight was possible. We contributed to keeping the peace by making sure we did not deliver that first blow. This approach frequently required controlling our reactions to others. No longer did we feed them knuckle sandwiches just because their clothes were "weird." We refrained from using our weaker playmates and siblings as personal punching bags. We became tolerant of the harmless actions and attributes of others. This tolerance extended to the property of our playmates as well. Taking or damaging their toys without their permission counted as "starting it." Lying to or about them also set the stage for mortal combat. Consequently, our commitment to keeping the peace required us not only to be tolerant, but also to be honest with others and to respect property that was legitimately theirs. We refrained from threatening "first strike" force, theft, and fraud. This was our first step in bringing peace to our own tiny corner of the galaxy.

The second step was just as important. If we struck others, took their toys, or lied about them, we tried to repair the damage we had

Thou shalt not kill.... Thou shalt not steal. Thou shalt not bear false witness against thy neighbor. Thou shalt not covet...anything that is thy neighbor's.
—THE HOLY BIBLE
Exodus 20:13–17

Men have the right to use physical force only in retaliation and only against those who initiate its use. The ethical problem is simple and clear-cut: it is the difference between murder and self-defense.
—Ayn Rand
author of ATLAS
SHRUGGED

done. We replaced the damaged toy out of our meager allowance, perhaps purchasing one just a little better to make up for the distress we had caused. We advised those who had heard our lies that we had misinformed them. We carried books for the playmate whose arm we had bruised. By restoring the balance that we had upset, we hoped to diffuse the tension our actions had generated. *Our program for peace, therefore, had two parts: (1) honesty, tolerance, and respect toward others and their property (i.e., refraining from threatening first-strike force, theft, or fraud); and (2) repairing any damage we had caused. We will refer to this dual approach of honoring our neighbor's choice and righting our wrongs as the practice of "non-aggression."*

As we became adults, our playmates became our neighbors. The degree of tranquillity in our community depended on how many of us practiced the principles of non-aggression learned in childhood. Property values tended to parallel the peace. Where theft and fighting were rampant, property values plummeted. We learned that *prosperity is possible only when aggression is the exception, not the rule.* Our immediate experience suggests that the way to a peaceful and prosperous world is to practice non-aggression and to encourage others to do the same.

On a one-to-one basis, we do exactly that. We would never steal from our next door neighbor, whom we'll generically refer to as "George." As adults, we feel no more entitled to his car and money than we did to his toys when we were kids. We practice non-aggression by *respecting property* that is legitimately his. Maybe George likes to wear things we wouldn't be caught dead in, but we wouldn't take a swing at him just because he doesn't conform to our standards. We practice non-aggression by being *tolerant.* If George doesn't contribute to our favorite charity, we wouldn't tell him his donation was going elsewhere just to get it. We practice non-aggression when we deal *honestly*. If we accidentally damaged George's property or person, we'd make it right again. We practice non-aggression by *repairing any damage that we have caused.*

We wouldn't join or hire a gang of our neighbors who wanted to steal from George, hurt him physically, or deceive him. If George had an encounter with such a gang, he would probably retaliate, perhaps with a gang of his own. The cycle could repeat itself indefinitely. Aggression begets aggression, and those involved alternate as victims and aggressors. "Starting it" is a prescription for neighborhood warfare, with a loss of both peace and prosperity. We practice non-aggression by saying "no" when others ask us to use aggression against another individual or group. Because we practice non-aggression naturally when dealing with our neighbors, it seems that selfish others must be responsible for aggression and the war and poverty it begets.

KNOWING OURSELVES

Before we absolve ourselves of responsibility for the world's woes, let us look more closely. In the 1960s, Stanley Milgram at Yale University conducted a series of studies to determine if gentle, considerate, everyday people could be persuaded—not forced—to hurt their fellow human beings. In one study, the scientist-experimenter strapped himself in a chair that was supposed to deliver electrical shocks of increasing severity to be administered to him by a naive volunteer. Whenever the scientist failed to learn a series of word pairs properly, the volunteer was supposed to shock him, using a higher voltage each time. A male experimenter went "undercover" and pretended to be a second volunteer.

The scientist did not actually receive any shocks; he was only pretending. The naive volunteers did not know this, because each of them had received a very real, low-voltage test shock as a demonstration. When the shocks reached a third of the maximum level, the scientist cried out that he could take no more and the experiment should end. The undercover volunteer tried to convince the real one that the experiment should continue. However, in every one of the 20 tests, the naive volunteers refused to keep shocking the experimenter. Apparently, the average person could not be convinced by a peer to force the scientist to continue against his will.[1]

In another study, however, the results were very different. The two experimenters switched places so that the scientist stood beside the naive volunteer and shocks were administered to the undercover one. When the "victim" cried out at one-third the maximum voltage, only 20% of the naive volunteers withdrew from the experiment. The others, at the insistence of the scientist, continued. At two-thirds maximum voltage, the victim cried out that he had a heart problem and feared for his life. Another 15% of the naive volunteers refused to continue, even though the scientist claimed that the shocks weren't severe enough to cause permanent damage. A full 65% of the volunteers continued to shock the victim even after he made no other sounds. Because the victim was hidden in a nearby room, some of the volunteers feared he might be unconscious and were extremely concerned for his safety. Yet, at the insistence of the scientist, they continued to shock him until they had administered the highest voltage three full times![2]

The scientist didn't need to force the volunteers at gunpoint; only verbal commands were required. *Even when the volunteers feared for the safety, even the life, of the victim, they were willing to proceed as long as an authority figure, but not a peer, urged them to.*

When the naive volunteers were interviewed afterward, certain trends emerged. The 20% who refused to continue as soon as the victim wanted to quit felt that they were responsible for shocking him. Administering the shocks was acceptable only if the victim agreed to it. They obviously believed in honoring their neighbor's choice—regardless of what anyone else told them to do. Those who continued shocking the victim were more likely to place the responsibility for his pain on the shoulders of the scientist or the victim himself for being a slow learner. Yet they surrendered their responsibility only when an authority figure, the scientist (second study), not a peer (first study), urged them to. A typical comment made by the volunteers was "I was just doing what I was told."[3] Similar statements have been made by those who executed Jews in the Nazi concentration camps in World War II or massacred women and children at My Lai in Vietnam.

We defer to authority figures because they are supposed to know more than we do. If a mistake is made, it's easy to lay the blame at their feet. Ultimately, however, we are responsible for choosing the authority figure we defer to. *Choosing to defer to one who urges aggression against others still puts the responsibility on us.*

Each of us would like to believe that we would be in the small group that refused to be persuaded by the authority figure to go on shocking the victim. When Milgram surveyed people who were unaware of the results to predict where they would stop, none believed they would go past two-thirds of maximum shock.[4] *Clearly, what we believe we would do and what we actually would do are quite different.*

We believe that we consistently practice non-aggression and that selfish others must be responsible for war and poverty. Milgram's studies teach us that our words and actions don't always match and that we can be unaware of this discrepancy. If we truly wish to help our world, we must first identify ways in which we may be causing the problem. Let us examine an instance of common, everyday aggression and see how we respond.

...civilization means, above all, an unwillingness to inflict unnecessary pain....those of us who heedlessly accept the commands of authority cannot yet claim to be civilized men.

—Harold J. Laski
THE DANGERS OF OBEDIENCE

In growing up, the normal individual has learned to check the expression of aggressive impulses. But the culture has failed, almost entirely, in inculcating internal controls on actions that have their origin in authority. For this reason, the latter constitutes a far greater danger to human survival.

—Stanley Milgram
OBEDIENCE TO AUTHORITY

HOW WE VIOLATE THE PRINCIPLE OF NON-AGGRESSION DAILY — WITHOUT EVEN REALIZING IT!

If we decided we wanted a new neighborhood park, how would we go about getting one? We could call together other individuals who want the same thing and could raise enough money to own and operate the park through donations, by selling stock in a corporation set up for that purpose, or through other voluntary means. If those who did not participate in the fundraising effort decide later to use the park, we might require them to pay an entry fee. Obviously, we would be relating voluntarily and non-aggressively with our neighbors. If George didn't want to be involved as either a contributor or a park visitor, we would honor his choice.

Of course, another way we could proceed would be to vote for a tax to purchase and maintain the park. If a large enough gang of our neighbors voted for it, George's hard-earned dollars would be used for a park he didn't want and wouldn't use. If he refused to pay what our gang dictated, law enforcement agents, acting on behalf of the winning voters, would extract the tax, at gunpoint, if necessary. If he resisted too vehemently, George might even get killed in the scuffle.

Wouldn't we be using a gang called "government" to steal from George? Wouldn't we be the first ones to turn guns on a neighbor who hadn't defrauded or stolen from us? Wouldn't George eventually retaliate by getting government to turn its guns on us for projects that he prefers but we want nothing to do with? Wouldn't we alternate as victims and aggressors, as minorities and majorities? Wouldn't we just be taking turns directing the law enforcement agents toward each other?

Through taxation, pacifists are *forced at gunpoint* to pay for killing machines; vegetarians are *forced at gunpoint* to subsidize grazing land for cattle; nonsmokers are *forced at gunpoint* to support both the production of

In matters of conscience, the law of the majority has no place.
—Mahatma Gandhi
father of modern non-violent resistance

How does something immoral, when done privately, become moral when it is done collectively? Furthermore, does legality establish morality? Slavery was legal; apartheid is legal; Stalinist, Nazi, and Maoist purges were legal. Clearly, the fact of legality does not justify these crimes. Legality, alone, cannot be the talisman of moral people.
—Walter Williams
ALL IT TAKES IS GUTS

tobacco and the research to counter its impact on health. These minorities are the victims, not the initiators of aggression. Their only crime is not agreeing with the priorities of the majority. Taxation appears to be more than theft; it is intolerance for the preferences and even the moral viewpoints of our neighbors. Through taxation we forcibly impose our will on others in an attempt to control their choices.

As individuals, we may not support taxation and other forms of aggression–through–government. However, the composite of our separate views, as reflected in our laws, indicates that as a nation, as a society, as a collective consciousness, we believe that aggression serves us. As we'll see in the next few chapters, just the opposite is true. Aggression creates poverty and strife in our city, state, and nation just as surely as it does in our neighborhood.

How could it be otherwise? Aggression could hardly produce peace and plenty simply because we use it as a gang instead of as individuals. Using the same means brings us the same ends. It's as plain as the nose on our face—and just as difficult to see! Only by looking at what is reflected back to us can we observe it.

Indeed, taxation and other forms of aggression–through–government are so taken for granted in our culture that one of our most popular sayings is that "nothing is certain except death and taxes." Yet slavery was once as universal. Taxation is thought to be indispensable to civilization today, just as slavery once was. Advocates of taxation claim that since most people pay assigned taxes before the guns show up, they have implicitly agreed to it as the price of living in "society." Most slaves obeyed their master before he got out the whip, yet we would hardly argue that this constituted agreement to their servitude. Today, we have an enlightened perspective on slavery, just as one day we will have an

A society that robs an individual of the product of his effort...is not strictly speaking a society, but a mob held together by institutionalized gang rule.
—Ayn Rand
THE VIRTUE OF SELFISHNESS

...while men usually recognize criminal acts when they are committed by an individual in the name of his own interest, they often fail to recognize the very same acts for what they are when they are committed by some large gang in the name of "social justice" or the "common good."
—Jarrett Wollstein
SOCIETY WITHOUT COERCION

enlightened perspective on taxes and other forms of aggression we now think of as "the only way."

Just as our ancestors rationalized slavery, we've created the illusion that taxation is legitimate. Like the volunteers who continued to shock the victim at the insistence of the scientist, we feel our actions are justified, perhaps even noble. We believe that we can create a world of peace and plenty if we are given a free hand to force those selfish others to do things our way. We feel taxation is indispensable for certain necessities (e.g., defense, clean air and water, helping the poor, etc.). Instead, as the following chapters illustrate, aggression *in any form* only hurts others—and ourselves. *We reap as we have sown.*

In Part II (*Forgive Us Our Trespasses: How We Create Poverty in a World of Plenty*), we'll see how our well-meaning aggression has created poverty, compromised our health, destroyed our environment, and fostered monopolies and cartels that manipulate us. Special interests chuckle at our naivete as they use our fears of selfish others to pit us against each other for their benefit. *In trying to control others, we find ourselves controlled.*

Having seen the folly of using aggression ourselves, Part III (*As We Forgive Those Who Trespass Against Us: How We Create Strife in a World of Harmony*) details a better way to deal with those who trespass against us. This "other piece of the puzzle" gives us power to create peace and plenty in our communities, our nation, and the world. First, however, we must take responsibility for the acts of aggression that we unwittingly commit. Like the volunteers who refused to shock the victim at the whim of the authority figure, we too must first honor our neighbor's choice. Only when we are innocent of aggression can we deal effectively with those who are guilty of it.

Aggression hides in our culture under many names. Taxation is only an example,

...we are living in a sick Society filled with people who would not directly steal from their neighbor but who are willing to demand that the government do it for them.
—William L. Comer
AVOIDING THE HIGH COST OF DYING (AND MANY OTHER FINANCIAL DILEMMAS)

...the moral and the practical are not in conflict, provided one knows what is, in fact, moral.
—Nathaniel Branden
JUDGMENT DAY

but one of the most widespread and uneconomical. If this concept seems incredible to you, consider the shift in awareness that it implies. Are we like children, accepting five pennies for our dime?

CHAPTER 2

WEALTH IS UNLIMITED!

Wealth is created when we use existing resources in new ways. Since such creativity is virtually limitless, wealth is too.

To determine whether we shortchange ourselves by choosing taxation and other forms of aggression as a means to our ends, we must understand what wealth is and where it comes from.

We usually equate money with wealth, but they are really very different things. Imagine a person stranded on a desert island without food, water, shelter, or medicine, but with a billion dollars in gold coin. Is this person wealthy?

Hardly! Food, water, shelter, and medicine—prerequisites for physical survival—are true wealth. Money is valuable only if it can be exchanged for something of value, such as goods or services. Money is only a measure of how much of the available wealth a person has access to. If no wealth is available, money is worthless.

Just how much wealth is available? Imagine the total wealth in the world 2000 years ago. Did even the richest of the ancients have access to antibiotics, anesthetics, or surgery when their children had appendicitis? Could their entertainers give them the same quality, selection, and special effects that are now available on television? Could they find out about events on the other side of the globe a few minutes after they occurred? Could they "reach out and touch" family members who had migrated to faraway lands? Could they visit their distant relatives after a few hours in the "friendly skies"?

Even the wealthiest of the ancients did not have many things we take for granted. A greater number of people than ever before now enjoy a lifestyle that our ancestors could not even imagine. Our wealth has increased greatly.

Where did we get all this wealth? The earth certainly did not get an additional endowment of natural resources between ancient times and the present. Instead, we discovered new ways to use existing resources. Coal, oil, and natural gas give us an unprecedented amount of power. We transmit this power over electrical wires and send communications via satellite. The antibiotics produced by fungi have been harnessed to fight infectious bacteria that invade our bodies. We stimulate our immune system with vaccines so that the ancient plagues have all but vanished. Artificial wings fly us all over the globe. Mass production, assembly lines, and robotics help to replicate the wealth–creating ideas. The new wealth allows creation of still greater wealth. For example, the energy trapped in fossil fuels lets us create new metal alloys that require higher smelting temperatures than wood can provide. One idea leads to the next.

We see that specific ideas on better uses for existing resources and the replication of these ideas are the real source of wealth. Natural resources are like seeds that grow into wealth when they are nurtured and developed by individuals acting alone or in concert. For example, oil was once considered a nuisance that contaminated good farmland. Not until enterprising individuals discovered how to pump, refine, and use it did oil turn into "black gold." Even water must be "developed" (drawn from a stream, well, or reservoir) before it can quench our thirst.

The amount of wealth a country produces does not depend primarily on its endowment of natural resource "seeds." Japan has almost no mineral wealth, while Mexico is well endowed, yet the Japanese are certainly more affluent than the Mexicans.[1] Similarly, North Korea is poorer than South Korea.[2] East Germany created much less wealth than West Germany before reunification in 1990.[2,3] Obviously, resource endowment is not the primary factor that determines a country's wealth. Population density cannot be the dominating factor either: both Japan and West Germany have a greater population density than their poorer neighbors Mexico and East Germany.[3]

When we consider that resources will one day be mined from planets other than the earth, that matter and energy are totally interchangeable, and that basic chemical elements can be transmuted, we realize that resource seeds are so abundant that they do not impose practical limitations on the creation of wealth at all. Even if our fossil fuels should be foolishly exhausted, for example, energy is abundantly available in each and every atom if only we knew—as we one day will—how to tap it safely. Even if we foolishly devastated our home world by unsound environmental management, a universe of other planets are available to us when we learn—as we one day will—how to reach them. Human resources, our "how to" ideas, and the replication of these ideas, determine how much available wealth there is at any one time. Since human creativity appears unbounded, the amount of wealth possible is virtually infinite! Truly we live in a "no limit" world!

The realization that resources do not limit the creation of wealth is a liberating one. Our country's wealth does not depend on the happenstance of its geographical boundaries, but on the self-determined thoughts and creativity of its populace. We create our world.

What secrets do the countries that enjoy great wealth possess? How are their populations different? As this book will demonstrate, *cultures with a strong belief in the practice of non-aggression, individually and collectively, enjoy the highest level of peace and prosperity.*

The United States has historically fostered a strong cultural belief in non-aggression in both collective and individual interactions. As we'll see in the next few chapters, this belief made the United States the wealthiest nation

...most real wealth originates in individual minds in unpredictable and uncontrollable ways.

—George Gilder
WEALTH AND POVERTY

PAST WEALTH

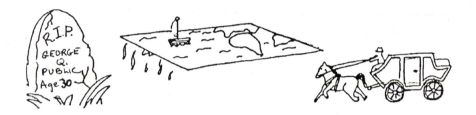

PRESENT WEALTH

FUTURE WEALTH

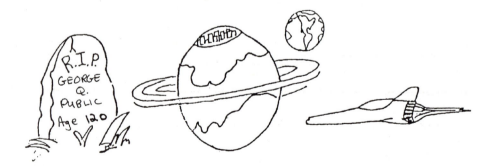

on earth. Unfortunately, while we continue to abhor aggression perpetrated by individuals, our belief that aggression is an effective way to deal with each other on a more collective (i.e., group-to-group) basis is growing. Most often, this aggression is sanctioned by the authority of the majority and implemented through government. *Aggression-through-government is the primary reason our country is experiencing a decline in the rate of wealth creation.*

We've seen how wealth is created by individuals, working alone or as part of a team. New ideas are implemented or reproduced. Our imaginary neighbor, George, for example, may work in a factory where he makes chairs. The factory owner gets the lumber from a tree farmer who planted and harvested the trees. These three individuals create new wealth in the form of chairs. They share the resulting wealth by exchanging it for money. They then trade their money for the wealth (food, clothing, etc.) that others have created.

Wealth belongs to its creators. All three individuals helped to create the chairs. Without their effort, the new wealth would not exist. When dealing with other individuals, we instinctively recognize this fact and act on it. We would never dream of going to George's house with a gun to steal the wealth he has created. He'd retaliate and we would take turns being victims and aggressors. With continual "warfare," a jungle-like atmosphere would pervade our neighborhood, and property values would plummet as wealth was consumed in the struggle. Effort would be directed at making war instead of wealth. Enlightened self-interest gives us strong incentives to practice non-aggression individually.

If we personally steal from George, we create havoc in our neighborhood. Nevertheless, we believe we can avoid this outcome if the government enforcement agents, acting on our behalf, perform the identical action. We believe the act of stealing is ennobled if the authority of the majority deems it to be for "the common

...Amnesty International's listing of human rights abuses shows a definite pattern where those nations with the least respect for human rights are also the poorest. By contrast, those with the greatest respect for human rights tend to be the richest.

—Walter Williams
ALL IT TAKES IS GUTS

good." As we'll see in the next few chapters, the laws of cause and effect still apply. The consequences of aggression are the same, whether perpetrated by an individual or a group. When *groups* of neighbors ask their government to steal from other *groups* of neighbors, we take turns being majorities and minorities, victims and aggressors. A jungle-like atmosphere prevails as effort is directed toward making war instead of wealth. Enlightened self-interest directs us toward the practice of non-aggression collectively—if we would only *realize* it!

THE MARKETPLACE ECOSYSTEM

The founders of our country recognized the importance of non-aggression. They realized that the "marketplace" was really an invisible interactive network of voluntary exchanges that take place among people in their communities, states, and nations. The marketplace has many similarities to nature's rainforest and oceanic ecosystems. Left to their own devices, the marketplace and the earth's ecosystems are self-regulating. Neither requires our forceful intervention to establish a holistic balance in which a diversity of complementary niches can evolve. Aggression in the marketplace or destruction in a natural ecosystem upsets this balance. Some of the niches are destroyed along with their occupants. Diversity is lost.

...the free market is a society in which all exchange voluntarily. It may most easily be conceived as a situation in which no one aggresses against person or property.
—Murray Rothbard
POWER AND THE
MARKET

The "free market" is the name given to describe the marketplace ecosystem when it is *free from aggression*. In the 1800s, our country came closest to this ideal. As a consequence, penniless immigrants flocked to our nation to make a better life for themselves and their loved ones. America became known as the "land of opportunity" and the richest nation on earth. Wealth was the natural by-product of a marketplace ecosystem free from aggression. As detailed in Chapter 19 (*The Communist Threat Is All in Our Minds*), democracies tend to have less aggression than the Communist ones. This is why North Korea and East Germany, before unification, created much less wealth than their "free world" counterparts.[2,3]

Even in the early days of the United States, the marketplace ecosystem was not entirely free from aggression, however. If a drug company sold untested products or if doctors misrepresented their training, the distraught consumers or their survivors had minimal recourse. Some forms of aggression, notably fraud, were widely practiced by individuals.

Our ancestors knew how to practice non-aggression themselves. *What they did not know was the most effective way to deal with those who aggressed against them.* Consequently, this aggression persisted. Eventually, people began to believe that freedom from aggression was an unattainable ideal because selfish others were always ready, willing, and able to take advantage of their neighbors. They adopted the belief that the aggressors enjoyed "too much freedom." People instructed their government to strike first and use aggression to prevent aggression. Their motto became "do unto others *before* they do unto you." *To fight the "evil" of aggression, they became aggressors themselves, with consequences more terrible than those they sought to prevent.* Let's see exactly how this happened in our own land of opportunity.

The trouble with people isn't their ignorance—it's the number of things they know that just ain't so.

—Mark Twain
American humorist
and novelist

PART II

FORGIVE US OUR TRESPASSES

How We Create Poverty in a World of Plenty

CHAPTER 3

DESTROYING JOBS

When we use aggression to increase the wealth of disadvantaged workers, we succeed only in making them poorer.

The previous chapter explained how wealth is created by individuals acting alone or in concert while working at an occupation or job. Wealth is virtually infinite, yet we commonly hear that the means to that end—jobs—are limited. Let's examine how this seeming contradiction has been created by aggression-through-government.

THE MARKETPLACE ECOSYSTEM: HONORING OUR NEIGHBOR'S CHOICE

In the early days of our country, new immigrants were at a disadvantage in the established marketplace ecosystem. Usually, they couldn't speak English. Their customs were different and disquieting. Frequently, they were unskilled and could produce little wealth. Employers had little incentive to hire them. The immigrants decided to change that.

The immigrants created a niche for themselves in the marketplace ecosystem by offering employers who would take a chance on them a greater-than-usual share of the jointly created wealth. By helping their employer, they also helped themselves. Instead of paying for expensive schooling to learn new skills, they got on-the-job training by accepting, for a time, lower wages than the experienced, American-born workers. Once they learned the language, trade, and customs, they could create much more wealth than before. The immigrants were either given a greater share of the jointly created wealth by their employers, or they took their experience and moved on. Sometimes they opened their own shop, sometimes they went to an employer with

greater appreciation for their newfound expertise. Some eventually became quite wealthy. *In
offering to serve their first employers well, they
ultimately served themselves.*

Young Americans sometimes use the same
technique to get that important first job. For
example, as an undergraduate, I worked in the
laboratories of various scientists after class.
Sometimes there was a little pay involved,
sometimes course credit, sometimes no visible
compensation at all. The scientists who hired
me really didn't have a job to give, so like the
immigrants, I created my job, my niche in the
marketplace ecosystem, by offering them a
better deal than any of my classmates would
even consider.

My peers thought I was crazy working for
"slave wages." A few years later, they changed
their minds. The experience I gained, plus the
recommendations of my mentors, turned out
to be quite valuable. These intangibles gave
me an edge over those with comparable formal
education when I applied for more advanced
positions. Offering my first employers a good
deal resulted in later employers offering *me* a
good deal. Letting myself be "exploited" was
one of the smartest career moves I ever made.

The balance of the marketplace ecosystem
evolves naturally. Workers without experience
who are willing to create a low-wage job can
gain the necessary experience and skills to
create more wealth. Almost everyone is able to
create some wealth, so everyone can find a
starting niche. As expertise evolves, so does
the niche—one way or the other. In serving
their first employer well, unskilled workers
serve themselves.

Usually, an employer will reward workers
as their capacity to create more wealth increases. By providing an improved work space,
more benefits, and/or increased wages, employers provide positive feedback, appealing to
the employees' own self-interest to create even
greater wealth. More wealth creation means
more profit for the employer and the employee

to split. By helping each other, they help themselves. *Both serve their own interest best by making sure that their partner in creating wealth is taken care of.*

Unenlightened employers who don't reward their workers for increased productivity lose them to employers who do. Employers who choose employees on the basis of color or sex or anything other than ability to create wealth find that their shop creates less wealth than it could. Less wealth means less profit for the employer and employee to share. Lower profits provide the employers with negative feedback. Discrimination on any basis other than productivity is costly. Employers reap as they sow.

We can observe this "yin-yang," or balance, of the ecosystem within the marketplace right in our own community. Our fictitious neighbor George decides to hire a neighborhood youth, Elaine, to paint his house because of her willingness to work for a very nominal sum.

Elaine created a job by giving her employer a better deal than the other teens in the neighborhood. Had Elaine not made such an offer, George would have let the house go unpainted for another few years. The creation of wealth in the form of a well-kept house would have been delayed. By offering to serve George well, Elaine also helped beautify her neighborhood. In the process, Elaine helped herself as well.

In the fall, Elaine asked George to put in a good word for her with the corner grocer. As a result of George's glowing recommendation, Elaine was hired instead of other youths with no one to vouch for them. The following summer, Elaine's references from the grocer helped her get a temporary job with a nearby factory. When Elaine graduated from high school, she was offered a well-paying job by a local banker. Elaine was chosen because her former employers could vouch for her conscientious performance. Her friends, who had mocked her as she worked for a "pittance," were rejected because they had no experience. By serving her employers well, Elaine also served herself.

AGGRESSION DISRUPTS THE MARKET-PLACE ECOSYSTEM

We'd never dream of putting a gun to George's head and threatening him if he didn't pay Elaine more than what they had jointly agreed on. After all, our neighbors know better than we do what will work for them. Pointing a gun at George would probably end any feeling of camaraderie we might have shared in the past. There's something about looking down the barrel of a gun that isn't consistent with "loving our neighbor." George is likely to call his local sheriff and have us arrested or make sure that he retaliates with sufficient force to prevent us from threatening him again. In trying to control George, we might very well find ourselves controlled.

Even if we successfully intimidated George, he might decide not to hire Elaine, rather than pay her more than he wished to. Without George's recommendation, Elaine might never get the grocery job. Without experience at the grocer's, Elaine might not be picked to work at the factory. Without these part-time jobs, Elaine would not have the experience so valued by the bank. Our attempt to protect Elaine from George's exploitation by using aggression would probably backfire and hurt the person we most wish to help.

The marketplace ecosystem operates in our neighborhood if we let it work its magic. We wisely refrain from threatening our neighbors when they are interacting and contracting with each other without using force or fraud. The individuals, after all, know their situation better than we do.

Exactly the same principles apply in the national work force, but somehow we see it differently. We view low wages as evidence of employer "stinginess" instead of schooling with pay for the unskilled. We try to correct the behavior of these selfish others by voting to *force* employers to pay a minimum wage—*at gunpoint, if necessary.* Through our government, we become aggressors, the first party to threaten violence. Our aggression yields the same results on a national scale as it does in our neighborhood.

For example, in the chair factory where George works, employees are paid at different levels ($4 or $5 per hour) depending on their experience. If the minimum wage is raised to $5 per hour, several things could happen.

If the employer pays the least experienced people $5 per hour, he will have to raise the price of the chairs. The people who were earning $5 will probably complain because they are being paid the same wage as the novices. The employer will have to give them a raise too. The price of the chairs goes even higher. Fewer people can now afford to buy the chairs, so the factory will cut back production. Workers will be laid off; the least experienced will be the first to go. Instead of earning $4 per hour, some of the inexperienced workers will be unemployed, while others will be making $5 per hour.

Some employers will be able to replace the unskilled workers with machines that cost $4.50 per hour instead of the $5 now mandated by law. The workers from the factory that makes the new machines are very skilled and already make well above the minimum wage. They now have extra orders for machines, so their factory must hire more skilled labor. At the chair factory, some of the more experienced workers make $5 per hour, while some of the unskilled workers are unemployed and make nothing. The machine factory hires more skilled labor.

Other employers might simply eliminate part or all of the job that the people earning $4 per hour once did. Maybe their job was to paint the chairs; now finishing is left to the buyer. More unskilled employees are laid off.

Every 10% increase in minimum wage makes the worker 2% worse off because companies must offset increased cost with reductions in other parts of the"payment bundle" such as hours, bonuses, etc.
—Albert Wessels
MINIMUM WAGES:
ARE WORKERS REALLY
BETTER OFF?

...a 20 percent increase [in minimum wage] makes approximately 81 percent of South Carolina workers worse off than before the change.
—James Heckman
and Guilherme
Sedlacek
REPORT OF THE
MINIMUM WAGE STUDY
COMMISSION

Some employers will not be able to use any of these options. There may be no substitute for the unskilled labor and no way to raise prices without losing too many customers. To comply with the law, these employers may cut back on other employee benefits, such as health insurance, vacation time, etc. The unskilled workers make $5 per hour, but lose some benefits that may have been worth more to them than the wage increase.

If none of these options are available, employers may have to forgo some of their profits. To avoid cutting their profits, these employers may close their factories and either retire or switch to a business that needs only skilled workers. In either case, the employees will be laid off. The skilled workers will have an easier time becoming employed again, because they are needed in places such as the machine factory that is expanding because of the demand for labor-saving devices. The unskilled workers will find themselves in less demand and will have more difficulty.

Each employer will react differently to the minimum wage increase, but the result is always the same. Fewer inexperienced employees will have a job. Instead of making $4 per hour, some will make $5 per hour, and others will make nothing. The best of the low-paid workers get a raise, but the most disadvantaged are forbidden to create what wealth they can.

If we support minimum wage laws, we destroy jobs, especially those that would have gone to the unskilled or disadvantaged. By using aggression, we limit wealth by destroying the jobs that create it. No wonder welfare to the newly unemployed increases when the mandated minimum wage goes up![1]

The Poor Get Poorer: Discrimination Against the Disadvantaged

Because minimum wage laws hurt the disadvantaged the most, they are frequently used to "legalize" discrimination. In South

Africa, white unions lobby for minimum wages (called "rate-for-the-job") in order to "reserve" particular jobs for whites.[2] If the unskilled blacks are forbidden by law to negotiate a training wage, they can never gain entry into these professions and are effectively barred by law from creating wealth in those occupations.

The same thing happens in the United States. Minimum wage laws hurt the very people they are supposed to help. Many disadvantaged workers are black; the most unskilled blacks are, of course, the young. As the percentage of jobs covered by minimum wage laws has increased (Figure 3.1A), black teenage unemployment has increased much more than white unemployment (Figure 3.1B). *What is particularly distressing is that black teenage unemployment was almost identical to white unemployment before the 1950s!* By trying to help the disadvantaged with aggression, we've hurt them more than the selfish employers ever did!

The inexperienced are not the only victims. The elderly and handicapped are adversely affected as well. This was vividly brought home to me in the mid-1980s while renovating low-income housing in the city of Kalamazoo. A young, unskilled man, who was partially disabled, had been watching our progress and asked if he could do some cleaning and yard work for $2 per hour. He was willing to accept such low wages because he could walk to the work site. He also hoped I might be able to give him a recommendation so others would "give him a chance." I explained to him that minimum wage laws prevented me from hiring him for anything less than $3.35. We both knew that I could hire an able-bodied person at that rate who would do more work per hour. We both would have been satisfied to settle on $2 per hour, but we were forbidden by law from doing so. Had we gone ahead, government enforcement agents could have "fined" me (i.e., taken my created wealth)—at gunpoint, if necessary.

The minimum wage law is one of the major causes of spiraling unemployment among young blacks.
—Walter Williams
THE STATE AGAINST BLACKS

A rising minimum wage broadens the income gap between blacks and whites, leaving black families proportionately further behind than ever.
—Robert Meyer and David Wise
REPORT OF THE MINIMUM WAGE STUDY COMMISSION

Past studies by and large confirm the prediction that higher minimum wages reduce employment opportunities and raise unemployment, particularly for teenagers, minorities, and other low-skilled workers.
—Masanori Hashimoto
MINIMUM WAGES AND ON-THE-JOB TRAINING

...low income workers as a group are the major victims of minimum wage legislation.
—Keith B. Leffler
ECONOMICS OF LEGAL MINIMUM WAGES

Figure 3.1 Temporal Relationship Between Increases in Minimum Wage and Decreases in Black Youth Unemployment

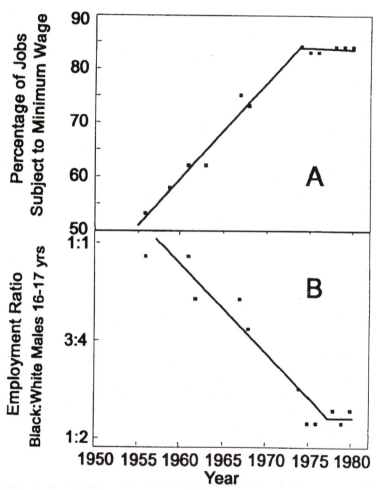

The percentage of jobs subject to minimum wage legislation increased as the unemployment ratio of blacks:whites decreased, until both leveled off after 1975.

Sources:
Masanori; Hashimoto, MINIMUM WAGES AND ON-THE-JOB TRAINING, (Washington: American Enterprise Institute for Public Policy Research, 1981) p.2.
Walter Williams, STATE AGAINST THE BLACKS, (New York:New Press, McGraw Hill, 1982) p 37.

Why shouldn't this young man have been able to make his own choices? He viewed working for $2 per hour in the same way I had viewed working in the laboratory—as a stepping stone to something better. Surely he could decide what a particular job was worth to him. By supporting minimum wage laws, we've condemned many of the disadvantaged to life "on the dole." Being dependent on others is surely more "degrading" than starting at the bottom and working one's way up!

When we use aggression to control the marketplace ecosystem with minimum wage laws or other mandated "benefits," we set in motion a destructive chain reaction. Instead of providing the disadvantaged with a better financial base, we prevent them from obtaining what they need most: on-the-job training in the art of creating wealth. Because they cannot work, they cannot get ahead. They cannot entice a reluctant or prejudiced employer into giving them an opportunity to show their worth when they cannot offer such employers a better deal.

THE RICH GET RICHER WITH OUR HELP!

If minimum wage laws so obviously hurt those they were intended to help, why do our legislatures keep passing them? Do minimum wage laws benefit someone else with power and influence? Of course they do!

With minimum wage laws, the skilled and educated no longer have to compete with the ambitious disadvantaged workers who are rising through the ranks. Only those who can afford to *pay* for training can get hired when the disadvantaged are forbidden from creating training jobs for themselves. When fewer skilled people are available, the experienced workers can command higher wages. Unions frequently lobby for minimum wage laws because such laws favor their skilled membership at the expense of unskilled workers, the handicapped, and minorities.[3]

...the responsiveness of labor supply to wage changes seems to be greater among the disabled than among the nondisabled...

—Andrew Kohen
REPORT OF THE
MINIMUM WAGE STUDY
COMMISSION

One of the most serious effects of minimum-wage legislation is the impairment of on-the-job-training for young workers.

—Masanori Hashimoto
MINIMUM WAGES AND
ON-THE-JOB TRAINING

Does this mean that the unions are full of selfish others who need to be put in their place? Not at all! Those who propose minimum wage laws know we have supported aggression in the past when we thought it was for the common good. Perhaps the last time we used aggression, union members were the victims.

Unions and other special interest groups that desire minimum wage laws do not use aggression themselves. Like the proverbial serpent in the Garden of Eden, they tempt *us* to practice aggression against our neighbors for their benefit. They only kindle the flames of poverty and strife—*we* control the final outcome. *We* fan the flame when we direct our government enforcement agents to carry out their wishes. We could choose differently. We could say "No!" to those who advocate minimum wages, just as Adam and Eve could have said "No!" to the serpent. Without our consent, the unions (and the serpent) are powerless. The choice—and responsibility—belongs to us.

A LOSE–LOSE SITUATION

Usually we agree to the aggression of minimum wage laws because we believe in a win-lose world, where wealth and jobs are limited, where gain can be had only at another's expense. When our choice is between winning and losing, aggression appears to be a useful tool. We don't notice that our aggression is limiting wealth and jobs because we take these limitations as a given. Our beliefs become self-fulfilling prophecies.

For this reason, the gains that the skilled worker makes when minimum wage laws disenfranchise the disadvantaged are largely an illusion. People who lobby for minimum wage laws, who enforce them, or who are unemployed because of them produce no wealth. Their activities create no new goods or services. The world as a whole is poorer, and so are we. Our money cannot purchase what does not exist, any more than it could in our desert island example from Chapter 2 (*Wealth Is Unlimited!*). In a world producing less wealth than it could, we are proportionately deprived. Because the lobbyists, enforcement agents, and unemployed produce no new wealth, part of what we create goes to support them. In trying to control others, we find ourselves controlled.

Wealth is only the smallest part of the price we pay, however. We've encouraged the disadvantaged to think of their plight as someone else's fault rather than a condition best rectified by their own efforts. By supporting minimum wage laws, we've taught the disadvantaged to turn the law enforcement agents on those still employed to feed, clothe, and shelter them. We take turns being victims and aggressors, minorities and majorities. Instead of taking responsibility for our choices and letting others do the same, we point fingers at each other. Self-improvement becomes equated with turning the guns of government on others, begetting "war" as we struggle for control of the enforcement agents. Our belief that selfish others are the problem has turned into a self-fulfilling prophecy.

By ignoring the voluntary choices of the individuals involved, we presume that we know what is best for them. On the average, however, individuals make better choices for themselves than we can by making a uniform choice for everyone. Some employees prefer to accept a lower hourly wage in return for more benefits, better working conditions, more flexible hours, proximity to work, congenial colleagues, etc. On the average, individuals know better than we how to choose the best combination of wages and benefits for their particular situation and temperament. With minimum wage laws, we decrease further the limited choices available to the disadvantaged.

THE EASY WAY OUT

We have a choice. We can just say "No!" to the aggression of minimum wage laws and

smother the flame of poverty and strife kindled
by special interests. No detailed evaluation of
the law or the proponents' motives is necessary. When we find that our enforcement
agents will be directed against those who are
interacting voluntarily with each other without
deceit or violence, we know that poverty and
strife will follow. The means and ends are
intimately related. Nationwide aggression is
every bit as destructive as neighborhood aggression is.

Many people believe that minimum wage
laws and other legal restrictions on employer-
employee bargaining helped to eradicate the
deplorable working conditions that existed
during the Industrial Revolution. They fear
that doing away with minimum wage laws
could recreate this dire situation. In fact, just
the opposite is true.

Nineteenth-century workers and their
families had to choose between a dangerous,
uncertain, and backbreaking existence on
their small farms or long hours and low pay in
crowded, poorly maintained factories. The
creation of wealth was so inefficient in those
times that almost every waking moment was
spent in creating enough wealth to barely
survive. The majority of the choices available
to our ancestors would look barbaric by today's standards. Our modern, efficient production of life's necessities has enabled us to
work 40-hour weeks, dispense with child
labor, and support those who create no wealth
at all. These choices were not realistic options
for most people until the latter half of this
century. If we continue to decrease wealth
production with increases in minimum wages
and other forms of aggression, we will find
ourselves faced with these harsh choices once
again.

Without minimum wage laws, what will
prevent employers from colluding to pay only
slave wages to workers, even when they learn
to create more wealth? The natural balance of
the marketplace ecosystem keeps employers'

greed in check automatically by simply allowing them to reap as they sow. If it didn't,
employers would be able to pay low wages to
workers even when they had experience!
Because employers voluntarily pay more than
90% of the workers who are 24–65 years of age
more than the minimum wage,[4] the marketplace ecosystem is obviously regulating the
marketplace well without aggression.

Without minimum wage laws, young,
inexperienced, or disadvantaged workers could
create niches (jobs) for themselves in the
marketplace ecosystem by offering employers
a greater share of the jointly created wealth in
return for training and experience. *Since
everyone can create some wealth, everyone
could be employed.* Instead of exploiting disadvantaged workers, this win–win arrangement lets them create some wealth, prove
themselves, and obtain a recommendation.
Instead of using their limited resources for
expensive schooling, they are paid to get both
training and experience!

Most job seekers find that the first question a prospective employer wants answered is
"How much experience do you have?" Employers know that past performance is the best
barometer of future success. In many cases,
on–the–job training is more valuable than
education of any kind. Without the aggression
of minimum wage laws, this opportunity would
be within everyone's reach.

After becoming proficient, employees could
seek higher wages, another employer, or businesses of their own. Few people stay where
they start. Most employee performance improves with experience. Low-paying jobs are
most often a beginning, *not* a dead end. The
self–regulating marketplace ecosystem protects the efficient worker by providing other
options. These opportunities make it difficult
for employers to exploit their employees.

An example of this type of regulation
occurred after the Civil War. Many Southern
landowners didn't want to have anything to do

with the newly freed blacks. However, wealth creation on their plantations was much more profitable with hired hands than without them. Blacks offered to work for less than whites would, making plantation owners choose between their prejudice and their pocketbook. Many chose to hire blacks to maximize their creation of wealth.

At first, the landowners tried to collude to pay the blacks as little as possible. Even though such action was perfectly legal, the marketplace ecosystem foiled such plans with its self-regulating magic. A few landowners soon found that if they paid the best workers a little bit more than everyone else did, they had their pick of the skilled blacks. Experienced workers created more wealth for the plantation than unskilled ones, so profits increased. Landowners who paid low wages were alarmed to see their best workers leaving to work for these more enlightened employers. They either offered higher wages or found themselves without help.[5] Even whites with deep prejudices found themselves persuaded by their pocketbook to treat their black hired hands better than they wanted to. Exploitation of newly emancipated slaves was limited by the employers' own greed. They were still able to discriminate (and many still did) but they paid dearly for it. By allowing them to reap as they sowed, the marketplace ecosystem taught them the hazards of exploitation and discrimination.

Blacks dissatisfied with working for landowners had other options as well. They migrated to Northern factories, opened their own shops, or simply offered their skills to the community as plumbers, electricians, etc. The marketplace ecosystem protected blacks from exploitation by the variety of niches (jobs) through which they could create wealth. As blacks began to gain respect and affluence, however, these avenues for creating wealth were closed to them by our well-meaning aggression, as described in the next chapter.

CHAPTER 4

ELIMINATING SMALL BUSINESSES

"Only in America" could penniless immigrants become affluent by starting their own businesses. Today, our aggression keeps the disadvantaged from following in their footsteps.

THE MARKETPLACE ECOSYSTEM: HONORING OUR NEIGHBOR'S CHOICE

In the previous chapter, we learned how enlightened employers paid higher wages, attracted the best workers, and were rewarded with the positive feedback of profit. Blacks who felt that no employer paid what they were worth often had the option of going into business for themselves as printers, plumbers, carpenters, or stone cutters.[1] Frequently, blacks found this latter route was the most rapid way to affluence. Many immigrants discovered the same thing.

The natural balance of the marketplace ecosystem also determined whether or not new ventures would stay in business. Business people who pleased their customers with better service and/or low prices got referrals and repeat business. Profit was a direct reflection of how well they served their neighbors. If they charged their customers excessively, other entrepreneurs began providing the product for a lower price, voluntarily accepting less profit to attract more customers, and ultimately more profit. Greedy competitors lost consumers. Profit and loss gave the tradespeople feedback that told them when they were—and were not—serving others adequately. Service providers reaped as they sowed. The customers voted daily with their purchasing dollars to supply this feedback. They directly regulated the marketplace ecosystem, keeping it in balance without aggression. The customer was the final authority. The customer was king.

Take care of your customers and take care of your people and the market will take care of you.
—Tom Peters and Nancy Austin
A PASSION FOR EXCELLENCE

Wealth comes from successful individual efforts to please one's fellow man...that's what competition is all about: "outpleasing" your competitors to win over the consumers.
—Walter Williams
ALL IT TAKES IS GUTS

If our fictitious neighbor George thought his employer was exploiting him, George might decide to create wealth by going into business for himself. We'd never dream of stopping George at gunpoint from providing service to willing customers because he hadn't gotten our permission to do so. The business that George and his customers voluntarily agree to transact is up to them. We simply honor our neighbor's choice.

We know that trying to tell George—at gunpoint—what he can and cannot do is likely to destroy any feelings of concern and trust that George may have for us. Brotherly love seems to dissolve when looking down a gun barrel.

Of course, if we "start it," George will probably fight back. Perhaps he'll call the local sheriff and have us arrested. Perhaps he'll retaliate with sufficient force to make us unlikely (or unable) to threaten him again. "Starting it" is a prescription for warfare, whether we're adults or children.

If we prevent George from creating wealth for himself, how would he survive? Chances are that he would feel justified in stealing the wealth we create, perpetuating the conflict between us. Just as our interference with George and his willing customers would wreak havoc with our neighborhood, so would the same actions create animosity and beget poverty in our city, state, and nation.

AGGRESSION DISRUPTS THE MARKET-PLACE ECOSYSTEM

Some whites were well aware that as long as the marketplace ecosystem was free from aggression, blacks, immigrants, and other minorities would have the opportunity to better themselves. Therefore, they clamored—successfully—for us to condone the aggression of licensing laws to destroy the small minority businesses.

Licensing laws instructed the government enforcement agents to stop, at gunpoint, if necessary, individuals from providing a service to a willing customer unless they have permission from a licensing board. By requiring high licensing fees, written examinations for manual occupations, and excessive schooling or apprenticeships, licensing boards were able to exclude blacks and other disadvantaged minorities. Blacks were almost entirely forced from the trades, even the specialties in which they had been well represented. U.S. citizenship was frequently required to exclude new immigrants as well.[2]

While minimum wage laws prevented the disadvantaged from getting that first job, licensing laws prevented them from starting their own businesses. Prevented from being an employer or an employee, disadvantaged individuals frequently found themselves unable to legally create wealth for themselves and their loved ones.

In New York City, for example, would-be taxi drivers must purchase a "medallion," or license, before they can legally carry customers. The number of medallions is limited and has not been increased since 1937. A new driver must purchase a medallion from someone who is retiring. In 1986, these medallions were selling for more than $100,000.[3] Many people who have a car and would be capable of creating wealth for themselves and their loved ones are forbidden, by law, to do so, because they can't afford the medallion. Those who are prosperous enough to purchase one must charge their customers more to make up for the extra expense. Thus, the first requirement for a successful cab driver in New York City is not pleasing the customer. Having money or the ability to borrow it is more important. Customers are no longer king.

The Poor Get Poorer: Discrimination Against the Disadvantaged

The licensing laws prohibit the disadvantaged from creating wealth by providing cab service even if they have a car, are capable drivers, and have willing customers. Most of the licensed taxi drivers can make a good living servicing only the better parts of the city. Few venture into the ghetto areas. Consequently, when those too poor to afford a car need to go to the doctor, legal taxi service is usually unavailable. Fortunately, residents able to purchase their own vehicle eventually decided that they would offer such service illegally.

By 1979, these "gypsy" operatives were believed to be more numerous than the number of medallion holders.[4] As long as they stayed in the ghetto areas, the government enforcement agents looked the other way. When the gypsy cabs came into the better areas, however, medallion holders insisted that the government enforcement agents prevent the gypsy drivers from servicing customers—at gunpoint, if necessary.[5]

We can learn several important lessons from the New York experience. First, the gypsy drivers were almost exclusively minorities, mostly black and Puerto Rican,[6] yet they were able to create a substantial amount of wealth, even in their impoverished areas, by providing a desperately needed service. When we don't interfere with the marketplace ecosystem, even the ghetto residents are able to create a significant amount of wealth. Second, the licensing requirements excluded the disadvantaged from creating wealth in the better areas of town where more profit was possible.

The aggression of licensing laws simply made the rich richer and the poor poorer. Because many of the poor were minorities, these licensing laws were, in fact, discriminatory. Finally, the customers suffered as well. In the better areas of the city, they paid more for taxi service, because the licensing laws increased the cost of doing business and limited the number of drivers to select from. The would-be customers in the ghetto frequently had no service at all!

OTHER EXAMPLES

The interstate trucking industry is regulated in much the same way as the New York City taxis. The primary criterion for permission to create wealth by moving goods across state lines is the ability to afford the license required by the Interstate Commerce Commission. Voluntary transactions between the trucker and the customer are forbidden, by law, without such approval. Needless to say, minorities and the disadvantaged are under represented in the trucking industry because of these restrictions.[7]

Licensing laws dealing with day care have severely impaired the ability of women with young families to create wealth. As mothers enter the work force, they select a child-care provider that best suits their standards and their pocketbook. Mothers who have no other marketable skills can create wealth by caring for the children of working mothers. Unfortunately for everyone, these natural child-care providers are often forbidden by law from providing this service, because they cannot afford to remodel their homes to meet licensing restrictions, pay for licensing fees, or deal effectively with the red tape required to get government permission to provide day care.[8]

We've supported this aggression to protect young children from unsafe and unscrupulous day-care providers. Obviously, most parents are better equipped than anyone else to evaluate the quality of care their child receives. Parents who are not competent or interested enough in their child's care to do so usually pose a much greater threat to their children than a sloppy day-care operator could! Our efforts are redundant at best.

At worst, licensing laws harm the very people they are meant to help. Licenses to operate day-care centers are not always easy to get. Some have been denied because the yard was deemed to be several feet too short! One center had to replace its four smoke

DAY-CARE LAWS LIMIT PRIVATE-HOME CENTERS THAT PARENTS LIKE BEST. For about 17 years, Susan Suddath kept other parents' children in her home....The state of Maryland...told her she would have to reduce the number of children, or close down ...her basement was too low in one place. Almost 6 feet tall herself, Mrs. Suddath assured the inspector she would be the tallest person in the room. But he couldn't bend the law.

—The Wall Street Journal
October 26, 1982

detectors with a five-detector interconnecting system, at a cost of $2,000. A prospective day-care operator had to remove a wall because the door was 36 inches wide instead of 38![9]

The women who succeed in upgrading their homes and working their way through the red tape (57 forms in Washington, D.C.)[10] must charge more for their services to make a profit. In North Carolina, 25% of the cost of day care is due to licensing-by-aggression.[11]

Some women, faced with these increased costs, can no longer afford to work outside the home. When they try to create wealth with a home business, licensing laws again hamper them. If they attempt to cut or even braid the hair of willing clients without getting several years of training to obtain a license, law enforcement agents will stop them, at gunpoint, if necessary.[12] In Chicago, hooking up a home computer to one owned by a business is illegal.[13] In Massachusetts, no goods and services can be produced in the home for a business located elsewhere.[14] Even in areas where home businesses are permitted, no employees may be allowed.[15]

Through my years as a landlady, I've watched my low-income tenants struggle with the aggression of licensing laws. Those who take in sewing or operate day care in their apartments live in fear that one day the government will stop them from creating wealth without a license. What callousness to demand that others get our permission before being allowed to put food in their children's mouths and a roof over their heads!

THE RICH GET RICHER WITH OUR HELP!

If the type of licensing laws described above hurt the disadvantaged without providing any consumer benefits, why do our legislatures vote for them? Sometimes home businesses are restricted because of the extra traffic they bring into a residential area. Except for the day-care center, however, none of the above examples creates extra traffic.

...Northrup cited an Eagle Comptronics Company incident near Syracuse where a group of women, who also were single parents, contracted to assemble electronic components in their homes. The State Labor Department, he said, closed them down under the anti-labor law, so the work is now contracted out of the country and the women, who were supporting themselves and their families, now are on welfare.
—Ithaca Journal
September 11, 1982

Home businesses have low overhead and so provide another avenue for the disadvantaged or part-time worker to create wealth. Because the overhead is low, products are frequently priced lower than similar items manufactured by skilled factory labor, giving consumers an option they wouldn't otherwise have. Although customers are pleased, factory workers are not. Many licensing laws are supported by skilled workers who want to keep the disadvantaged from offering to serve the customer better than they are willing to.[16]

Does this mean that skilled workers or union members are selfish others who deserve our wrath? Not at all! Those who propose licensing laws have seen our willingness to sanction aggression-through-government for "a good cause." Perhaps the last time we used aggression, skilled workers were its victims. In a system of aggression, we simply take turns being winners or losers. Instead of cooperative win-win scenarios, we perpetrate a win-lose game in which we are constantly at each others' throats.

The skilled workers do not use aggression themselves. Like the proverbial serpent in the Garden of Eden, they tempt us to practice aggression against our neighbors for their benefit. They only kindle the flames of poverty and strife. We choose to smother the flame by refusing to direct our government enforcement agents to do their bidding—or we fan it with our acquiescence. Without our consent, the skilled workers (and the serpent) are powerless. The choice—and the responsibility—belongs to us.

A LOSE-LOSE SITUATION

As in all cases of aggression, everyone loses. As we have already noted, blacks were forbidden to create wealth in their own businesses after the Civil War. Those restrictions left them vulnerable to prejudiced employers. Today, the unskilled mother is similarly discouraged by law from creating wealth through child care or a home business. The would-be truckers and taxi drivers who cannot afford a license cannot work in their chosen profession. Licensing laws, coupled with the minimum wage laws, frequently keep the disadvantaged from ever getting a start. *Infinite wealth through innumerable job possibilities is limited and made finite primarily through aggression-through-government.*

The Ladder of Affluence (Figure 4.1) illustrates this process. If our parents are on the upper rungs of the Ladder of Affluence, they probably have enough wealth to put us through college or professional training so that our first job is several rungs up on the Ladder. Disadvantaged individuals, however, have to start at the bottom and work their way up. Training jobs at low pay and home businesses are the first rungs of the Ladder.

Minimum wage and licensing laws destroy the lower rungs, giving the disadvantaged less opportunity than ever. Instead of being *paid* a low wage while getting training and experience, the disadvantaged must *pay* for training or an expensive license. Instead of having the opportunity to work their way up the Ladder of Affluence, they cannot get started. They are excluded from climbing the Ladder at all! If they wish to survive, they must rely on the charity of others or use aggression to wrest wealth from those legally permitted to create it. How can we claim to care for the disadvantaged if we are willing to put them in this position?

Those who manage to get that first job in spite of these handicaps find that the marketplace ecosystem cannot effectively protect them from exploitation. For example, when licensing laws excluded blacks from the trades, these would-be entrepreneurs swelled the ranks of those seeking employment. Employers had the upper hand when the former slaves were no longer permitted to start their own businesses. By supporting aggression, we

Figure 4.1 The Ladder of Affluence

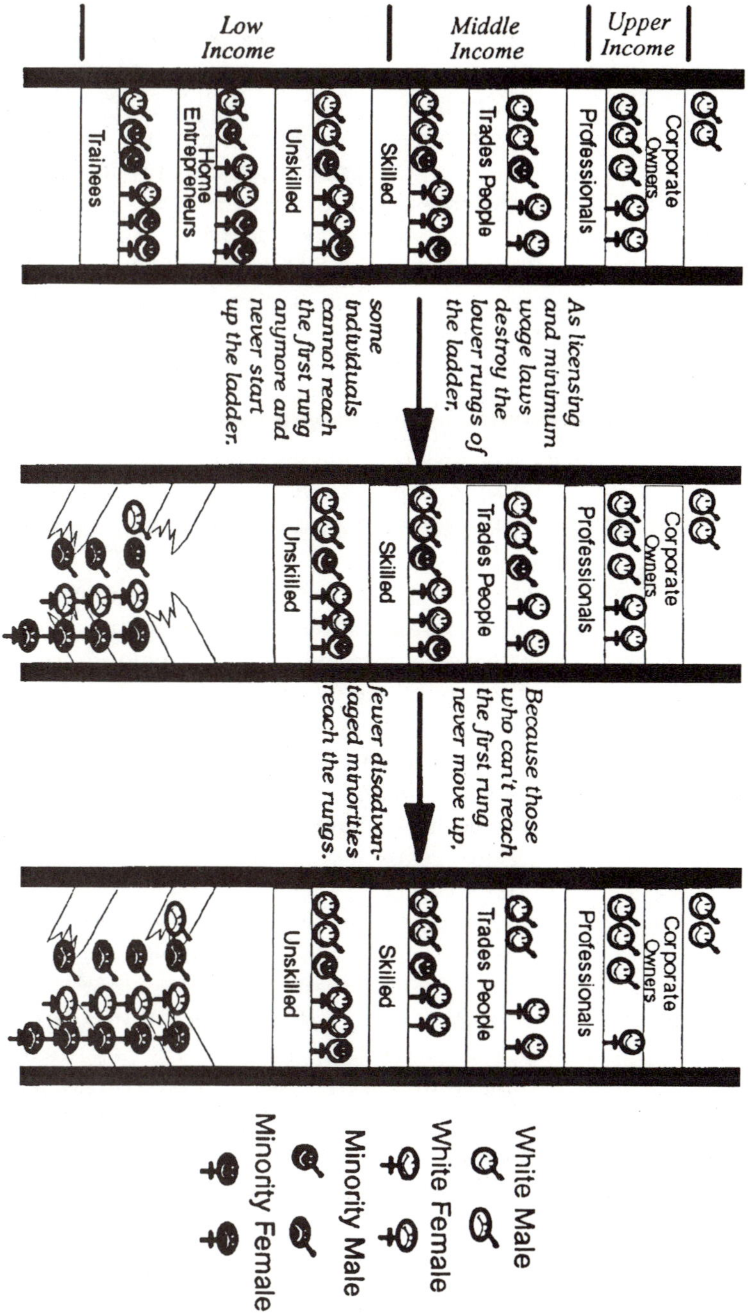

put blacks and other disadvantaged groups at the mercy of prejudiced employers. The disadvantaged workers were sacrificed for the benefit of consumers who received no net benefit at all!

As aggression is used to limit the creation of wealth by the disadvantaged and to augment the income of the advantaged, the gap between rich and poor widens. Since the disadvantaged create less wealth than they otherwise would, the society as a whole is poorer. Now we can begin to understand why the distribution of wealth is most even in countries with the highest GNP per capita (e.g., Switzerland and the United States).[17] *Countries can decrease poverty and uneven wealth distribution by abandoning the aggression that restricts the creation of wealth by the disadvantaged.*

Many disadvantaged Europeans immigrated to the United States because aggression-through-government in their homeland forbade them to create wealth for themselves and their loved ones. They wished to go where their children would not have to beg for permission to create wealth. Today, their descendants find themselves in the same trap, which they have helped to create by refusing to honor their neighbor's choice.

This situation is tolerated, even encouraged, by the well-to-do in the belief that widening the gap between themselves and the disadvantaged makes them winners. People in the trades saw their incomes rise as their licensing laws forced blacks out of business after the Civil War. Licensing laws prevent ambitious, unskilled workers from offering customers a better deal than highly paid union members could. Aggression appears to serve these special interest groups well.

However, this gain is largely an illusion as Figure 4.2 shows. When we look closely, we see that aggression is a lose-lose proposition for everyone!

Figure 4.2 The Wealth Pie

In the absence of aggression, everyone creates goods and services, so that the Wealth Pie and our Piece of it (shading) is as large as it can be for our current level of knowledge.

As licensing laws and minimum wage laws forbid the disadvantaged from creating wealth, the Pie shrinks accordingly. Our Piece (the goods and services our money can buy) is proportionately diminished.

Because those who lobby for and enforce these laws create no new wealth themselves, the Pie shrinks once again, making our Piece smaller as well.

As skilled workers, we may see our Piece of the Pie increase *relative* to everyone else's with these changes, but the *absolute* size of our Piece is smaller than it otherwise would have been. We cannot buy wealth that does not exist, no matter how much money we have relative to everyone else. Even with the extra dollars, we have much less purchasing power than we would have had in the absence of aggression.

The enforcement agents who keep the disadvantaged from producing wealth produce none of their own. Consequently, they must take some of ours in the form of taxes. Our diminished Piece shrinks further.

To survive, those who are not legally permitted to create wealth demand that the law enforcement agents take some of ours—at gunpoint, if necessary—as taxes to provide welfare. Our Piece of the Pie shrinks accordingly.

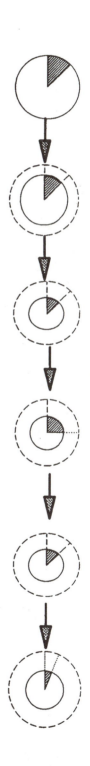

Both the employed and the unemployed battle to control the force of law to gain an advantage. Each group attempts to have the guns of the law enforcement agents pointed at the other, taking turns being victims and aggressors. This is not brotherly love; this is war! The only difference between this war and conventional ones is that both sides take turns "capturing" the only weapon—the government. Because each side occasionally "wins," both have the illusion of gain. The cost of the weaponry of aggression (lobbying, limiting the creation of wealth, supporting those who create no wealth) is so high that both sides lose in the long run.

Hostility is created and wealth is not; other fallout occurs as well. Against the background of chronic unemployment, a belief emerges among the advantaged that some people are simply not competent enough to ensure their own survival. The disadvantaged, trapped by aggression and told that only more aggression–through–government can save them, begin to believe in their own impotence. While one segment of society justifies its aggressive actions on the basis of its own alleged superiority, another segment cringes with loss of self–esteem.

THE EASY WAY OUT

In a society without minimum wage or licensing laws, disadvantaged individuals would not be excluded from creating wealth, as they are today. Opportunity for on–the–job training *with pay* would be readily available. If employers did not give adequate pay raises to individuals who performed well, the employees would have the option of starting their own businesses, possibly competing with their former employer. In this way, the marketplace ecosystem protects a worker from exploitation.

Approximately 80% of all new jobs are created by small businesses.[18] Destroying small businesses through the aggression of licensing laws is the fastest way to destroy jobs. As small businesses are thwarted, *large* companies dominate. As jobs are destroyed, *employers* get the upper hand. As people become even poorer, dependence replaces self-sufficiency.

If small businesses were not stopped at gunpoint from creating goods and services, consumers would have more options and lower prices. No one would need to support enforcement agents, lobbyists, or the unemployed. Available wealth would be increased greatly and everyone's piece of the pie would be correspondingly larger.

If we truly wish to narrow the gap between rich and poor, while increasing the wealth of all, the most effective thing we can do is to say "No!" to the aggression of minimum wage and licensing laws. Instead of interfering in the voluntary transactions of others, we simply honor our neighbor's choice! It's that simple!

What do we do about those who would exploit or discriminate against the disadvantaged? When no physical force, fraud, or theft is involved, we simply let them reap as they sow. Employers who treat their employees poorly will lose them to the many other opportunities available when the marketplace ecosystem is free from the aggression of minimum wage and licensing laws. Employees who stay with an unenlightened employer are either happy where they are or they aren't sure how to make a move. If we want to help them, we can encourage them to apply elsewhere, show them how to improve their skills, or hire them ourselves. Such actions require us to get personally involved with the disadvantaged and to truly show our concern and care. Surely, action of this type bespeaks brotherly love more than pointing guns at selfish employers!

In working with the disadvantaged in this way, I have discovered that they frequently prefer a steady, safe job with low pay to the rigors of job hunting, interviewing, and the uncertainties that come with a new position.

Some choose to accept low pay for jobs they are overqualified for in return for a low-stress, supportive environment. Those who really want to get ahead usually know what they need to do.

A common belief in our society is that aggression can be used to rectify destructive social attitudes, such as prejudice and discrimination. Many people supported minimum wage laws because they were supposed to help, rather than hurt, the disadvantaged. As we've seen, such aggression hurts those it was intended to help.

Some licensing laws were supposed to protect the consumer rather than the worker in areas where a mistake can be life-threatening, such as electrical or medical work. In the next chapter, we'll see again that aggression, as usual, harms the very people it is supposed to help.

CHAPTER 5

HARMING OUR HEALTH

Licensing of health care services gives us the illusion that we are protected against selfish others who would defraud us. Instead, our aggression boomerangs back to us, costing us our wealth, our health, and our very lives.

We've tolerated, even encouraged, the aggression of some licensing laws. We believe that they protect us from selfish others who would otherwise give us low-quality service, especially when a mistake can be deadly. The available evidence, however, suggests that our aggression in the form of licensing laws hurts us, rather than helps. Quality is most often compromised, not improved, by licensing laws.

To understand how this happens, let's review what we know about the impact of licensing laws. Licensing always lowers the *number* of service providers by imposing extra requirements, such as citizenship, schooling, monetary payments, or apprenticeship for those wishing to create wealth. In the previous chapter, we saw how licensing limited the number of taxi drivers and home child-care providers while increasing the prices charged by those still legally permitted to create wealth in those professions. Studies show that whenever the number of service providers goes down, more people, especially the disadvantaged, either do without the service or do it themselves. For example, when the number of plumbers decreases because of licensing laws, retail sales of plumbing parts go up as people attempt to make their own repairs. Dental hygiene is poorer in states with the most restrictive licensing requirements for dentists, because fewer people can afford regular check-ups. For the same reason, the incidence of blindness increases in areas with the most stringent licensing for optometrists. Accidental

...mainly the research refutes the claim that licensing protects the public.

—Stanley Gross
Professor of
Psychology,
Indiana State
University

...most of the evidence suggests that licensing has, at best, a neutral effect on quality and may even cause harm to the consumers.

—S. David Young
RULE OF EXPERTS

electrocutions go up when licensing requirements for electricians increase.[1] Licensing laws intended to protect us can—and do—kill.

By limiting availability, licensing laws lower the overall amount of quality service delivered. The negative impact of decreasing availability far outweighs any increase in quality that may occur, as the above studies indicate. Evidently, few people attempt to do work for which they are totally unqualified. Licensing laws prevent many more people who have some qualifications from performing simple services at affordable prices. The observation that licensing laws lower the overall quality of services delivered takes on a very personal meaning when we realize that one of the most highly regulated (licensed) sectors of our economy is the health care network.

For most of us, state-of-the-art knowledge of how to stay well and get well will be the primary factor in determining how long and how well we live. Licensing limits the availability of a service, thereby lowering the overall quality delivered. Thus, we would expect our health care to be of substantially lower quality than it could be in the marketplace ecosystem undisturbed by our aggression. Let's examine two major aspects of health care regulation—licensing of physicians and pharmaceuticals—to see if we have chosen a cure that is worse than the disease.

THE MARKETPLACE ECOSYSTEM: HONORING OUR NEIGHBOR'S CHOICE

In the mid-1800s, doctors learned their profession in medical schools, by apprenticing with another practitioner, and/or by developing their own therapies.[2] Many individuals limited their practice to specific areas, such as midwifery, preparation of herbal remedies for common ailments, or suture of superficial wounds. This diversity in the training and type of practice encouraged innovation and allowed individuals to patronize the health care provider who seemed best suited to both their

The higher entry standards imposed by licensing laws reduce the supply of professional services....The poor are net losers, because the availability of low-cost service has been reduced. In essence, the poor subsidize the information research costs of the rich.
—S. David Young
THE RULE OF EXPERTS

needs and their pocketbooks. Good healers were recommended by their clients, while those unable to help their patients soon found themselves shunned. Physicians reaped as they sowed. The patients voted with their dollars, thereby regulating the quality of health care. The customer was king.

AGGRESSION DISRUPTS THE MARKET-PLACE ECOSYSTEM
Lowering Quality

As long as health care providers did not lie about their qualifications and past successes, the marketplace ecosystem evolved a natural balance. Some individuals, however, misrepresented their skills to attract patients. By lying about their expertise, they disrupted the marketplace ecosystem with the aggression of fraud. Patients who entrusted themselves to such individuals sometimes risked their very lives.

Americans were in a quandary. They wished to continue to honor their neighbor's choice but didn't know how to deter aggressors. Had they understood the other piece of the puzzle—the power of having aggressors compensate their victims—as described in Chapter 13 (*The Other Piece of the Puzzle*), the balance of the marketplace ecosystem would have been rapidly restored.

Unfortunately, even today the powerful impact of this second principle of non-aggression is not recognized or understood. In Part III (*As We Forgive Those Who Trespass Against Us: How We Create Strife in a World of Harmony*), we'll learn more about this principle and how its application would have defused the practice of medical fraud. For now, however, let's focus on the high price Americans paid by choosing to fight aggression by becoming aggressors themselves.

By the early 1900s, every state had agreed to the aggression of physician licensing. To obtain a license, healers had to meet the requirements of the licensing board. Without permission to practice, they would be stopped—at gunpoint, if necessary—from treating patients who still wanted their services. If our neighbors didn't choose as the licensing board did, their choices would no longer be honored, even if the unlicensed healer could cure them![3] The consumer was no longer king; the licensing boards were.

The licensing boards in each state soon began refusing licenses to health professionals who had not been trained at one of the "approved" medical schools. Only half of the existing medical schools were approved, so most of the others had to close their doors by 1920.[4] By 1932, almost half the medical school applicants had to be turned away.[5] Those who apprenticed, went to unapproved schools, or developed their own therapies were stopped—at gunpoint, if necessary—from healing.[6] As a result, the number of medical doctors per 100,000 people dropped from 157 in 1900 to 125 by 1929.[7] Specialists, such as midwives, were usually forbidden to practice unless they had a full-fledged medical degree.[8]

As medical knowledge expanded, a smaller number of physicians were available to perform an ever-widening range of services, so that the shortage created by licensing became even more pronounced. Just as more people die of electrocution when licensing requirements restrict the number of electricians, the decreased number of physicians in the early part of this century almost certainly resulted in poorer health care, especially for the disadvantaged.[9] Until 1970, the physician to population ratio remained below what it had been in the early 1900s![7] By 1985, this figure had risen to 230 per 100,000,[10] but the time required for each patient had dramatically increased as well because of a more extensive array of procedures, preventative annual physicals, and more involved diagnostic procedures. Naturally, with more work and fewer physicians, the price of medical care soared.

One measure of the doctor shortage is the average work week, estimated at 60 hours for practicing physicians and 80 hours for those in training.[11] Because of their fewer numbers, physicians today tend to see a whirlwind of patients in their long working hours. A transplant surgeon with whom I was collaborating once asked why I had elected research instead of medicine. My reply, only half-joking, was that I was unable to function competently after 48 hours without sleep. He admitted in all seriousness that one needed such an ability to get through hospital training and to practice in the more demanding specialties such as his own.

Such a long workweek can result in serious oversights. My own mother, in her late fifties, went to her doctor with a small breast lump. The doctor, although aware that five of her relatives had died of cancer, did not even order a mammogram. Embarrassed by the professional brushoff, my mother did not confide in anyone until the tumor was unmistakable—and had just begun to metastasize (spread). A few short years later, my mother drew her last breath.

The saddest part of this story is that it is not unique. My mother's best friend and my own ex-mother-in-law had almost identical experiences and met the same premature fate. Another friend survived a rapidly growing oral cancer only because his dentist insisted on its removal in spite of his physician's advice to "wait and see."

Only heart disease kills more Americans than cancer.[12] Any practicing physician can certainly identify it if he or she takes the time and trouble to investigate. Were the doctors whom my family and friends visited just too harried to provide that care? Is physician overwork causing major medical mistakes?

Some Californians think so. In 1990, they attempted to pass a law stopping the hospital physician—at gunpoint, if necessary—from working longer than 80 hours a week![13] More aggression is not the answer, however.

Inhibiting Innovation

Shortages and erratic care are only the tip of the proverbial iceberg. Quality care is compromised in ways other than restricting the number of physicians. By determining who can practice, the M.D.-dominated licensing boards define what constitutes legitimate medicine. In 1938, students of homeopathic, osteopathic, and chiropractic medical schools could no longer qualify for licensing as medical doctors.[14] Hospitals or medical schools that dared to employ them risked losing their approved status. Since licensing required internship from an approved hospital, loss of this status caused loss of students and interns necessary to run the hospital.[15] M.D.s who associated with the "cultists," shared facilities with them, or referred patients to them would be judged "unethical," thereby risking their own professional standing.[16] Relying on the advice of licensed M.D.s, insurance companies sometimes denied reimbursements to alternative practitioners, making their service much less affordable.[17] Alternative practitioners were frequently denied other privileges as well.[18] So blatant were these discriminatory practices that in 1987 the American Medical Association (AMA) was found guilty under the antitrust laws of having "conspired to destroy the profession of chiropractic in the United States" by using the political power afforded them by licensing laws.[19]

Were we being protected from "quacks" by licensing laws that suppressed alternative therapies? My own experience suggests just the opposite. After suffering back pain for several years and having several M.D.s advise me to take muscle relaxants and live with the discomfort, a coworker recommended an osteopath who had helped him with a similar problem. My spine had been locked in an unnatural position, probably as a result of an accident that had occurred some years before. The osteopath was able to relieve the tension with a gentle adjustment. Although spinal manipulation used to be common practice among osteopaths, the chiropractors do most of it today. When my osteopath retired, he turned over his practice to a chiropractor. When an automobile injury resulted in whiplash some time later, I was very grateful to have this alternative therapy.

Several studies of workers' compensation records have indicated that chiropractic can be superior to medical treatment with respect to lost work time and expense of care for certain types of injury.[20] Chiropractic manipulation, like surgery and drug therapy, is an important medical specialty.

Evidently, the M.D.s have belatedly come to the same conclusion. Some physicians are beginning to learn and practice the spinal manipulation techniques developed by alternative practitioners.[21] In the 1960s, osteopaths were once again permitted to practice in approved hospitals,[22] possibly because the M.D.s had fled to the lucrative medical specialties, leaving a lack of general practitioners.[23] With such tacit admissions that these alternative specialties have a place in medical practice, one wonders how many people suffered needlessly over the past 75 years because licensing laws have suppressed alternative therapies.

The suppression of different medical practices by licensing laws can be overt, as with the osteopathic and chiropractic professions described above. The subtle suppression of new therapies may be even more devastating, however.

The role of nutrition in health and disease is a good illustration. After 20 years in medical research, seeking causes and cures, I've seen how difficult it is to give laboratory animals our most troublesome diseases. For example, when studying the protective effects of prostaglandins on alcoholic liver disease, an M.D. collaborator suggested that we use a diet deficient in key nutrients to produce a similar syndrome in rats.[24] A great deal of evidence suggests that alcohol damages the liver by inducing nutritional deficiencies.[25] Most of our peers, however, believed that a single study had conclusively shown that baboons fed a supposedly adequate diet could still develop liver damage when given alcohol.[26] The control animals gained weight during the years of the study, while the baboons getting alcohol did not. Nevertheless, few physician–researchers realized that the failure of the baboons to thrive suggested that the diet was not adequate. The laboratory that performed this study demonstrated many years later that lecithin, a component of many foodstuffs, was able to partially prevent the alcohol–induced damage and maintain normal weight![27]

Such minimal awareness of nutritional basics is probably due to the poor training doctors receive in this area. Indeed, in 1990, only 34 of the accredited medical schools required a course devoted exclusively to nutrition.[28] Cardiovascular disease, which kills more people in the United States than any other ailment, is thought to be intimately linked with diet and lifestyle. We obviously need more doctors trained in nutrition, but licensing laws have prevented us from having significant choices other than those the medical monopoly lets us have.

The damage done by licensing laws is augmented further by the aggression of taxation, which is used to provide funding for medical research. Instead of allowing individuals to target the wealth they create toward the medical research that appeals to them, we have directed our government enforcement agents to confiscate it—at gunpoint, if necessary—in the form of taxes. Research proposals are evaluated by committees composed of established scientists and physicians.

Having served on such committees, I have seen why innovative ideas that do not fit mainstream thinking never get funded. Each

...restricting the practice of what is called medicine and confining it...to a particular group, who in the main have to conform to the prevailing orthodoxy, is certain to reduce the amount of experimentation that goes on and hence to reduce the rate of growth and knowledge in the area.
—Milton Friedman
Nobel Prize winner,
Economics

...by proper orthomolecular measures, mostly nutritional, it is possible for people to extend the length of the period of both life and well–being by about 25 years.
—Linus Pauling
Nobel Prize winner,
Chemistry

evaluator gives the proposal a score; even a single low rating is enough to prevent funding. Research in osteopathy or chiropractic, therefore, receives little funding. Research in therapeutic nutrition is also severely limited. Even Linus Pauling, winner of the Nobel Prize for chemistry and for peace, has had difficulty obtaining federal funding for his research on the use of Vitamin C to treat cancer.[29]

Medicine is not as definitive as most people think. Less than 25% of medical procedures have been demonstrated to be useful in controlled clinical trials.[30] Such trials are time-consuming and expensive, and physicians are hesitant to withhold any therapy that might be beneficial just for the study's sake. This is why surgery involving coronary bypass, the most frequently performed major surgery in the United States, has only recently been shown to be worthwhile, and then only in a select group of heart patients.[31] As a result, many people over the years have undergone needless pain, expense, and risk by having an unnecessary bypass.

To some extent this situation is unavoidable, since rigorous proof of a procedure's efficacy takes time, which some patients do not have. However, through the licensing process, certain types of unproven procedures (e.g., surgery) are permitted, while others are arbitrarily banned as quackery. Such unscientific selection has often led to the comical situation of yesterday's quackery becoming tomorrow's cure!

Medicine is still in its infancy; there is much that we do not know. Like it or not, we are human guinea pigs for medical doctors and alternative practitioners alike. The aggression of licensing laws limits our options without protecting us from unproven cures.

HISTORY REPEATS ITSELF AS THE RICH GET RICHER WITH *OUR* HELP!

The dangers of licensing laws were well known to our ancestors who left Europe and

Phony "youth cures" ... include products to soften the skin, to "make the person feel young again," to remove brown spots and cellulite. Of course, there is no product that will work in this way any more than there is a product known to medical science that retards baldness or helps grow hair back on a bald scalp.
—CONGRESSIONAL REPORT ON QUACKERY, 1982

Upjohn has introduced Rogaine...as the "first prescription medication proven effective for male pattern baldness."
—Scrip, 1986

its guild–style licensing system to settle in America, the "land of the free" (i.e., "free" from aggression). Licensing of doctors evolved in the early years of the United States, but was abandoned in the mid–1800s. Licensing had been found to exclude competent healers, hinder the development of alternative therapies (e.g., herbal medicine), create a monopoly of established practices (e.g., bleeding!), and retard innovative research.[32] Isn't this reminiscent of the above description of today's medicine? If history clearly repeats itself with the aggression of licensing laws, why were they instituted once again in the twentieth century?

Licensing of physicians was largely a result of lobbying by the AMA. This is not at all unusual: licensing laws are usually requested, not by consumers complaining about the quality of service, but by the professionals themselves! Indeed, professional organizations are frequently founded with the sole purpose of lobbying for licensing laws.[33]

...state licensing boards, particularly for medicine, but also for other professions, have instead become first and foremost devices for protecting the monopolistic position of the professionals.
—Marie Haus
REGULATING THE PROFESSIONS

Why would service providers desire licensing laws designed to regulate them? Legislators turn to established service providers to determine what requirements new entrants must satisfy. Not surprisingly, the established practitioners suggest giving licenses to those already in practice, setting high standards for new entrants, and denying approval to practitioners who use different techniques from theirs. Most physicians supported such measures in the belief that the quality of health care would be improved. After all, the surgical and pharmaceutical therapies of modern medicine have indeed contributed to the 25-year increase in life expectancy gained in this century.[34] Nevertheless, some of the AMA leadership appeared to be well aware that fewer physicians meant higher income for those allowed to practice.[35] Evidence suggests that the pass–fail rate of qualifying examinations may even be adjusted by the licensing boards to keep numbers of service providers

...an oversupply of doctors threatens.... perhaps there is need for professional birth control.
—Journal of the American Medical Association, 1932

(including physicians) low.[36] Choice is diminished, and fees rise accordingly.

Since the AMA controls the licensing boards, it can influence the behavior of practicing physicians by threatening to revoke their licenses. Medical doctors giving discounts have been censured by the AMA to keep physicians' incomes high.[37] When acupuncture was introduced into the United States, the AMA attempted to restrict its use to licensed medical doctors.[38] Other practices that are just as adequately and more economically performed by paraprofessionals have been grounds for turf battles.[39]

Should we then blame the negative effects of physician licensing on those selfish others who set AMA policy? Of course not! The AMA leaders simply observed our willingness to use aggression–through–government for a good cause. Perhaps the last time we used aggression, the M.D.s were the victims. Like the serpent in the proverbial Garden of Eden, the AMA tempted us to use aggression against our neighbors. They only provided us with the spark—the suggestion—of aggression. We fanned the flame into a raging inferno by instructing our government to enforce the decisions of the AMA-dominated licensing board. We were ready to deny our neighbor George access to the medical service of his choice because of our belief that better service for ourselves would result. We were content to have practitioners who did not follow the dictates of the licensing boards labeled as quacks even if their clients wanted their particular mode of healing. We yielded to the temptation to benefit ourselves by initiating force against others. The responsibility belongs to us.

THE POOR GET POORER: DISCRIMINATION AGAINST THE DISADVANTAGED

As usual, the poor suffer most from the aggression of licensing laws. Indeed, one of the concerns of those who spoke against it was

As you increase the cost of the license to practice medicine, you increase the price at which the medical service must be sold and you correspondingly decrease the number of people who can afford to buy the service.
—William Allen Pusey
AMA President, 1927

that the poor would be deprived of medical care altogether as costs increased. Rural areas, which could no longer support a full-time physician, were abandoned.[9] The would-be practitioner coming from a disadvantaged background was also penalized. In 1910, there were seven medical schools specializing in training black physicians. By 1944, only two had survived.[40] Women were excluded from the medical profession in the same manner.

The proportion and absolute number of women physicians was greater in 1910 than in 1950.
—Stanley J. Gross
Professor of
Psychology,
Indiana State

Most medical schools that catered to the working class by providing flexible training regimens, such as night school and apprenticeship, were closed.[41] Without the ability to work while they trained, aspiring physicians from the lower classes found themselves unable to afford the schooling or the time.

A LOSE–LOSE SITUATION

As usual, we reap as we sow. Licensing laws for physicians operate in much the same way that other licensing laws do. Those privileged to create wealth as physicians command higher prices than they otherwise would. The disadvantaged, less able to pay for medical care, take their turn as aggressors. They instruct the government enforcement agents to take wealth from the advantaged—at gunpoint, if necessary—to pay for their health care. The enforcement agents create no new wealth, so they must also take enough wealth from us for their support as well. Our piece of the Wealth Pie shrinks further.

...the study of medical history indicates that quacks flourish whenever physicians are scarce or when their remedies are ineffective. Licensing laws may actually worsen this problem by artificially restricting the supply of practitioners.
—S. David Young
THE RULE OF EXPERTS

Although the plight of the poor is most visible, the aggression of medical licensing laws hurts everyone. The greatest loss—the creation of wealth by economical, accessible, innovative medical therapies—is an invisible one. When we watch our loved ones die from "incurable" diseases, we pay dearly because of our refusal to honor our neighbor's choice!

THE EASY WAY OUT

To expand our options for medical care, we need only to say "No!" to the aggression of licensing laws. We would then be faced with another concern: how would we evaluate the competence of our physicians or surgeons before placing our life in their hands?

Quality practitioners of many professions have realized that people will do without a service if they can't readily evaluate it, especially if a poor choice is associated with a high risk of injury. Therefore, enlightened service providers often seek voluntary certification or a "Seal of Approval" from a professional or consumers' organization. For example, the AMA might rate practitioners by a variety of criteria, giving "certification" or ratings to those who met their standards. If their ratings are appropriate, consumers will turn to them for guidance. Professionals seeking certification would happily pay a hefty fee for a certification that meant more business. The AMA would profit when it *expanded*, rather than *limited*, its membership! Truly, it's a win–win world!

However, the AMA would have to be careful not to certify carelessly. Otherwise, consumers would no longer give it credence, and professionals would seek another certifying organization that consumers trusted.

This natural regulation by the marketplace ecosystem *increases* the number of service providers in areas that use certification when compared to places without certification or with the aggression of licensing laws.[1] Since the number of practitioners appears to be the primary determinant of how much quality service is actually *delivered*, voluntary certification should increase the availability of quality health care. Even if this were the only benefit derived from abandoning the aggression of licensing laws, our national health would be greatly enhanced. However, more quality care is only the beginning.

The skyrocketing costs of health care would plummet without the aggression of licensing. Today, health care professionals spend much of their time involved in activities

Certification provides all the information of licensure while offering a wider choice set.
—Keith B. Leffler
Journal of Law & Economics

that fail to use their skills fully. For example, numerous studies have shown that nurses and other non–physicians are able to diagnose and treat common conditions as competently as licensed medical doctors.[42] The fees charged by these non–physician professionals would be more than they receive today, but less than those charged by a physician today.

Pediatric nurses, for example, are able to give proper medical care to approximately two–thirds of all childhood cases, referring the remainder to physicians.[43] Nurses and other non–physician medical personnel can competently decide whether a respiratory ailment is a cold, an infection, or a more serious problem that needs a doctor's attention.[44] Nurses and other medical personnel could economically run clinics to monitor blood pressure, serum cholesterol, and glucose tolerance and could provide feedback to patients as they alter their lifestyles. Even minor surgery, such as suturing superficial wounds, can be competently performed by trained non–physicians.

As an undergraduate, I met a man recently back from Vietnam who hoped to go to medical school once he graduated from college. Because the army never had enough physicians available for the large numbers of wounded, he often found himself performing emergency surgery in an attempt to save soldiers otherwise doomed to bleed to death. This individual was obviously quite capable of creating wealth by assisting in a hospital operating or emergency room, or by suturing superficial wounds. However, until he completed medical school, he was unable to use the skills he had. Many veterinary or laboratory personnel are competent surgeons but are currently forbidden by law to perform even the simplest procedures on people.

If these skilled individuals were able to assist surgeons or treat uncomplicated cases, the cost of routine medical care would go down. Lower cost would make health care more accessible, especially to the poor, thereby increasing the overall amount of quality care delivered. Quality would be maintained, because less skilled practitioners could refer difficult cases to those with more training. Instead of being overburdened with routine care, medical doctors could focus on pushing back the frontiers of medicine. They could still enjoy hefty fees for state-of-the-art medical skills, while *routine* medical services would be provided more economically by non-physician practitioners.

Hospitals and medical centers could hire individuals for their skills, regardless of where, when, and how they received their education. Training for medical practitioners of all kinds would be as diverse as potential job niches. Individuals could once again apprentice, attend part-time medical schools, or develop their own therapies.

Not only would traditional care become more readily available at a lower cost, but new paradigms of healing would be readily available. People whose conditions warranted treatment by a non-traditional medical practitioner would be able to accept the risks and benefits of doing so. Such individuals would *voluntarily* provide a valuable service to us all as they helped to determine the value of each new treatment.

Such people might be putting themselves at risk as they try new therapies. However, we all acknowledge that life is not risk free. Between 40,000 to 50,000 people are killed each year in automobile accidents,[12] yet we do not outlaw driving. Everyone decides whether the benefits of driving outweigh the risks. We should honor our neighbor's choice of new medical therapies as well.

By saying "No!" to the aggression of licensing laws, we increase the overall health care quality by increasing availability, decreasing price, encouraging innovation, and allowing full use of each individual's skills. How we benefit when we honor our neighbor's choice! It's truly a win-win world!

The benefits of health care deregulation could be sabotaged by the aggression of fraud. Practitioners who attempt to deceive patients by making false claims of certification or qualifications perturb the natural balance of the marketplace ecosystem, just as surely as aggression–through–government does. Chapter 13 (*The Other Piece of the Puzzle*) explains how to deal effectively with aggressors without becoming aggressors ourselves. We'll see how the second principle of non–aggression, righting our wrongs, restores the balance while rehabilitating and, more importantly, deterring aggressors. Before examining this concept in detail, however, more exploration of *our* aggression is in order.

In the next chapter, as we explore the harm done by licensing products instead of people, we'll find that we can measure the costs in thousands upon thousands of lives!

CHAPTER 6

PROTECTING OURSELVES TO DEATH

By using aggression to avoid medications that harm us, we lose access to life-saving drugs.

A MATTER OF LIFE AND DEATH

If our neighbor George were terminally ill, we'd never dream of entering his home at gunpoint to take away a medicine that might save him. Similarly, we'd be furious if a family member had an incurable disease, but George stopped our loved one at gunpoint from taking a medicine that might help. As individuals, we honor our neighbor's choice. If we think our friends are choosing poorly, we might try to dissuade them. However, the final decision has to be left to them, in consultation with a physician, if that's what they wish. After all, it is *their* health at stake, not ours. Most of the time, they will know better than we what is best for them, and we'll know what's best for us. We practice non–aggression by taking responsibility for our own choices and by letting others do the same. Forcing our choices on others is an attempt to take responsibility for their lives.

When we deal with our community, state, and nation, however, our attitude is entirely different. Somehow, we think that forcing our choice on others becomes transformed into benevolence. For example, we support laws that stop manufacturers—at gunpoint, if necessary—from selling medicine that has not been licensed or approved by the Food and Drug Administration (FDA). We refuse to honor our neighbor's choice; instead, we instruct our FDA to make up their minds for them—at gunpoint, if necessary. The effect is the same as if we used such aggression against George. Life-saving medicines are ripped out of the hands of our fellow Americans—literally!

AIDS AND THE DRUG LAG

Until July 1988, customs officials took dextran sulfate away from AIDS victims who were returning to the United States after traveling all the way to Japan to purchase it.[1] At the time, no one knew if dextran sulfate could cure AIDS, but it did prevent the HIV virus from attacking white blood cells in a test tube.[2] If dextran sulfate prevented this attachment in a person's body, it might have stopped the virus from destroying its victim's immune system. Until it was proven to work, the FDA kept it from being sold in the United States—at gunpoint, if necessary.

Many AIDS victims didn't feel that they had time to wait until all the testing was done. Since they were the ones most affected by a decision—right or wrong—they thought we should honor their choice. Unfortunately for the AIDS patients, our laws dictated otherwise. As the Customs officials confiscated their new hope at gunpoint, the true impact of our aggression was unveiled. Our food and drug laws can kill if they delay life-saving therapies from reaching terminally ill individuals.

The spectacle of the AIDS victims being denied drugs that might be beneficial to them has helped us to see the results of our aggression clearly. FDA Commissioner Frank Young courageously began allowing individuals under a doctor's care to import medications from other countries for personal use.[3] Many of these pharmaceuticals are not sold here because of the "drug lag" our laws have created.

We're not prepared to march into people's homes like the Gestapo and take drugs away from desperately ill people.
—Frank Young
former FDA
Commissioner

Thus, the United States gets most new medications long after they are available in other countries, because our licensing laws are the most aggressive in the world. The FDA requires manufacturers to perform many years of testing, with costs estimated at $200 million.[4] The manufacturer ships truckloads of data to the FDA, which then takes an average of two and a half years to decide if enough testing has been done.[5] Meanwhile, people whose lives might hang in the balance are prohibited—at gunpoint, if necessary—from buying the new drug. Like all licensing laws, regulations governing our pharmaceuticals decrease the availability of new drugs and increase their cost greatly.

We all want the medicine we take to be tested thoroughly to be sure it's safe and effective. We also want breakthrough therapies as soon as possible to alleviate pain and suffering. Testing takes time and delays the availability of a new medicinal drug. If we wait for testing, we may suffer (or even die) for lack of treatment. If we don't wait for testing, we may take a cure that's worse than the disease. How do we decide what's best?

THE MARKETPLACE ECOSYSTEM: HONORING OUR NEIGHBOR'S CHOICE

Before 1938, Americans decided by themselves, or in consultation with their physician or pharmacist, which medicines were best for them. To aid the consumers and their physicians in evaluating pharmaceuticals, independent groups, notably the American Medical Association and Consumers' Research, first began evaluating and then testing pharmaceutical products. Other evaluations by physicians and pharmacists were reported in their trade journals and special lay publications as information about specific remedies emerged.[6] Intermittent articles appeared in *Ladies' Home Journal* and *Collier's* to alert readers to the dangers of specific products,[7] as did books written for the same purpose.[8] In 1904, the General Federation of Women's Clubs sent out thousands of letters, promoted lectures and exhibits, and distributed information to educate the public about specific problems.[9] Even when the modern pharmaceutical industry was in its infancy, the marketplace ecosystem responded naturally to protect the consumer. On the basis of these independent opinions, Americans made choices about which medications to take and honored their neighbor's choice.

Much of the drug toxicity observed in those days dealt with side effects that were not predictable from state-of-the-art knowledge. For example, we now know that some drugs are perfectly safe when given once or twice, but can be quite toxic if taken often. Earlier in this century, however, the frequency of this effect was not appreciated. As a result, more than 100 people who repeatedly used local antiseptics containing silver salts developed a blue-gray caste to their skin.[10] Thallium, a component of rat killer, was successfully used to treat ringworm. When applied routinely as a depilatory cream, however, at least 32 women died of its toxic effects.[11] Because of such incidents, multiple doses of modern pharmaceuticals are tested in animals before recommending even a single dose to humans.

Unfortunately, drug toxicity cannot always be predicted by animal testing. Animals can be unaffected by drugs that can cause devastating side effects in people. Dinitrophenol, used as a diet pill in the early 1930s, caused cataracts in 177 women, but none in the test animals.[12] In the early 1930s, amidopyrine killed 1,600 people in the United States, while the Spanish, with different genetic ancestry, were unaffected.[13] Because of a genetic sensitivity, paraphenylenediamine caused blindness in 1 out of every 120 women who colored their eyelashes with Lash Lure.[14] These idiosyncratic effects are not seen in animal studies and are not readily predictable even today.

The bottom line is that there is no such thing as a drug that is safe for everyone. Even life-saving penicillin has killed those who were allergic to it. The risk of experiencing an unpredictable side effect has to be weighed against the benefits each individual hopes to get. Before the aggression of FDA licensing laws, every individual did exactly that, and let others do the same. Individuals honored their neighbor's choice. Some people were willing to take more risks than others; some did not like the idea of taking any drugs at all. Each person took responsibility for his or her choice and honored the choices of others.

Most manufacturers realized that killing the customer was bad for business, and did safety testing before marketing their drugs. Careful manufacturers wooed the public and increased profits by advertising that "We have never yet had reported a case of sudden death following the use of our Antitoxin," or that their products had been tested and approved by various outside laboratories.[15] Brand name loyalty rewarded the drug manufacturer who always gave the customer what was promised. Manufacturers reaped as they sowed. Producers of questionable products simply had too few customers to stay in business.[16]

However, a few manufacturers were not so careful. Elixir Sulfanilamide was the most tragic example of this. It contained a safe drug, dissolved in an unsafe solvent, which was not tested before its sale in 1937. As a result, 107 people died.[17] The AMA had not granted the Elixir its Seal of Approval;[18] the marketplace ecosystem protected those who cautiously awaited further testing, while honoring the choice of those who believed the risk of taking a product that had not been independently evaluated was warranted.

This incident showed Americans how important a critical evaluation of pharmaceuticals could be. Had the marketplace ecosystem been kept free from aggression, the AMA and other independent evaluators probably would have extended their drug evaluations in the wake of the Elixir Sulfanilamide tragedy. Charging manufacturers a fee for examining their products could have funded such a system. Careful consumers could choose to buy only approved products.

Manufacturers who fraudulently misrepresented their products should have been required to compensate victims or their families as described in Chapter 13 (*The Other Piece of the Puzzle*). Such compensation would not only help to undo the damage, but it would deter future aggression. Even in the case of death, a monetary settlement to the victim's family is better than no restitution at all! Unfortunately, Americans took another tactic. They decided to try to deter aggressors by becoming aggressors themselves. In doing so, they created a cure worse than the disease.

AGGRESSION DISRUPTS THE MARKET-PLACE ECOSYSTEM

In 1938, laws were passed demanding that each manufacturer obtain approval from the FDA (i.e., a license) before selling each drug.[19] The FDA relied primarily on its evaluation of the safety testing performed by the manufacturer. If individuals wanted to buy the drug before the FDA was satisfied, government enforcement agents would stop the manufacturer—at gunpoint, if necessary—from selling it to them. As the FDA demanded more and more testing, many small manufacturers of folk remedies closed their doors, eliminating diversity of products and favoring larger firms. As a society, we no longer honored our neighbor's choice; instead, we used aggression to force others to do things our way "for their own good." As the number of tests grew, so did the time taken to perform them. As with all licensing restrictions, the *availability* of new therapies decreased.

The Illusion of Protection: Thalidomide

New drugs usually appeared on U.S. pharmacy shelves many years after they had been sold overseas in countries with less-aggressive licensing laws. Sometimes this drug lag protected us from pharmaceuticals with side effects that were difficult to predict through animal studies. Thalidomide, for example, was marketed in Europe for several years as a sedative while its manufacturer sought approval to sell it in the United States. In the early 1960s, the sensitivity of an unborn child to drugs that are quite safe for the mother was not widely appreciated, so doctors began prescribing thalidomide to pregnant women, even though no safety testing had been done in pregnant animals. Thalidomide prevents normal development of arms and legs in unborn humans, monkeys, and a single strain of rabbit.[20] If animal testing had been performed in standard test animals (rats and dogs), thalidomide probably would have appeared to be safe. Unfortunately, for human babies, it was not. Approximately 12,000 European children were born with deformed limbs.[21] Few American babies were affected, because only a few test samples had been distributed in this country. The FDA physician who had delayed its approval was given a presidential award.[22] By such feedback, we instructed the FDA to give us safety by aggression—at the cost of our very lives.

While other countries did not react to the thalidomide tragedy by changing their licensing laws substantially, Congress gave the FDA a mandate to use more aggression. Manufacturers had to complete extensive human tests to demonstrate that their drugs were effective.[23]

Naturally, manufacturers already did such tests, but not the elaborate way that the FDA demanded. Longer and larger studies had to be undertaken. Foreign testing was only infrequently considered acceptable to the FDA, forcing manufacturers to repeat studies that had been done elsewhere. In the meantime, manufacturers would be stopped—at gunpoint, if necessary—from selling such drugs.

Did these additional tests save us from drugs that were ineffective? Apparently not! Studies suggest that consumer waste from purchasing ineffective drugs changed little after the additional studies were mandated in 1962.[24] Evidently, patients and physicians are usually able to tell if a drug has the desired effects and will stop using it if it doesn't work. Companies desiring the positive feedback of profit quickly find that they must please their customers.

...the penalties imposed by the marketplace on sellers of ineffective drugs before 1962... have left little room for improvement by a regulatory agency.
—Sam Peltzman
REGULATION OF PHARMACEUTICAL INNOVATION: THE 1962 AMENDMENTS

...the U.S. system of approval, in spite of greater restrictiveness and insistence on detail, has not proved markedly superior in the prevention of marketing drugs that are subsequently discontinued in light of safety questions.
—Olav Bakke et al.
Center for the Study of Drug Development, University of Rochester, N.Y.

Did the 1962 regulations save us from more side effects? Apparently not: the percentage of newly approved drugs taken off the market in the United States was the same as in Great Britain, which did not substantially change its licensing procedures in the immediate aftermath of thalidomide.[25]

Paying with Our Lives

...rarely, if ever, has Congress held a hearing to look into the failure of FDA to approve a new entity; but it has held hundreds of hearings alleging that the FDA has done something wrong by approving a drug.... The failure to approve an important new drug can be as detrimental to the public health as the approval of a potentially bad drug.
—Alexander Schmidt, former FDA Commissioner

... according to George Hitchings, co-winner of the 1988 Nobel prize in medicine, FDA's five-year delay in approving the antibacterial drug Septra cost 80,000 lives.
—Sam Kazman
Competitive Enterprise Institute

While the British continued to enjoy many new drugs to treat their illnesses, only half of these were available to Americans, and only after many more years of waiting.[26] One of these new drugs denied to Americans was propranolol, the first beta-blocker to be used extensively to treat angina and hypertension. In the three years between introduction into the United Kingdom and the United States, approximately 10,000 Americans died needlessly every year,[27] because it was against the law for their doctors to treat them with propranolol. Even in 1968 when propranolol became available in the United States, it was approved only for minor uses. Advertising propranolol as a treatment for angina or hypertension was illegal until 1973 and 1976, respectively, so countless other Americans died because their doctors hesitated to prescribe the drug for a use that was still unapproved by the FDA. When the FDA finally gave approval, it was criticized by a congressional committee for exposing the American public to a drug with potential side effects![28] Since every drug has side effects in some individuals, asking the FDA to license only drugs that are completely safe is asking them to approve no drugs at all!

Our aggression, applied to this single drug, cost *at least* 30,000 American lives. Britain also practices the aggression of licensing laws, but to a lesser extent than the United States. Thousands more lives might have been saved if no aggression were present at all.

Deaths We Can Only Guess At

The more tests that a pharmaceutical firm has to perform, the longer it takes. Extra years of testing mean that drugs cannot be sold until the patent on them has almost expired. Thus, companies focus on drugs that can be used widely, and do little research on cures for less widespread diseases. Unpatentable therapies, such as vitamin and mineral regimens, are not studied or developed, because the manufacturer cannot recover the cost of FDA-mandated testing without some exclusivity.

As a researcher in a major pharmaceutical firm, I have been intimately involved with the licensing laws governing the marketing of therapeutic drugs. Some of my work dealt with the natural prostaglandin hormones or their synthetic analogs, which could partially prevent the deleterious effects of various toxins on the liver.[29] More than 100,000 people die each year from alcoholic liver disease for which bed rest and abstinence are the only, and often ineffective, treatments. I approached management with a win–win idea: test whether prostaglandins added to alcoholic beverages would lessen the chance of alcoholic liver disease. My employer would profit while it helped to prevent illness and death.

Unfortunately, the FDA would never permit such a thing, for it would appear as if we were encouraging people to drink. A major distiller was reputed to have tried to add vitamin B-1 to alcoholic beverages with the same end in mind and was met with a negative reception by the regulatory agencies.[30] We might be able to develop the prostaglandin as a pill to be taken daily by the drinker, but it would require a prescription; people who were ashamed to tell their doctor they drank a lot might forgo the medication. If we decided to go ahead, we still had to do the studies that the FDA required to show that it worked with 95% certainty. Since alcoholic liver disease

...the pattern of intervention into science from a combination of local, state, and federal sources has moved from reasonable control to something close to chaotic strangulation.

—Donald Kennedy
former FDA
Commissioner

takes years to develop and probably many years to cure, we would have to study hundreds of individuals over several years. Not only would this be costly, but heavy drinkers don't always take their medicine regularly. To ensure that we had enough individuals who actually got the prostaglandin, we'd need even more study participants. Furthermore, we weren't sure exactly how to measure our progress, other than waiting for people to die, because no other drugs had been successful in alleviating this damage. We might collect data for years only to find out that we had only enough patients to show that it worked with only 80% certainty—not good enough for the FDA. Meanwhile, our patent would be close to expiration. Without patent protection, we could not recover the cost of all these studies. Generic manufacturers would undersell us because they would not need to recover the gargantuan cost of testing. The win–win situation evaporated with the aggression of licensing laws, since we could not legally sell the prostaglandin as a drug that *might* work. My employer lost only a source of profit; people with alcoholic liver disease continue to lose their lives, perhaps needlessly.

Unfortunately, this story is not unique. Aspirin deforms the unborn young of almost every animal species but humans[31] and could not be marketed today if it had to go through FDA evaluations as a new drug! Penicillin, digitalis, and fluroxene might have met a similar fate,[32] costing thousands upon thousands of lives. *Many more lives have probably been lost by the aggression of licensing laws than have been saved.*

A LOSE–LOSE SITUATION

We never intended that licensing laws should kill. We wanted only to protect ourselves from selfish others who might sell us something that would kill instead of cure. What went wrong?

We chose the aggressive means of licensing laws, which led us to health care poverty. Just as physician licensing limits the number of practitioners, and thereby lowers the quality of care delivered, so too does licensing of drugs lower the availability and raise the cost of life-saving pharmaceuticals.

A two-year delay in a cancer therapy that reduces mortality by only 10% would cost a-bout 66,000 American lives[33]—many, many more than have died from all the drug toxicity in this century. The great loss of life caused by the delay of the single drug, propranolol, was a tragic, real-life example of the fruits of aggression. Before licensing laws, the largest example of manufacturer neglect was the unnecessary deaths of 107 people taking Elixir Sulfanilamide. The marketplace ecosystem, when free from aggression, is the best consumer protection of all.

Just as physician licensing created a cartel that excludes innovators and keeps fees high, so too do large pharmaceutical firms profit at the expense of the small ones. The increasing cost of development imposed by our aggressive regulations puts the smaller firms at a disadvantage.[34] As requirements increase, mergers become necessary and the number of firms decreases. A few large firms dominate the industry when newcomers are excluded by the high cost of satisfying the FDA. The price of each drug that is marketed reflects these incredible costs.

The advantage of the large pharmaceutical firms is largely an illusion, however. Their taxes are increased to pay the salaries of the law enforcement agents, who produce no new wealth. Creation of wealth is compromised as the health of the nation deteriorates. Even if the large manufacturers have a bigger piece of the Wealth Pie, its absolute size is less than it would be without aggression. Nobody wins.

The real tragedy affects everyone, including those in the pharmaceutical cartel and the

FDA itself. *When our loved ones are dying of "incurable" diseases, we all pay the ultimate price for our aggression.* Perhaps we should consider a better way.

THE EASY WAY OUT

If licensing laws do us more harm than good, how do we ensure that our drugs are safe and effective?

If the aggression of licensing laws ended, patients and their physicians could buy whichever drugs they felt might be helpful, regardless of the stage of testing. Since they could not competently evaluate every drug for themselves, they would probably rely on a professional or consumer's group for a status report on pharmaceuticals they were considering. Patients and physicians could *choose* to defer to one of these "authorities," but none could *force* adherence to their verdict.

Such advisory groups operated in this country before the introduction of the licensing laws. The AMA's Seal of Approval Program and Consumers' Research actually tested pharmaceuticals and cosmetics in their own laboratories instead of simply reviewing manufacturer testing, as the FDA does now. Elixir Sulfanilamide had not been approved by the AMA;[18] patients and/or their doctors who waited for the Seal of Approval before purchasing new drugs were protected from its lethal effects. The marketplace ecosystem protected them without aggression and without denying access to life-saving pharmaceuticals that they may have chosen before AMA approval.

Modern testing or evaluation groups might be funded by concerned citizens such as the Women's Clubs of the past, operate for the benefit of its members as the AMA and Consumers' Research did, charge the manufacturer an evaluation fee, or provide information to individuals for a small charge. The positive feedback of profit would encourage testing by several groups. We would have independent evaluations, rather than an examination of the manufacturer's data by the FDA alone.

An example of modern day independent drug evaluations is the *Medical Letter on Drugs and Therapeutics*, whose revenue is derived totally from subscriptions to doctors, medical students, pharmacists, and pharmaceutical companies.[35] By reversing the aggression of licensing laws (i.e., deregulation), we would enjoy a much wider range of safe and effective therapeutic drugs than we do today.

However, the benefits of deregulation can be sabotaged by the aggression of fraud. Drug companies that attempt to deceive consumers by falsely claiming that they have certification or seals of approval perturb the natural balance of the marketplace ecosystem. In Chapter 13 (*The Other Piece of the Puzzle*), we'll learn how the second principle of non-aggression—righting our wrongs—restores the balance while *deterring* future aggression. Before examining this concept in detail, however, we need to explore more fully the problems that our own aggression creates.

CHAPTER 7

CREATING MONOPOLIES THAT CONTROL US

Most monopolies are not created by selfish others, but by our own aggression.

In the last few chapters, we've seen how the aggression of licensing laws restricts the number of service providers. The disadvantaged individual, no longer able to get medical training through night school or apprenticeship, finds obtaining a medical license arduous, if not impossible. Small pharmaceutical firms find it increasingly difficult to meet the costs of FDA requirements. Well-to-do individuals and businesses move toward a monopoly on wealth creation.

This aggression-through-government has other fallout too. The rich not only get richer, they also have more power over our choices —and our lives. In trying to control selfish others, we find ourselves controlled by those hired to protect us! Like a fly caught in the spider's web, further aggression only entraps us more.

THE PYRAMID OF POWER

This concept is graphically illustrated by the Pyramid of Power (Figure 7.1). In the absence of aggression, the Base of the Pyramid is as broad and wide as our choice of goods and services. Our cost is low when aggression is absent. In addition, when we honor our neighbor's choice, it's more difficult for any one person or group to dictate *our* choices.

When we add a layer of aggression in the form of licensing laws or regulations, some goods and services are outlawed by the licensing agencies. As a result, First Layer goods and services are not as broad and wide as the Base. Prices go up as availability goes down. Consumers' choices are limited to licensed items or those they can provide themselves.

Figure 7.1 Pyramid of Power

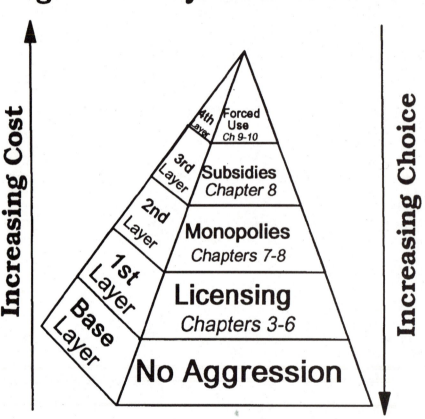

First Layer aggression, described in the previous two chapters, gives the AMA and FDA control of our health care options. When we are ill, they literally have the power of life and death over us.

Licensing is *exclusive* when all but a single monopoly provider is stopped—at gunpoint, if necessary—from serving consumers. When this Second Layer of aggression is added to the First, costs go up further as the choice of goods and services becomes even narrower. Consumers must buy the monopoly service, do without, or provide their own. Utilities are the most common example of Second Layer aggression. Later in this chapter, we'll see how giving utilities an exclusive monopoly has created our energy dependency. With every layer of aggression, those privileged by the licensing laws gain more control over our choices.

A Third Layer of aggression is added to the Pyramid when those people who don't use the Second Layer monopoly service are forced—at gunpoint, if necessary—to subsidize those who do. Usually, such services are provided by a government department rather than a private firm. Part of their cost is subsidized by the taxpayer. Public services usually cost *twice* as much as those provided by a private firm, for reasons we'll explore shortly. Even if consumers choose to do without or provide their own service, they must still subsidize the monopoly! The most devastating effect of Third Layer aggression, its environmental impact, is detailed in the next chapter.

The Fourth Layer of aggression is added to the Pyramid when consumers are forced—at gunpoint, if necessary—to *use* the subsidized monopoly service. Doing without or providing their own is no longer an option. With every layer of aggression, consumers have fewer choices until finally they have no choice at all! Chapters 9 (*Banking on Aggression*) and 10 (*Learning Lessons Our Schools Can't Teach*) show how *our* desire to control others creates

Monopoly: A right granted by a government, giving exclusive control over a specified commercial activity to a single party.
—AMERICAN HERITAGE DICTIONARY, 1982

Bureaucratic Rule of Two: Removal of an activity from the private to the public sector will double its unit cost of production.
—Thomas Borcherding
BUDGETS AND BUREAUCRATS: THE SOURCES OF GOVERNMENT GROWTH

the Pyramid of Power, giving others control over every aspect of our lives!

Aggression-through-government is the tool through which each successive layer of aggression is added. That's why Ralph Nader and his associates refer to government as "Uncle Sam, the Monopoly Man."[1] This contrasts with the popular belief that the free market creates and sustains monopolies. Let's take a look at history and examine this belief further.

THE MARKETPLACE ECOSYSTEM: HONORING OUR NEIGHBOR'S CHOICE

We must ever remember we are refining oil for the poor man and he must have it cheap and good.
—John D. Rockefeller

...the richest people in the world are those who've done best at pleasing others, especially the common man ....Henry Ford became richer than Bentley; Ford made cars for the common man....The pursuit of profits is the activity most consistent with human needs.
—Walter Williams
ALL IT TAKES IS GUTS

Occasionally, consumers vote with their dollars to give their business almost exclusively to one service provider. John D. Rockefeller, for example, through efficiency and innovation, helped lower the price of kerosene from $0.58 to $0.08 per gallon between 1865 and 1885.[2] His workers were loyal, hard working, and well paid; Rockefeller, an enlightened employer, was one of the first to initiate a retirement plan.[3] Because he shared the jointly created wealth with his workers, they were highly motivated. Standard Oil scientists developed better refining methods (e.g.,"cracking")[4]; found a way to use culm, a by-product of coal mining, for fuel;[5] and learned how to purify oil contaminated with sulfur.[6] Before these developments, only the well-to-do could afford the expensive candles or whale oil for nighttime illumination. With these innovations, kerosene, for a penny per hour, transformed evening activities for Americans of more limited means.[7] Americans voted with their dollars to make Rockefeller's Standard Oil their kerosene provider; by 1879, it had 90% of the refining business.[8]

In spite of its prominence, Standard Oil was unable to raise prices without encouraging fledgling competitors to lure customers away by selling for less. The marketplace ecosystem, free from the aggression of licensing laws, protected the consumer from being overcharged. Rockefeller tried to organize pendent oil refiners to keep the price of oil high[9] in much the same way that Southern landowners had colluded to pay slave wages to blacks after the Civil War. Just as some land-owners found they could profit by paying their workers a little more than anyone else, refiners who lowered their prices were able to attract more business. Without the help of govern-ment enforcement to make the oil refiners cooperate, Rockefeller found that the market-place ecosystem, when free from aggression, regulated his attempts to exploit his custom-ers.

Having failed to fix prices, Rockefeller tried to buy out his competitors. Since he did not have the help of government to *force* them to sell, he had to make them an offer they would not refuse.

Encouraged by Rockefeller's story of rags to riches, young hopefuls tried to gain part of the giant's market share by offering to take less profit so customers would be attracted by their lower prices. Naturally, many consumers were willing to take a chance on a new refiner that offered them a better deal than Standard Oil would.

Barely four years after attaining 90% of the market, Standard Oil's competitors had dou-bled their volume.[8] In 1884, almost 100 refin-eries were processing 23% of the crude.[10] Com-petition also began to stiffen on the interna-tional front. In 1882, Standard refined 85% of the world's oil; by 1888, Russian oil had cut Standard's world market share to 53%.[11]

In the early 1900s, natural gas also began to be used as a substitute for kerosene.[12] Without the aggression of licensing laws to prevent competition and innovation, Rocke-feller could keep his monopoly only as long as he served consumers better than anyone else. Obviously, few companies can accomplish this feat for extended periods of time.

Of course, being large gave Rockefeller certain advantages. The railroads gave Rocke-feller special shipping rates because of the volume and steadiness of his business. Although his competitors objected, the railroads offered the same discounts to any other firm who could give them as much business.[13] No other companies could match the volume of Standard or get the discount.

Price wars to undersell competitors were also easier for the industry giant. They were not entirely successful, however. Rockefeller stopped letting the public know when he acquired an independent firm, since some consumers had begun to shun Standard Oil because they did not wish to further the mammoth's influence.[14]

Without permission from the American citizenry to use law enforcement agents to stop his competitors—at gunpoint, if necessary—Rockefeller was unable to maintain his monopoly—even if he practiced deception. By 1911, Standard refined only 64% of the available petroleum in contrast to the 90% it refined 32 years earlier. The competition included Gulf, Texaco, Union, Pure, and Shell.[15] More and more consumers turned to natural gas and electricity. The marketplace ecosystem, free from the aggression of licensing laws, ensured that Rockefeller could keep his monopoly only as long as he could serve consumers best. Like other natural ecosystems, the marketplace ecosystem is *self*-regulating.

The antitrust conviction in 1911 against Standard Oil, paid for with our tax dollars, was rather redundant. Consumers had already chosen to give a large share of their business to other firms with new technologies, possibly in response to Rockefeller's own unsavory tactics.

...economists have long known that business (that is, non-governmental) monopolies are short-lived.
—Peter Drucker
INNOVATION AND
ENTREPRENEURSHIP

As Rockefeller's monopoly rose and fell, Bell Telephone, which eventually evolved into AT&T, learned a lesson from Standard Oil. Instead of trying to serve consumers best, Bell asked American consumers to use aggression against its competitors.

Before 1894, Bell Telephone's patents protected it from competition by other firms.

Its growth averaged 16% per year; annual profits approached 40% of its capital.[16] Bell catered primarily to the business sector and the wealthy. When the patents expired, other companies began providing affordable telephone service to the middle class and rural areas.[17] The independents charged less since customers could call only those serviced by the same company. Consumers were evidently pleased to make such a tradeoff; by 1907, some 20,000 independents controlled half of all the new telephone installations. The number of phones zoomed from 266,000 in 1893 to 6.1 million in 1907. The independents matched Bell's monopoly market share in 14 short years.[16,18]

Competition from the independents had caused annual Bell profits to plummet from 40% to 8%[16] as many consumers chose the independents who served them best. The marketplace ecosystem was again protecting consumers from monopoly profits.

As telephones went from a curiosity to a standard household utility, the independents began developing a plan for sharing each other's lines to avoid duplication and to increase the number of phones each customer could call.[19] The marketplace ecosystem was again working to promote cooperation for the benefit of the consumer, without aggression. Service providers voluntarily sought to give the customer better service because they would, in turn, be rewarded by more business and the positive feedback of profit.

AGGRESSION DISRUPTS THE MARKETPLACE ECOSYSTEM
The Big Get Bigger

Theodore Vail, Bell's new chairman, was determined to regain a monopoly market. He asked Americans to use the aggression of exclusive licensing against the independents that had served them so well. He claimed that competition caused duplication and penalized the customer (i.e., telephone service was a

It has been in periods of untidy, tumultuous competition that products have been democratized and have gone through their most rapid rate of growth and innovation.
—Peter Samuel
UNNATURAL
MONOPOLIES

Firms receive their income, in the final analysis, from serving consumers. The more efficiently and ably the firms anticipate and serve consumer demand, the greater their profits; the less ably, the less their profits....
—Murray Rothbard
Professor of
Economics,
University of Nevada

"natural" monopoly).[19] Had this been true, the independents would never have been able to lure customers from the established Bell monopoly in the first place!

If our neighbor George asked us to stop—at gunpoint, if necessary—everyone other than himself who tried to provide services to willing customers, we'd probably be very suspicious of his motives. Nevertheless, by 1910, Americans were lulled into a false sense of security when Bell made a similar proposal. The government of each local community would allow only one telephone company to operate in that region. Other companies would be stopped—at gunpoint, if necessary—from providing service to willing customers. Since Bell was the largest single company, it was in the best position to lobby the state utility commissions effectively and was almost always chosen over the independents.

Consumer Exploitation

How were consumers to be protected from predatory pricing by the new AT&T monopoly? The licensing law allowed the company to charge enough to cover all costs and to generate a fixed profit. With costs and profits guaranteed, AT&T paid top dollar for its research staff, who then developed patents in radio, television, movies, and electronics. AT&T had little incentive to innovate in the telephone market, since technology that would lower costs to customers generated no new profit for the company. Consumers paid for research that allowed AT&T an edge in other industries where its competitors did not have a monopoly enforced at gunpoint.[20]

During the depression of the 1930s, AT&T stock continued to pay handsome dividends.[21] If subscribers didn't like subsidizing AT&T's new ventures and investor portfolios, they were not free to choose another telephone company whose prices didn't reflect such extras. People could protest only by not having phone service. Evidently, many people elected

The dominant fact of American political life at the beginning of this century was that big business led the struggle for the federal regulation of the economy.
—Gabriel Kolko
THE TRIUMPH OF CONSERVATISM

to do just that. From 1914 to 1934, annual growth rate slowed to less than 5% compared to 27% between 1894 and 1907 when the marketplace ecosystem was less dominated by aggression.[22] Since there was only one phone per ten people, this lower growth rate probably reflected consumer choice, rather than market saturation.[23]

Our aggression cost more than excessive charges for phone service. As the wealth of AT&T increased and its research had an impact on other industries, the Justice Department brought antitrust suits with our tax dollars to keep AT&T out of radio, television, and movies.[24] In addition to paying higher prices, Americans paid taxes to regulate the monopoly (estimated costs of $1.1 billion per year).[25] In the marketplace ecosystem free from aggression, none of these expenses would be necessary.

In 1984, an antitrust suit, paid for with our tax dollars, eliminated AT&T's 75-year monopoly in long-distance service. As new long-distance companies served the consumer better for less, rates plummeted 30% over the next five years.[26] The marketplace ecosystem protected consumers well when aggression was outlawed. However, the cost of local service, still monopolized by exclusive licensing, went up 50% during the same period![27] Seven of the "Baby Bells," which were split off from AT&T by the antitrust ruling, earned 25% more than the top 1,000 U.S. firms in 1987.[28] Why? Local phone companies were allowed to charge extra fees as compensation for loss of AT&T's long distance monopoly![28] Not only do we pay higher prices to the local phone monopoly, we also pay for its regulation, for antitrust suits to break it up, and compensation for no longer getting monopoly status! Is this consumer protection?

Although other companies cannot sell local phone service, they are allowed to bypass AT&T's network by using their own phone lines, microwave routing, or satellite systems.

Monopoly favors the rich (on the whole) just as competition (on the whole) favors the poor.
—George Watson
Journal of Economic Affairs

By the late 1980s, more business phones were serviced through private exchanges than by conventional phone lines.[29] Businesses find these systems more economical, suggesting that once again the consumer is being over-charged by the local telephone monopoly. Even the Federal Communications Commission, the government agency in charge of regulating AT&T, bypasses the local phone network![30] What a shame that the aggression of licensing laws keeps the average consumer from taking advantage of the cost savings of these innova-tive technologies!

The telephone industry is just one example of a natural monopoly that is not so natural after all. If an industry profits by being large, smaller companies will find it in their best interest to merge or cooperate with each other as the independent telephone companies did. The aggression of monopoly licensing is nei-ther necessary nor desirable. When consumers are not allowed to vote with their dollars for the service provider that pleases them the most, customer-pleasing goes down and costs go up. The regulator of the marketplace eco-system, the consumer, is bypassed.

Even when we lower the guns of govern-ment just enough to permit one other choice of service provider, the consumer is empowered. Quality service costs less. For example, in the few cities that license two power companies instead of one, prices are lower than regions where only one company is permitted to pro-vide service.[31] Unfortunately, higher costs are only a small part of the price we pay for our aggression.

Aggression's Environmental Impact

Phone books and newspapers are a large part of the 40-50% of waste paper in land-fills.[32] The French are well on their way to eliminating this refuse through videotext, an electronic phone directory and newspaper delivered through the phone line.[33] AT&T would like to make this service available to

Americans, but it has been stopped from entering the information services area for the same reason it was prevented from engaging in TV and radio—as a legal monopoly it enjoys an unfair advantage over independent service providers. In trying to control others, AT&T now finds itself controlled!

Monopoly-by-aggression has contributed greatly to our dependence on fossil fuels. In the early 1900s, for example, several paper companies used cogeneration to produce cheap electricity from steam. These efficient producers were told they would be stopped—at gunpoint, if necessary—from selling their electricity because of the monopoly licensing bestowed on public utilities.[34] Small plants using alternative energy sources were also banned.

Centralized energy production was best accomplished by fossil fuels. Utilities had no incentive to conserve on fuel or develop alternative energy methods because their profit was determined by politicians, not by the consumers they served.

THE EASY WAY OUT

Fortunately, the financial and ecological costs of monopolies maintained by aggression are so obvious and devastating that they are beginning to be dismantled. For example, in 1978, Congress decided that the utilities' monopoly in *generation* of electricity would end, even though the monopoly in *distribution* would continue. Public utilities must now buy electricity at favorable rates from power plants that rely on renewable sources such as wind, water, or cogeneration from steam. Small local power plants are springing up that run on fuel as diverse as cow dung and old tires![35] Before this time, if you had wanted to put up a windmill and sell your extra electricity to George and other neighbors, you would have been stopped—at gunpoint, if necessary—to protect the "natural" utility monopoly. In some locales, you can now sell your extra electricity, but only to the company that has the local monopoly. Even rejecting some of the aggression that we've supported in the past can make a significant impact on our energy dependence. As we reverse the aggression of licensing laws further (i.e., deregulate), we'll enjoy the benefits of honoring our neighbor's choice.

Adding that Second Layer of aggression carries some hefty costs in terms of selection, cost, and environmental quality. As we'll see in the next chapter, however, adding Third Layer aggression makes Second Layer environmental insults look like tender loving care!

CHAPTER 8

DESTROYING THE ENVIRONMENT

We are more likely to protect the environment when we own a piece of it and profit by nurturing it.

In earlier chapters, we learned how First Layer aggression of licensing laws allowed the FDA and AMA to dictate our health care options and increase their cost. The previous chapter showed us how Second Layer aggression, *exclusive* licensing, creates monopolies that overcharge us and promote our dependence on fossil fuels. With the addition of the Third Layer, however, we are forced—at gunpoint if necessary—to *subsidize* the monopoly service—even if we choose not to use it! Most often, the subsidized monopoly service is provided by a government agency or department. This transfer to the public sector has its own hidden costs—including large-scale environmental destruction.

INCREASING COSTS

Public services on the average cost *twice* as much as the same service provided by the private sector.[1] Bureaucrats have little incentive for efficiency when consumers must pay for the service, whether they use it or not. The proof of this inefficiency is the enormous savings enjoyed when public services are contracted out to private firms instead of being performed by government employees. California cities save between 37% and 96% by contracting out their street cleaning, janitorial services, trash collection, traffic signal repairs, grass cutting, and street maintenance/overlay construction.[2] Private municipal transit service saves taxpayers 30–50%.[3] Savings have also been realized in various locales by contracting out fire protection,[4] emergency ambulance service,[5] building or operation of water and

If we can prevent the Government from wasting the labors of the people under the pretense of caring for them, they will be happy.

—Thomas Jefferson
author of the
Declaration of
Independence

sewage treatment plants,[6] and solid waste recycling.[7] The monopoly services are still subsidized, but to a lesser extent.

ENCOURAGING WASTE

Whenever people do not pay the full costs for something they use, they have much less incentive to conserve. For example, when people pay the same amount of taxes for solid waste disposal whether they recycle or not, fewer people are inclined to conserve. As a consequence, more waste is generated and disposal problems increase.

Forces which impede innovation in a public service institution are inherent in it, integral to it, and inseparable from it.
—Peter Drucker
INNOVATION AND
ENTREPRENEURSHIP

Conversely, when subsidies decrease, conservation automatically follows. In Seattle, during the first year that customers were charged by the volume of trash they generated, 67% chose to become involved in the local recycling program.[8] Since about 18% of our yearly trash consists of leaves, grass, and other yard products,[9] composting coupled with recycling can dramatically lower a person's disposal bill. As less waste is generated, fewer resources are needed to dispose of it. What could be more natural?

DISCOURAGING CONSERVATION

Ownership and distribution of water is most often a government monopoly subsidized by our tax dollars. In California's San Joaquin Valley, 4.5 million acres of once–desert farmland is irrigated by subsidized water. Our tax dollars, taken—at gunpoint, if necessary— were used to construct dams for irrigators, pay many of their delivery costs, and support zero–interest loans so that farmers pay only about 10% of the water's market value![10] These subsidies encourage wasteful over–irrigation, resulting in soil erosion, salt build–up, and toxic levels of selenium in the run–off. Kesterson Wildlife Reservoir has been virtually destroyed by irrigation–induced selenium build–up, which now threatens San Francisco Bay as well.[11]

As long as our tax dollars subsidize the irrigators, however, they have little financial incentive to instill drip sprinkler systems or other conservation devices. As a result, less water is available for other uses, so prices increase for everyone else. Without subsidies, irrigators would be motivated to conserve water, which is desperately needed in California's coastal cities for domestic use.

DESTROYING THE ENVIRONMENT

The above examples of Third Layer aggression deal with exclusive monopolies where service is provided by a public works department, subsidized in whole or in part by taxes. Strictly speaking, the grazing rights, timber sales, and park operations by governmental units are not exclusive monopolies. No one is stopped at gunpoint from creating wealth by providing these same services to willing customers. Rather than exclusive licensing, another form of aggression—forcible prevention of homesteading—made the U.S. government the largest single provider of such services. In addition, these services are subsidized by tax dollars, making them similar to the other examples in this chapter.

Homesteading is a time-honored way of creating wealth. An individual or group improves previously unused land by clearing it for agriculture, fencing it for grazing, making paths for hikers, building a home, etc. To own the wealth they have created, the creators lay claim to the property on which it resides.

Much of our country was settled this way. On 42% of U.S. territory, however, the government prevented the creation of wealth through homesteading—at gunpoint, if necessary, by making these lands "public."[12] Such widespread aggression has an impact similar to the exclusive licensing characteristic of the Second Layer of the Pyramid of Power. Adding subsidies through the aggression of taxation gives public holdings of range land, forests, and parks many of the characteristics of Third Layer aggression.

If the guns of government were used *only* to prevent homesteading (Second Layer), the lands would simply be left in their natural state. Some wealth would be consumed protecting the lands from squatters, just as would happen with individual homesteaders. However, the land could not be used constructively or sustainably to create new wealth. No trees would be harvested for wood. No cattle would be raised for food.

Sometimes we equate wealth creation on rangelands and in forests with their ultimate destruction. These natural ecosystems, however, are renewable and sustainable if they are properly cared for. Individual homesteaders or owners have incentive to do just that, because they will profit most if the creation of wealth is able to continue year after year. An individual who wishes to leave wealth to children and grandchildren is more likely to care whether the property continues to be fruitful.

Overgrazing the Range

The incentives are very different for the congressional representatives who oversee the Bureau of Land Management. To appreciate their perspective, we should listen in on an imaginary conversation between a congressman and some of his constituents.

"Mr. Congressman, we represent the ranchers in your district. Things are pretty tough for us right now, but you can help us. Let us graze cattle on all that vacant rangeland the government has in this area. We'll be properly grateful when it comes time to contribute to your campaign. As a token of our good will, we'd like to hire your out-of-work daughter as the assistant manager of our association."

The congressman has twinges of conscience. He knows that the ranchers will overstock the government lands, even though they carefully control the number of cattle on their own. Since they can't be sure of having the same public range every year, however, they cannot profit by taking care of it. They cannot pass it on to their children. They profit most by letting their cattle eat every last blade of grass. When he shares his concern with the ranchers, they reply:

"Mr. Congressman, we will pay a small fee for 'renting' the land. Renters don't take as good care of property as owners do, it's true, but the land is just sitting there helping no one. All those people who want to save the land for the next generation must not have the problems we do just keeping food on the table so there will be a next generation. *Your* next generation benefits most if you allow us to give her a job and you keep yours. If you don't help us, sir, neither of you will have a job. We'll find someone to run against you who knows how to take care of the people he or she represents. We'll make sure that you're defeated."

The congressman sighs and gives in. After all, the ranchers gain immensely if allowed to graze cattle on the land he controls. They have every incentive to make good their threats and their promises. The people who might prefer to let the land simply remain *au naturale* do not benefit financially from doing so. While the ranchers will share the money they make from the rangeland with the congressman, no profit is generated by maintaining the status quo. If anyone objects, the congressman and the ranchers can use the money generated from the range to finance its own destruction.

The congressman tries to get a coalition of his colleagues together to encourage changes in the way the Bureau of Land Management (BLM) operates. He finds that some of *their* constituents have similar desires for the construction of a dam, access to timberland, etc. He agrees to help them change the policies that control resources in their area in return for their agreement to help him with the Bureau of Land Management, which controls an area almost twice the size of Texas,

The most entrepreneurial, the most innovative people behave like the worst time serving bureaucrats or power hungry politicians 6 months after they have taken over the management of a public service institution, particularly if it is a government agency. Forces which impede innovation in a public service institution are inherent in it, integral to it, and inseparable from it.

—Peter Drucker
INNOVATION AND
ENTREPRENEURSHIP

including nearly all of Alaska and Nevada.[13] Naturally, these changes set precedents for *all* the resources controlled by the BLM, not just the ones in this congressman's district.

Because of these skewed incentives, almost half of these lands are rented out to ranchers for grazing cattle at one-fifth to one-tenth the rate of private grazing land.[14] By 1964, three million additional acres had been cleared by "chaining"[15] to create more rentable rangeland. Because the ranchers and their representatives cannot profit by protecting the land, they have little incentive to do so. As early as 1925, studies demonstrated the inevitable result: on overgrazed public ranges, cattle were twice as likely to die and had half as many calves as animals raised on private lands.[16]

Are the ranchers and their representatives selfish others whom we should condemn? Not at all! Had ranchers been permitted to homestead these lands in the first place, the rangeland would now be receiving the better care characteristic of private grazing. Our consent to aggression has taken the profit out of caring for the environment. When this aggression is even partially removed, the situation improves.

What is common to many is least taken care of, for all men have greater regard for what is their own than what they possess in common with others.
—Aristotle

For example, in 1934, Congress passed the Taylor Grazing Act to encourage ranchers to care for the public grazing land by allowing them ten-year transferable leases.[17] Essentially, ranchers were allowed to homestead or own the land for ten years. Ranchers who cared for the land were given the positive feedback of good grazing or a good price when selling their lease. As a result, almost half of the rangeland classified as poor was upgraded.[17] However, in 1966, leases were reduced to only one year, giving ranchers less incentive to make improvements. As a result, private investment in wells and fences in the early 1970s dropped to less than a third of their 1960s level.[18]

Logging the Forests

As subsidies increase, so does the environmental destruction. Most of the trees in our national forests wouldn't be logged without subsidies, because the cost of building the roads necessary to transport the timber exceeds the value of the lumber. Once again, however, the special interests found a way to use the aggression of subsidy to their own advantage. Let's listen to an imaginary conversation between the timber companies and their congresswoman.

"Ms. Congresswoman, the U.S. Forest Service has money in its budget for hiking trails. Now we're all for hiking; we just think we should get our fair share of the forest and our fair share of the subsidy. Some of that money for trails should be used to build logging roads. Consumers will benefit by increases in the supply of timber. We'd profit too and see that you got your 'fair share' for your campaign chest. We'd pay some money for replanting too, so the environmentalists will be happy."

The Congresswoman considers their offer. She knows that the loggers, like the ranchers, have little incentive to log sustainably on public lands. She also knows that if the hikers complain, she can ask for a larger subsidy for the U.S. Forest Service. Some of that subsidy can be channeled to more logging roads and more campaign contributions. If anyone objects, the profit from the forests can be used to lobby for their own destruction.

Special interests reap high profits with subsidies, so it is worth their while to spend large sums of money to protect them. If the congresswoman doesn't agree to the timber companies' demands, they'll put their considerable money and influence behind her opponent. The timber companies will be able to log the forests. The only question is which congressional representative will reap a share of the profits. The congresswoman sighs and agrees to fight for more logging subsides.

As a result, the U.S. Forest Service, which has custody of forest and rangeland covering an area larger than Texas, uses our tax dollars to log the national forests. By 1985, almost 350,000 miles of logging roads had been constructed in the national forests—eight times more than the total mileage of the U.S. Interstate Highway System![19] Construction of roads requires stripping the mountainous terrain of its vegetation, causing massive erosion. In the northern Rockies, trout and salmon streams are threatened by the resulting silt. Wildlife and fragile ecosystems are disturbed.[20]

The Forest Service typically receives 20 cents for every dollar spent on roads, logging, and timber management.[21] Even though the timber companies are charged for the cost of reforestation, 50% of these funds go for "overhead."[22]

While logging vehicles are encouraged, hikers are discouraged. Even though the number of backpackers increased more than ten times between the 1940s and the 1980s, trails in the national forests dropped from 144,000 miles to under 100,000.[23]

Should we blame the timber companies and their congressional representatives for this travesty? Hardly! After all, if we sanction aggression to prevent homesteading, we take the profit out of protecting the forest. The nation's largest private landowner, International Paper, carefully balances backpacking and other forest recreation with logging. In the Southeast, 25% of its profit is from recreational use.[24] When we honor the choices of others, they profit from honoring ours.

Slaughtering Wildlife

Unfortunately, vour tax subsidies have also been responsible for the extermination of wildlife, sometimes to the point of near extinction. While state governments were encouraging the shooting of hawks (Pennsylvania paid hunters a bounty), Mrs. Rosalie Edge began a sanctuary for them with voluntary contributions. She bought what is now known as Hawk Mountain, an eastern Pennsylvania area of the Appalachians that was ideally suited to bird watching. Before she established the Hawk Mountain Sanctuary in 1934, sportsmen had used it to shoot the magnificent birds.[25]

In 1927, the owner of Sea Lion Caves, Inc., the only known mainland breeding and wintering area of the Stellar sea lion,[26] opened it to visitors as a naturalist attraction. Meanwhile, Oregon's tax dollars went to bounty hunters who were paid to shoot sea lions. The owners of Sea Lion Caves spent much of their time chasing the hunters off their property. While the owners of Sea Lion Caves and Hawk Mountain Sanctuary were protecting the wildlife that inhabited their land, they were also forced—at gunpoint, if necessary—to pay the taxes that rewarded hunters who endangered it!

Not everyone in a group wants resources treated in the same way. When all people treat their property as they think best, one owner's careless decision is unlikely to threaten the entire ecosystem. When bureaucrats control vast areas, however, one mistake can mean ecological disaster. In addition, special interest groups struggle for control.

For example, Yellowstone, the crown jewel of the national park system, has been torn apart by conflicts of interest. In 1915, the Park Service decided to eradicate the Yellowstone wolves, which were deemed to be a menace to the elk, deer, antelope, and mountain sheep that visitors liked to see.[27] Park employees were permitted to keep or sell hides from wolves they had trapped as an inducement to hunt them. Eventually, the fox, lynx, marten, and fisher were added to the list.[28] Without predators, the hoofed mammals flourished and began to compete with each other for food. The larger elk eventually drove out the white–tailed deer, the mule deer, the bighorn sheep, and the pronghorn. As their numbers increased, the elk ate the willow and aspen around the river banks and trampled the area so that seedlings could not regenerate. Without the willow and aspen, the beaver population dwindled. Without the beavers and the ponds they created, water fowl, mink, and otter were threatened. The clear water needed by the trout disappeared along with the beaver dams. Without the ponds, the water table was lowered, decreasing the vegetation growth required to sustain many other species. When they realized their mistake, the Park officials began removing the elk (58,000 between 1935 and 1961).[29]

Meanwhile, the elk overgrazed, greatly reducing the shrubs and berries that fed the bear population. In addition, the destruction of willow and aspen destroyed the grizzly habitat, while road construction and beaver loss reduced the trout population on which the grizzlies fed. When the garbage dumps were closed in the 1960s to encourage the bears to feed naturally, there was little left for them to eat. They began seeking out park visitors who brought food with them. Yellowstone management began a program to remove the problem bears as well. In the early 1970s, more than 100 bears were removed. Almost twice as many grizzlies were killed.[30]

Subsidies create tension between special interests with different views. Yellowstone visitors wanted to see deer and elk. Some naturalists would have preferred not to disturb the ecosystem, even if it meant limiting visitors and disappointing some of them. Since everyone is forced—at gunpoint, if necessary—to subsidize the park, each person tries to impose his or her view as to how it should be run. The resulting compromise pleases no one.

Contributors to private conservation organizations, in contrast, choose to donate to

...government owner-ship has another kind of impact on society: it necessarily substitutes conflict for the harmo-ny of the free market.
—Murray Rothbard
POWER AND THE MARKET

a group that shares their common purpose. For example, at Pine Butte Preserve, the Nature Conservancy replanted overgrazed areas with chokecherry shrubs for the grizzlies and fenced off sensitive areas from cattle, deer, and elk, animals that thrive in the absence of predators.[31] The Nature Conservancy has preserved more than 2.4 million acres of land since 1951.[32]

The Audubon Society also uses ownership to protect the environment. The Rainey Wildlife Sanctuary is home to marshland deer, armadillo, muskrat, otter, mink and snow geese. Carefully managed natural gas wells and cattle herds create wealth without interfering with the native species.[33] Other private organizations investing in wilderness areas for their voluntary membership include Ducks Unlimited, National Wild Turkey Federation, Inc., National Wildlife Federation, Trout Unlimited, and Wings Over Wisconsin.

The story of Ravena Park illustrates how aggression compromises the care given to the environment. In 1887, a couple bought up the land on which the giant Douglas firs grew, added a pavilion for nature lectures, and made walking paths with benches and totems depicting Indian culture. Visitors were charged admission to support Ravena Park; up to 10,000 people came on the busiest days.

Some Seattle citizens weren't satisfied with this non-aggressive arrangement. They lobbied for the city to buy and operate the park with tax dollars taken at gunpoint. In 1911, the city took over the park, and one by one the giant fir trees began to disappear. Concerned citizens complained when they found that the trees were being cut into cordwood and sold. The superintendent, later charged with abuse of public funds, equipment, and personnel, told the citizens that the large "Roosevelt Tree" had posed a "threat to public safety." By 1925, all the giant fir trees were gone.[34] The superintendent could personally profit from the beautiful trees by selling them.

Power Corrupts

The above example illustrates why layering aggression upon aggression forms a Pyramid of *Power*. Licensing laws (Layer 1) give a group of professionals the *power* to limit our choices. Exclusive licensing (Layer 2) gives a single firm the monopoly *power*. Subsidizing (Layer 3) allows a tiny handful of bureaucrats the *power* to trade public assets for personal gain. Unlike the personal power that comes from wisdom, inner growth, and hard work, this power comes from the point of a gun. This power of aggression corrupts those who use it, impoverishes those who have little, and destroys the earth that supports us. We ask for these results when we vote for subsidies.

THE EASY WAY OUT

In earlier chapters, we saw that the aggression of exclusive licensing inhibited innovation, increased costs, and lowered the quality of service. Subsidies encourage inefficiency and waste as well.

Ironically, we often sanction the aggression of subsidized, exclusive, government-run monopolies because of the erroneous belief that they promote improved efficiency and prudent use of resources. Subsidies are sometimes tolerated in the equally mistaken belief that they allow the poor access to services they otherwise couldn't afford. The cost of aggression, however, is so great that the poor are harmed instead of helped.

For example, those too poor to own property pay no property taxes *directly*. Instead, they rent from property owners, who raise rents to compensate for tax increases. The municipal services that these taxes fund will cost considerably more than they would in the absence of aggression. The tax increases, therefore, are higher than the cost of the services would be. The poor end up paying higher rents to subsidize inefficiency and waste—even for services they do not use!

Socialist countries abound with exclusive, subsidized government-run monopolies. Not surprisingly, many are reacting to this new knowledge by privatizing subsidized government-run monopolies, including railways and highways, by selling them to individuals or corporations.[35] In New Zealand, the post office has been privatized. Without increasing rates, the private postal service was still able to maintain service to all addresses, increase on-time delivery of first-class mail from 84% to 99%, and transform an annual loss of $37 million to a profit of $76 million![36] Since this yearly $37 million loss was usually made up by the taxpayer, *real* postal rates actually went down as quality went up!

How can privatizing decrease costs so quickly? When provision of services is not restricted to a subsidized government agency, the profit motive spurs businesses to adopt the latest, most efficient technology possible. For example, instead of dumping refuse into landfills, waste disposal companies find ways of turning trash into cash. Recomp, Inc. (St. Cloud, Minnesota), and Agripost, Inc. (Miami, Florida), use composting whenever possible and sell the resulting loam to landscapers, Christmas-tree farms, and reclamation projects. Other projected uses for the nutrient-rich compost include topsoil replacement for the farms, rangelands, and forests[9] that have been devastated by Third Layer aggression.

Better quality at lower cost is only the beginning of the natural beauty of the market-place ecosystem, however. Private companies, unlike public ones, can offer ownership to employees through stock options. Government employees sometimes become owners of newly privatized firms. Surly employees whose jobs were guaranteed by subsidies are transformed overnight into dedicated workers whose profits depend on serving their customers efficiently and well. Saying "No!" to the aggression of subsidies reduces waste and encourages employees to take pride in their work, while benefiting the poor and the consumer.

Doing away with subsidies means doing away with the aggression of taxation that generates them. As aggression decreases, prosperity increases. Studies of the U.S. economy show that a measure of wealth creation, our Gross National Product (GNP), plunges when taxes increase.[37] The economic growth of individual states is also highly dependent on how heavy a burden of taxation they place on their populace.[38] We can hardly expect to prosper if we subsidize inefficiency and waste!

Privatization of public lands and waterways holds a special bonus for the American populace. Although its value is difficult to estimate, a substantial percentage of the national debt could likely be retired with the proceeds!

In 1989, 15% of our federal expenditures went to pay the interest on the national debt.[39] If the debt were repaid and the taxes lowered, tremendous economic growth would result.

Some people don't worry much about the national debt because they believe we simply "owe it to ourselves." In a way, that is true. The government I.O.U.s are held by individuals, corporations, and pension plans (including Social Security) throughout the land. For our pension plan to pay us, taxes will have to go up to pay off the I.O.U. We will have to pay more taxes so that our pension plan can pay us. The net result is that we may have no pension at all!

To understand how we came to such an impasse, we should look at the apex of the Pyramid of Power—the money monopoly.

CHAPTER 9

BANKING ON AGGRESSION

We established the "money monopoly" in the hopes of creating economic stability. By using aggression as our means, we created boom- and-bust cycles instead.

In the previous chapters, we've seen how the Pyramid of Power we've created controls us more with each layer of aggression. The First Layer of licensing laws stops us—at gunpoint, if necessary—from choosing whoever serves us best. The Second Layer, exclusive licensing, creates monopolies that exploit us. The Third Layer forces us to subsidize these monopolies, often to the detriment of the environment. The Fourth Layer then forces us to *use* the subsidized service.

One example of Fourth Layer aggression is the money monopoly. To understand why it is the apex of the Pyramid of Power, we must first understand how money works.

THE DIFFERENCE BETWEEN MONEY AND WEALTH

Earlier we learned that wealth consists of goods and services, not money. Money is a claim check on the goods and services that constitute wealth. The more money people have, the larger a percentage of the goods and services they are able to claim or buy for themselves. Historically, gold and silver were commonly used as money because they could easily and accurately be coined or weighed. Moreover, in societies where precious metals were made into jewelry or used industrially, gold and silver were goods as well. They constituted a form of wealth as well as money.

As people prospered, carrying their metallic money or protecting it against theft became burdensome. People began to deposit their gold and silver with bankers equipped to guard it well. Some bankers simply charged a fee for this service. Others found that if they could loan part of the gold to someone else, interest could be collected and shared between the bank and the depositor.

The banker gave the depositor a promissory note, which was a promise to return the gold to the depositor whenever the note was returned to the bank. A bank with many customers could usually count on being able to make this promise good, because it was unlikely that everyone would want to withdraw his or her money at the same time. In the interim, the depositor could exchange the promissory note for goods and services as if it were gold. Thus, these notes began to function as money or claim checks for the available goods and services. Our U.S. dollars were once promissory notes of this type, which were redeemable in the gold and silver that people had stored with their local banker.

THE CAUSE OF INFLATION AND DEFLATION

Since people did not want their gold and silver all at the same time, banks kept a fraction of the precious metal on reserve and loaned the rest. In doing so, they created money. Today's banks can create money the same way, although they have other methods at their disposal as well.

For example, assume that your bank needs to put 20% of its funds on reserve to operate optimally. You deposit $100 in your favorite bank; the bank puts $20 into reserve and loans out the other $80. The person who borrowed the $80 deposits it in his or her checking account. That person's bankbook says he or she has $80. Yours says you have $100. Together, the two of you have $180 in the bank. But wait! Only $100 is there to begin with! The bank has created the $80 it lends out!

The process continues. The bank then puts 20% of the newly deposited $80 (i.e., $16) in reserve and lends out the remaining $64, which is then redeposited and goes through the same process. When the reserve is 20%, the $100 eventually becomes $500. The lower the reserve requirement, the more money is created. For example, when the required reserve is 10%, every deposit is multiplied by 10 instead of 5. How amazed I was when my father, a bank manager and economics teacher, first explained this process to me!

Creating this extra money can cause price inflation when there is no compensating increase in goods and services. In the board game Monopoly®, each player starts out with $1,500 and struggles around the board several times before being able to acquire enough property and enough money to build houses and hotels. If players each had $7,500 at the start instead, the houses and hotels could be built much earlier in the game. A boom in building would result. When the starting money was only $1,500, players might sell some properties to other players to get enough money to build their hotels and houses on the remaining ones. When starting with $7,500, property owners might not need to raise the cash. Players without property would probably have to pay owners more in order to entice them to sell. Real estate prices would rise with inflation in Monopoly just as they do in the real world.

On the other hand, price deflation can occur when the money supply decreases without a compensating loss in goods and services that people want. Banks can cause deflation by increasing their reserves, keeping money out of circulation instead of lending and creating it. In our Monopoly example, deflation would be simulated by everyone returning a percentage of his or her cash to the bank.

Now players are much more likely to be caught short when their mortgages or rent comes due. If players try to sell their properties, they find others with less money to buy them. Real estate prices fall, just as they do in the real world.

THE RICH GET RICHER

In real life, the inflation and deflation caused by changes in the money supply don't affect everyone equally, as in our example above. When the bank creates new money, it increases its claim checks on wealth relative to everyone else. The bank is like a Monopoly player who gets more money than the other players to start with. If you and another player were bidding on the same property at auction, and the other player's pile of cash increased while yours stayed the same, the other player would likely top your best bid and get the property.

When the other player is sure to outbid you with new money, the auctioned property will probably sell for a slightly higher price than it otherwise would have. The sellers would thereby acquire some of the newly created money. As they spend that extra money, by outbidding other players for property, it slowly diffuses into other hands by increasing each seller's profit. Several turns may pass before some players get access to the new money. Those who have no property may never get part of the new money. They are worse off relative to the other players than they would have been if no new money had been created at all!

In real life, the banks that create money use it first. Those wealthy enough to put up collateral can borrow the money and use it next. Since governments are the biggest borrowers, they benefit at the expense of those who have little property and savings. As we've seen, government officials tend to support special interests with the wealth they control. Deficit spending, which occurs when the government needs to borrow, is really a redistribution of wealth from the poor to the rich.

By a continuous process of inflation, governments can confiscate, secretly and unobserved, an important part of the wealth of their citizens....The process engages all the hidden forces of economic law on the side of destruction, and does it in a manner which not one man in a million is able to diagnose.
—John Maynard Keynes
English economist and board member of the Bank of England

THE POOR GET POORER

The longer Monopoly players wait for a share of the new money, the worse off they are. In real life, prices rise before wages do, as more money is created. People who do not get the new money at all (those on a fixed income without savings or property) must contend with rising prices without an increase in income.

Those who get the new money last are worse off than if there had been no inflation at all. Inflation through new money creation *artificially* increases the claim checks on goods and services for the wealthy, but not for the poor. This redistributing of wealth to the banks and the well-to-do by increasing the claim checks (money) that these groups have is frequently referred to as the *inflation tax*.

The U.S. banking system alternates inflation with deflation. Without alternating the cycles, inflation would run rampant, as it has in several Latin American countries. In nations that inflate rapidly, getting the new money even a few hours later than someone else makes a person very much worse off. That is why workers in such countries rush to buy goods and services as soon as they receive their paycheck!

Alternating inflation and deflation creates other problems. When the rate of new money creation slows, people and businesses cannot borrow as readily as before. Consumers cannot buy goods; businesses must cut back production; workers get paid less or are laid off. Those who have little savings find themselves unable to make their mortgage payments. As a result, banks repossess many more homes in times of deflation.

The same people who were hurt by inflation usually find themselves crippled by deflation as well. People without property and without savings suffer the most. Alternating inflation and deflation bankrupts those living on the edge. Creditors repossess the homes and belongings of these unfortunates. The rich get richer and the poor get poorer.

THE MARKETPLACE ECOSYSTEM PROTECTS THE CONSUMER

Luckily, the marketplace ecosystem regulates banks in the absence of aggression so that the destructive boom–bust cycles are minimized. The banking system in Scotland between 1793 and 1845, for example, was almost entirely free from aggression.[1] Each bank issued its own notes, promising to return depositors' gold on demand. In other words, each bank issued its own money.

This could be a very confusing situation unless every bank and service vendor accepted each note at face value. In Scotland, everyone did so because banks had to make good on their promises. If a bank ran out of reserves, its owners (stockholders) had to pay the depositors out of their own pockets. Each bank was thus highly motivated to limit the amount of new money it created to what was truly needed. Limiting inflation attenuated deflation as well. In the marketplace ecosystem free from aggression, the poor would be protected from the devastating effects of alternating these two policies.

Occasionally, a bank would foolishly print so many notes that it could not meet depositors' demands. If the stockholders of a failing bank were unlikely to be able to pay off their debts, sound banks sometimes did so to retain the confidence of the Scottish people and gain grateful new customers. Scottish prosperity was attributed in part to the efficient banking system that evolved in the marketplace ecosystem free from aggression.

Across the border, the English depositors did not fare so well. In 1841, total losses to Scottish depositors over the preceding 48 years were estimated at 32,000 pounds, while public losses in London were twice that amount for the previous year alone![2] Although records do not allow a precise correction for differences in population and per capita deposits, English citizens appeared to be exposed to 24 times more risk than the Scots.[3] The English were at the mercy of the central bank, an exclusive monopoly–by–aggression. Unfortunately, we are too!

AGGRESSION DISRUPTS THE MARKET-PLACE ECOSYSTEM

In 1914, the Federal Reserve (Fed) received an exclusive monopoly to issue U.S. currency. Like AT&T, the Fed is a private corporation, owned by its member banks. The Fed is a powerful institution; some believe it is the most powerful in the world. Let's find out why.

Before the creation of the Fed, banks found they needed reserves of approximately 21% so that they would have enough money on hand when their customers wanted to make a withdrawal. When the Fed took over the reserves of the national banks, it lowered the reserve requirement to half that.[4] The Fed itself used a reserve system: it kept only 35% of the reserves entrusted to it by the member banks![5] The balance was loaned out, mostly to the government, with the wealth of the American people as collateral.

Lowering reserves resulted in the creation of more money. As a result, the money supply doubled between 1914 and 1920[6] and once again from 1921 to 1929.[7] In contrast, gold in the reserve vault increased only 3% in the 1920s.[8] The bankers would obviously be unable to keep their promise to deliver gold to depositors if a large number of people withdrew their money at the same time.

Businesses could not use all the newly created money the banks wished to loan, so stock speculators were encouraged to borrow.[9] Many people got heavily into debt, thinking that the boom would continue.

In 1929, the Fed started deflation by slowing the creation of new money.[10] People who had counted on renewing their loans to

When the President signs this bill, the invisible government of the Monetary Power will be legalized....
—Congressman Charles A. Lindbergh 1913, referring to the Federal Reserve Act

Depressions and mass unemployment are not caused by the free market but by government interference in the economy.
—Ludwig von Mises
THE THEORY OF MONEY AND CREDIT

cover stock speculations or other investments found they could no longer borrow. They were forced to sell their securities, and a stock market plunge ensued. The mini-crash in October 1987 also may have been triggered by the Fed's slowing the creation of new money.[11]

People who lost money spent less on goods and services; business began to slow. With banks unwilling to renew loans,[12] businesses began to reduce their work force. People nervously began withdrawing their gold deposits as banks in other countries quit honoring their promise to return the gold. Rumors circulated that the Federal Reserve would soon be bankrupt as well.[13] Naturally, there was no way for the banks to exchange the inflated dollars for gold.

As people withdraw their bank funds, the money supply decreases—just the reverse of what happens when they deposit it. The banks' failure to loan coupled with massive withdrawals, caused even greater deflation. People lost their savings and their purchasing power; in turn, businesses lost their customers and laid off workers. Each loss contributed to the next, resulting in the most severe depression Americans had ever known.

Had this happened in Scotland between 1793 and 1845, bank owners (stockholders) would have to make their promises good by digging into their own pockets. In our country, however, the government enforcement agents were instructed to come after the American citizenry instead! Franklin Roosevelt convinced Congress to pass a bill making it illegal for Americans to own gold.[14] Everyone had to exchange their valuable gold for Federal Reserve notes, which had no intrinsic value. Gold was still given to foreigners who brought their dollars to be exchanged for gold, but not to Americans!

While U.S. banks failed in the early 1930s and Americans were shorn of their gold, no Canadian banks failed. Between 1921 and 1929, American depositors lost an estimated

If the American people ever allow banks to control the issuance of their currency, first by inflation, then by deflation, the corporation that will grow up around them will deprive the people of all of their property until their children will wake up homeless on the continent their forefathers conquered.
—Thomas Jefferson author of the Declaration of Independence

This great government, strong in gold, is breaking its promises to pay gold to widows and orphans....It's dishonor, sir.
—Senator Carter Glass 1933, principal author of the Federal Reserve Act

$565 million, while Canadian losses were less than 3% of that.[15] Canada enjoyed a banking system similar to the one described earlier for Scotland—few licensing laws and no central bank with an exclusive monopoly on currency issue.[16] Each bank issued its own notes and protected itself and the public by refusing to loan to inflating banks. Just as in Scotland, the stockholders of the banks were obligated to make good the inflated currency. Unfortunately for Canada, the aggression of licensing laws was instituted in 1935.[17]

Why did the Canadians switch from a system that protected them from bankruptcy? Why did England eventually impose its inferior system on Scotland? Why was the Fed introduced in the United States and relieved of its promise to return gold that was deposited by our great-grandparents and their contemporaries? Why did the Fed slow money creation in 1929, precipitating the stock market crash? Why does the Fed alternate inflation and deflation at the expense of the American public today?

Several authors have proposed that the evolution of central banks represents a collusion between politicians and a small elite with ownership/control of major banking institutions.[18] Bank owners want to create as much money as possible, without having to dig into their own pockets when depositors want their money. Politicians long to fulfill their grandiose campaign promises without visibly taxing their constituency. Central banking can give both groups what they want.

First, through the aggression of exclusive licensing, politicians give the central bank a monopoly on issuing currency. As long as banks must make good on their promises to depositors, however, they are still subject to the regulation of the marketplace ecosystem. The politicians encourage the aggressive practice of fraud by refusing to make banks and similar institutions (i.e., Savings & Loans, known as "S&Ls") keep promises to depositors.

The entire banking reform movement, at all crucial stages, was centralized in the hands of a few men who for years were linked, ideologically and personally, with one another.

—Gabriel Kolko
THE TRIUMPH OF
CONSERVATISM

Every effort has been made by the Fed to conceal its power but the truth is—the Fed has usurped the government. It controls everything here and it controls all our foreign relations. It makes and breaks governments at will.

—Congressman
Louis T. McFadden
1933, Chairman,
Banking and
Currency Committee

Instead, owners and managers who make risky loans can simply walk away from their mistakes, as former President Bush's son Neil did.[19] Depositors either lose their life savings or are reimbursed from taxes taken—at gunpoint, if necessary—from their neighbors.

The bankers, of course, must give the politicians something in return. When the ranchers, loggers, or other special interest groups want more subsides, our representatives need not incur the wrath of the populace by suggesting more taxes. Instead, they borrow some of the Fed's newly created money! When it comes time to pay the loan back with interest, the politicians pay it back with a bigger loan using our wealth as collateral. The special interest groups thank the politicians by funding their reelections.

As a result, our national debt has grown so big that the interest alone consumed 25% of 1989 federal outlays![20] The single largest holder of the national debt is the Federal Reserve itself. As mentioned in the previous chapter, our pension and investment plans often buy the government I.O.U.s. For our pension funds to pay us, we may first have to pay higher taxes to cover the I.O.U.s. How much higher will our taxes be? The 1989 national debt was more than $11,000 for every man, woman, and child![20]

Like any special interest group, the Fed is inclined to help the politicians who protect it. By manipulating the money supply to cause boom or bust at the appropriate times, the Fed controls the illusion of prosperity—an illusion that determines which politicians people will vote for or against. Like any other special interest group, the Fed can control our government to a significant extent.

For example, the exclusive monopoly of the Second Bank of the United States was scheduled to end in 1836. Andrew Jackson swore not to renew it if he were reelected president in 1832. Soon after his victory, he removed the government's deposits from the central bank. The bank's president, Nicholas Biddle, attempted to bring about a depression by cutting back on the creation of money, just as the Federal Reserve would do almost 100 years later. Biddle hoped to blackmail Congress into renewing the banks's monopoly by making the voters miserable. Fortunately, these tactics were not successful.[21] The American people were not fooled and the bank charter was not renewed. Unfortunately, this lesson was forgotten, and central banking was reestablished with the Federal Reserve.

A LOSE-LOSE SITUATION

The money monopoly is our first example of Fourth Layer aggression. The Federal Reserve has an exclusive monopoly on currency issue (Third Layer aggression). We subsidize the monopoly through the aggression of taxation and inflation (Fourth Layer aggression). Finally, we are forced—at gunpoint, if necessary—to use the Federal Reserve notes we call dollars. Clearly written on our Federal Reserve notes is the phrase "This note is legal tender for all debts, public or private." Our taxes, for example, must be paid for in the monopoly currency.

Forcing people to *use* a service prohibits them from providing it for themselves. Even though AT&T has an exclusive monopoly on local phone service, bypassing it is still a legal option. Even though many utilities are exclusive monopolies, we can still provide our own power and septic systems if we choose. Even though we must subsidize the municipal bus system, we don't have to use it. With the exclusive money monopoly, however, we are forced—at gunpoint, if necessary—to participate whether we want to or not. When everyone uses the money monopoly, it controls the financial fate of the entire nation. In trying to control others, we find ourselves controlled!

Without the money monopoly, politicians would be unable to borrow the large sums of money that create deficits. Without these

The bold effort the present bank had made to control government, the distress it had wantonly produced...are but premonitions of the fate that awaits the American people should they be deluded into a perpetuation of this institution or establishment of another like it.
—President Andrew Jackson

deficits, the enforcement of licensing laws and the provision of special interest subsidies could be financed only by more taxes. The American citizens would be unlikely to support subsidies and waste if the true cost of these items were reflected in their tax bills. The money monopoly makes this sleight of hand possible.

Destroying wealth or curtailing its creation makes the world poorer. By forcibly shunting the wealth toward special interests, the gap between the rich and the poor widens. New medicines, old–age cures, advanced space exploration, or a three–day work week with five–day benefits are just a few of the possible increases in wealth we forgo because of the money monopoly.

Even people who believe they benefit from the money monopoly are only fooling themselves. The bankers and politicians condemn themselves to a culture that is backward in comparison to what would otherwise be possible. They are like royalty in an ancient civilization, having more than their contemporaries, but less than they would otherwise have in a culture with more abundance.

We can hardly blame the politicians and bankers for this state of affairs, however. We elect politicians who promise to cater to our special interests without raising taxes. We encourage them to mask the true cost of the aggression we demand. They give us only what we have asked for.

How can we blame the owner–bankers of the Federal Reserve for asking that we favor them with an exclusive monopoly just as we favored AT&T? How can we blame them for seeking the same subsidies we are willing to give the ranchers and timber companies? Like our Biblical ancestors in the Garden of Eden, we want to blame the serpent because we ate the apple. As always, the choice and responsibility belongs to us. When we accept our role in creating the problem, we empower ourselves with the ability to solve it!

THE EASY WAY OUT

The demise of the Second Bank of the United States demonstrates that selfish others are capable only of igniting the flames of war and poverty. We control its growth, its very survival. When we say "No!" to the aggression of monopoly-at-gunpoint, we protect ourselves from selfish others who would exploit us.

A modern banking system free from aggression would be much like the Scottish system described earlier. Since owner/managers could be liable if the bank lost its depositors' money, they would probably buy liability insurance to protect themselves and their depositors. Unlike the Federal Deposit Insurance Corporation (FDIC) or the Federal Savings and Loan Insurance Corporation (FSLIC) of today, premiums would differ for each institution, depending on how well each bank invested its depositors' money. Poor managers would be saddled with high premiums, just as poor automobile drivers are today. As premiums go up and profits go down, poor managers would be fired.

Today, each bank pays the same premium regardless of the way it does business. Managers can make risky loans that generate high closing fees, and walk away if their loans turn sour. The taxpayer then picks up the tab. Estimates made in the early 1990s indicate that every man, woman, and child will pay an average of $6,000[22] to cover recent S&L defaults. This money is essentially a giant subsidy to the poor managers and investors. This is the cost of the Pyramid of Power created by our eagerness to control our neighbors.

The money monopoly has international implications as well. We'll learn more about these in Part IV (*Lead Us Not Into Temptation: Foreign Policy*). For now, let's examine another example of Fourth Layer aggression, the monopoly over our minds. Let's find out why we never learned in school about the way the world really works!

LEGAL

ILLEGAL

CHAPTER 10

LEARNING LESSONS OUR SCHOOLS CAN'T TEACH

How can our children learn to abhor aggression when we teach them in a school system built on it?

At the turn of the century, horses were still the mainstay of the transportation industry. Today, automobiles and planes take us all over the world. Most of our great–grandparents remember using Rockefeller's kerosene to light their homes. Today, electricity and natural gas provide light, heat, and power for innumerable appliances. Just a few generations ago, infectious disease was the most frequent cause of death. Today, most bacterial plagues are effectively controlled with antibiotic treatment. In most areas of our lives, radical progress has been made over the past century. Unfortunately, education is one of those rare exceptions.

In the early 1900s, our great–grandparents trudged off to the neighborhood school. For the better part of the day, the teacher stood in front of the class, chalk in hand, to expound on lessons contained in the school books. Today, our children might ride a bus to their neighborhood school, but once there, everything is very similar to the way it was for our great–grandparents. For the better part of the day, the teacher stands in front of the class, chalk in hand, to expound on the lessons contained in the school books. The facilities are newer and the curriculum includes some additional subjects, but the teaching methods have changed little.

The cost of doing things the same old way, however, has skyrocketed. Only national defense consumes more of our taxes than the public school system.[1] In spite of this great

In no other industry in U.S. history has there been so little technological change as in the field of public school education.
—National Center for Policy Analysis "The Failure of Our Public Schools: The Causes and a Solution"

Only 20 percent of job applicants at Motorola can pass a simple seventh-grade test of English comprehension or a fifth-grade mathematics test.
—Nation's Business, October 1988

Of the Aquarian Conspirators surveyed, more were involved in education than in any other single category of work....Their consensus: Education is one of the least dynamic of institutions, lagging far behind... other elements of our society.
—Marilyn Ferguson
THE AQUARIAN
CONSPIRACY

expenditure, a survey on education finds the United States "A Nation at Risk."[2] Almost 25% of our high school students do not graduate, and another 25% have too few academic qualifications to be placed in a job or college program.[3] Even those in the top 50% of their graduating class frequently find themselves classified as unskilled labor. After a 25-year decline in scholastic aptitude tests (SATs),[4] our best and brightest compare unfavorably to students from other nations.[5]

Perhaps we shouldn't be too surprised. After all, our grade school and high school educations are examples of Fourth Layer aggression. The educational system is basically an exclusive monopoly (Second Layer aggression). All schools, even private ones, must meet the requirements of the accreditation (licensing) boards. Such boards usually dictate the core curriculum, the list of acceptable textbooks, and the educational standards for teachers.[6] High prices, low quality, and lack of innovation are hallmarks of licensing laws, especially exclusive ones that create monopolies.

Education is heavily subsidized by taxes (Third Layer aggression). Subsidies cause waste, especially when services are provided by the government. Public schools consume twice as many dollars in operating costs as do private ones.[7] The amount of money spent per pupil, however, does not significantly affect educational quality.[8] The real waste is not money, however, but the minds of our children. A poor education means fewer skills with which to create wealth. As always, aggression breeds poverty.

School-age children are forced—at gunpoint, if necessary—to attend a licensed school (Fourth Layer aggression). Because we want all children to get a good education, we view tuition-free public schools and mandatory attendance as a way to ensure that neglectful parents are not allowed to deny their children this valuable asset. As always, aggression gives us results we'd rather not have. Specifically, Fourth Layer aggression allow others to control the way we think about our world, just as it allows an elite group to control our finances (Chapter 9: *Banking on Aggression*).

THE MARKETPLACE ECOSYSTEM: HONORING OUR NEIGHBOR'S CHOICE

Early in our country's history, Americans were considered to be among the most literate people in the world.[9] Schooling was neither compulsory nor free, although private "charity" schools provided education to those too poor to afford formal instruction.[10] Licensing requirements for teachers and schools were almost non-existent. In the early 1800s, Boston had schools that were partially tax-supported public institutions, but twice as many children attended the private ones. Admission to these public schools required that the students already have been taught to read and write either by their family, a tutor, or one of the private "dames" schools.[11] Nevertheless, a survey in 1817 revealed that over 90% of Boston's children attended the local schools! Evidently, only a few parents were too proud to take charity, didn't feel schooling was of much value, taught their children at home, or needed the extra income the child could make working.[12] Education was readily available for those who chose to take advantage of it. Not surprisingly, school attendance in New York City showed no change after the establishment of tuition-free public education.[13]

Parents had a variety of schools from which to choose, especially among institutions that were not restricted by conditions attached to state support. Some schools prepared students for the university and some taught the trades. Some schools provided a broad-based education, while others focused on a particular area of expertise. Private tutoring was available for those unable to attend ordinary day school. The marketplace ecosystem, free from aggression, quickly adapted to consumer needs. Parents voted with their dollars to support the educators who served them best. In this way, parents determined both the content and process by which their children would be educated.

AGGRESSION DISRUPTS THE MARKET-PLACE ECOSYSTEM

The diverse education available in the United States greatly pleased the immigrants, who came from societies where their children could not go to a school that taught the values they cherished. Some influential citizens, however, felt that society was disrupted, rather than enriched, by the different perspectives and faiths that the immigrants brought with them. With a uniform system of "American" education, they could mold children into what they perceived as proper citizens. They clamored to increase the aggression of taxation so that public schools wouldn't need to charge much tuition. Parents would be forced—at gunpoint, if necessary—to turn over their hard-earned dollars to the public schools. If they were wealthy enough to have any money left, their children could still go to the private school of their choice. Like the serpent in the Garden of Eden, the so-called reformers tempted the American citizenry to use aggression against the poor immigrants, ostensibly to create harmony throughout the land.

Many immigrants had come to the United States to escape this holier-than-thou attitude. In spite of the additional financial burden, impoverished immigrants made great sacrifices to educate their children as they saw fit rather than send them to inexpensive or even free public schools. Catholics saw the public schools as vehicles for Protestant propaganda and established parochial schools; German immigrants sent their children to private institutions when the public ones refused to teach them in German as well as in English. Immigrants who preferred that their

Historically, much of the motivation for public schooling has been to stifle variety and institute social control.
—Jack Hugh
Cato Institute

...public schooling often ends up to be little more than majoritarian domination of minority viewpoints.
—Robert B. Everhart
Professor of Education, University of California, Santa Barbara

children be taught in their native tongue and learn about their Old World heritage opted for private or parochial schools that catered to their preferences.[14]

The willingness of poor parents to send their children to private instead of public school tells us how highly they valued education, specifically, education that reflected their belief system and culture. Many people had come to the United States for a chance to pull themselves away from the poverty trap spun by Europe's guild-style licensing laws and other forms of aggression. Perhaps they didn't want their children in schools that were created by the kind of aggression from which they had recently fled. Perhaps they feared that schools built on aggression would teach aggression. If that seems farfetched, consider your own education. As you've read through the past few chapters, have you been saying to yourself, "That's not the way my teachers told me the world worked"?

Can you imagine a school system that is funded by taxation hiring a teacher who equated taxation with theft? Such a teacher would be unlikely to seek a job in the public school system in the first place. Obviously then, public school teachers are highly likely to believe that selfish others are the cause of war and poverty and that altering their behavior—at gunpoint, if necessary—is justified—even noble. From this perspective, children will be taught that first-strike force, fraud, or theft is acceptable as long as it's for a good cause. An obvious underlying assumption of this philosophy is that the ends are not influenced by the means used to obtain them. To parents with an enlightened view of how the world works, this is analogous to teaching their child that 2 + 2 = 5! Unfortunately, these are the beliefs that are being propagated. These are the beliefs that are keeping us from a world of peace and plenty.

We interpret facts according to our world view. If our interpretation is correct, we will do

A general State education is a mere contrivance for molding people to be exactly alike one another; and as the mold in which it casts them is that which pleases the predominant power in the government, whether this be a monarch, a priesthood, an aristocracy, or a majority of the existing generation; in proportion as it is efficient and successful, it establishes a despotism over the mind, leading by a natural tendency to one over the body.
—John Stuart Mill
English philosopher
and economist

the things that take us to our goal. We will be able to create peace and plenty in our hearts, our families, our communities, and our world. If our interpretation is faulty, we will create problems instead of solving them. No wonder parents who wanted the best for their children were willing to make great sacrifices to send them to a school that would complement their home instruction!

The immigrants not only wanted their children instructed according to their faith and culture, they wanted their children to develop readily marketable technical skills. Since school boards were drawn from the upper class and professional groups, curricula tended to be geared toward a liberal arts education as preparation for college.[15] Those who could not afford to pay public school taxes *and* private school tuition sometimes opted for informal instruction in the trades or home schooling.

Some immigrant children worked because their families needed their support.[16] Today, our society is wealthy enough that child labor is usually unnecessary, but this was not true in the 1800s. Immigrant children, especially those on farms, contributed substantially to their family's financial well-being. When the family's financial condition improved, the level of the children's education did too.[17] This pattern suggests that rather than being "exploitation," child labor was a matter of necessity and was dispensed with as soon as possible. Since schooling was not compulsory, children could mix work and school as necessary to strike a balance between creating enough wealth to survive and learning long-range wealth-creating strategies in school. Of course, working was also a form of education. It gave the child experience, skills, and accountability training. Employers look for experience. By forbidding children to work, we deny them an excellent educational opportunity.

Compulsory school attendance made it more difficult for children to obtain work experience. Children were less available for learning a trade or obtaining employment when they had to be in school for many months each year. Without the ability to mix work and school, private education became less affordable. Private education was an option only for children with parents wealthy enough to pay for private school tuition in addition to the taxes that supported free public schools.

As always, when we sow the seeds of aggression, we reap the bitter fruit. The reformers were successful in getting education by aggression—but the results have not been what they desired. Because children are required by law to be in school, the public institutions find themselves saddled with some individuals who have little motivation to learn. Although these children can be disruptive, sometimes even violent, expelling them is not a legal option. As attendance has risen, so has theft, drugs, and violence perpetrated by students unmotivated by the curriculum.[18] As attendance has increased, SAT scores have declined (Figure 10.1), suggesting that keeping problem students in school adversely affects learning for other students.

In response to schools that cannot educate or even guarantee student safety, many parents have chosen to keep their children out of schools and teach them at home. In many states, home schooling is legal only if a state-certified teacher is instructing. Parents without certification have been fined or jailed for home schooling, even when the education has been progressing well.

The Amish have been persecuted as well. These closely knit rural communities shun modern technology and embrace a simple, non-violent way of life. They found that standard curricula encouraged a materialistic and violent perspective that was incongruent with their spiritual beliefs. Certified teachers were ill-equipped to teach the Amish children the values the community cherished. In addition,

Yet some parents are now saying that deliberate withdrawal of their children from compulsory schooling —an illegal act in most states—is not unlike draft resistance in an immoral war.

—Marilyn Ferguson
THE AQUARIAN
CONSPIRACY

Figure 10.1 Relationship Between Student
Attendance and Performance

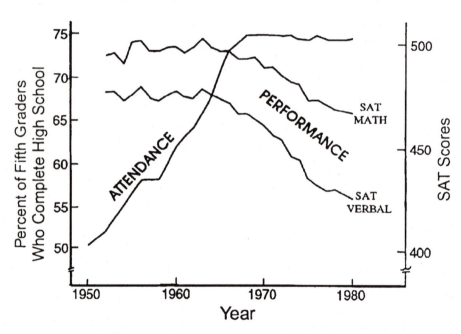

Reprinted with permission of the National Center for Policy Analysis

certified teachers were more expensive than their Amish counterparts.

The Amish believe secondary education should consist of learning agricultural and domestic skills, rather than the liberal arts and science. Instead of honoring their choice, aggression is used to herd their children into the schools of "the one best system." While we deplore historical references to the persecution of early scientists, such as Galileo, we feel comfortable in dictating the choices of those who prefer a life without technology. If the Amish tried to force our children to learn their ways, we'd be appalled; yet we feel justified in doing to them what we don't want done to us.

Of course, well-to-do parents needn't worry about persecution or home schooling or even paying private school tuition in addition to school taxes. They congregate in expensive neighborhoods where only "their kind" can afford to live. Their local public schools cater to their values. Indeed, the suburban public schools have become more exclusive than the private ones.[19]

On the other side of the tracks, parents too poor to move from the ghetto shudder at the prospect of sending their children to neighborhood public schools where violence prevails and learning is difficult. Through their rents, they pay a large portion of their income for the property taxes that support schools they dare not send their children to. Instead, they've started to enroll their children in the local parish or independent neighborhood schools— even if they have to pay tuition with their welfare checks![20] As a result, the proportion of minorities in private schools increased from the early 1970s to the early 1980s, even though tuition costs continued to rise.[21] In the late 1970s, more private school students came from families in which the parents earned between $5,000 and $10,000 a year than from families with incomes of $25,000 or better.[22]

The minorities and low-income families are not the only ones choosing private education

...the Plain Peoples' approach to education may be one of the most effective yet devised. Their success in training the young to be farmers has impressed many agricultural experts. Unemployment, indigence, juvenile delinquency, and crime are surprisingly infrequent. Amish prosperity and self-sufficiency are legendary. These are not the characteristics of a preparation for adulthood that has failed.
—Donald A. Erickson
Professor of Education, University of California, Los Angeles

*...when it (the State)
controls the education,
it turns it into a rou-
tine, a mechanical
system in which in-
dividual initiative, in-
dividual growth and
true development as
opposed to a routine
instruction become
impossible.*
—Sri Aurobindo
SOCIAL AND POLITICAL
THOUGHT

*Public educators, like
Soviet farmers, lack
any incentive to pro-
duce results, innovate,
to be efficient, to make
the kinds of difficult
changes that private
firms operating in a
competitive market
must make to survive.*
—Carolyn Lochhead
Insight, December 24,
1990

for their children, however. Public school
teachers, who ought to be best informed, are
twice as likely as the rest of the population to
send their children to private schools![23] What
does this tell us about public school quality?

Obviously, parents choosing private
schools do so for reasons other than their
religious beliefs or their concern for their
children's safety. Public schools are doing
such a poor job of teaching students, that
many children are being sent to private after-
school learning centers,[24] which were virtually
non-existent a generation ago. Private schools
nationwide are much more successful at
teaching students than public schools are.
This difference was obvious to me even as a
high school student. Students from the
Catholic schools took a higher proportion of
awards at the Science Fair than public school
students did. A 1987 study found the reason:
parents can choose to take their children and
their dollars elsewhere if schools don't meet
their standards.[25]

One innovative private institution charges
less than half of the dollars consumed by the
public system, even though it caters to students who are about to drop out of school.
Using computer technology and a low student
to teacher ratio, the school boasts an 85%
graduation rate.[26] The founder of this school
is a former public school teacher who just
couldn't convince the bureaucracy to try
something new.

The secret behind the success of private
schools is less aggression. Parents are not
forced—at gunpoint, if necessary—to send
their children to the neighborhood public
school. Instead, they can remove their child if
they are not satisfied with the educational
content or process and can enroll them
elsewhere. Removing even a tiny amount of
aggression from public education has a
beneficial effect. For example, public schools in
Harlem were encouraged to each take on an
individual specialty, one emphasizing science

and math, another encouraging the performing arts, and still another providing special attention for those with learning difficulties. Parents could choose which school their child would attend. If things didn't work, they could move to another. Schools had to either perform or lose their clientele. The results are impressive. Before "choice," only 15% of the district's students read at grade level; now 64% make the grade.[27] Similar results have been reported in other areas of the country.[28] No wonder the poor and the minorities are the strongest supporters of educational choice that is engendered by less aggression.[29]

THE EASY WAY OUT

If such a little freedom from aggression goes such a long way, what might we expect if we were willing to forgo it altogether? If we honored our neighbor's choice, what educational heights could we aspire? Let's try to imagine what a successful school might look like if education were totally deregulated (i.e., completely free from aggression).

Quest, Inc., might be such a school. Larger than most high schools before deregulation, it's still expanding to accommodate the large number of student applicants. Quest's success is largely due to its effective use of computers and audiovisual equipment, which have long been known to double a student's learning.[30]

Both of Carol's parents work and are easily able to pay her tuition at Quest. Some of Carol's classes begin with a professionally produced, entertaining video produced by a company that sells exclusively to schools. This company pays royalties to any teacher whose ideas for improvements or new subjects are incorporated. Continuous updating ensures that the videos use the best ideas and methods to maintain the student's interest.

After the video, students go into one of several "query" classrooms where the resident teacher answers any questions the students may have. Different students relate best to different teachers; letting the students gravitate to those who "speak their language" facilitates understanding. Not all Quest teachers have advanced degrees, but all instructors must facilitate students' learning. Teachers who can't attract students to their query sessions won't be at Quest very long. Teachers who do especially well are given bonuses and asked to share their techniques with other Quest faculty members. Teachers reap as they sow.

When their questions are satisfied, students proceed through an interactive computer program that tests their new knowledge gained from the video. Students who do not properly answer the computers' queries review the relevant part of the lesson on the computer in a different format, and the student is retested later in the session. Students may then opt for more sophisticated problems or mini-lessons to extend their knowledge.

The programming is designed according to a student's strengths and weaknesses. Carol excels in history and the social sciences and does poorly in math and the sciences. When she keys in her password on the computer, she accesses the math problems formulated in terms of historical events. Sometimes Carol finds the math video so confusing that she spends all her time in the query session, never getting to the computer at all. Since her family has a home computer, she can either take a disk home to catch up or stay after class, since Quest staff is available from 7 a.m. to 9 p.m. This format lets ambitious teens work and go to school part-time.

Some teens are actually placed in jobs by Quest. Students aspiring to be scientists or doctors, for example, cannot be sure they have made the appropriate choice until they actually find themselves immersed in the type of work they have chosen. Quest cultivates relationships with good employers/mentors to expose students to work environments (e.g., hospitals or laboratories) before students need to make definitive career choices. Before deregulation, students might be in their last year of college before they actually held the type of job for which they had spent so much time learning.

The instructors enjoy working at Quest, Inc., because they can do what they were trained to do—teach. The repetition is taken out of their jobs by the extensive series of professionally produced videos and computer learning programs provided for the students. Some teachers supplement their income by preparing audio-visual texts in their specialty. Teachers devote most of their time to answering students' questions, guiding them toward the curriculum most suited to their needs, or teaching essay writing and other skills that do not lend themselves to electronic instruction.

The computer summarizes each student's progress, so teachers can monitor what each child is learning on a regular basis and give special attention when needed. Since they are paid partially in stock certificates and they share in school profits, teachers make sure all students meet their predefined targets.

For example, Carol's counselor explained that her exceptional grasp of the social sciences and her average understanding of math and the sciences gave her several options. For example, she could spend more time on science and math to match her proficiency in other areas. Alternatively, she could elect to focus only on the basics in math and the sciences while earning college credit in her specialties. Most colleges expect applicants to take some of the privately administered national tests to be sure prospective students meet college standards. High school diplomas are a thing of the past. Instead, students continue until satisfied that their test scores indicate the proficiency level they had targeted. By age 12, most Quest students have the equivalent of an old-style high school diploma. Most also have at least one work reference from on-the-job training.

Problems with drugs or violence are virtually non-existent, since students are suspended for the first offense and expelled for recurrence. If they choose to, expelled students can still get a Quest education through the home-study program described below.

Social interaction is integrated into the curriculum. Children are instructed in how to tutor younger siblings and classmates, engage in constructive teamwork, and practice leadership by taking turns coordinating cooperative assignments. Some of this instruction is intertwined with physical education or work-study assignments.

Quest is less expensive overall than the old-style public school system, for a number of reasons. Because of the advanced technology, students learn faster and spend less time in school. Teachers are able to give whatever level of attention is needed to maximize each student's learning. Bureaucracy is minimized, and teachers are discharged if they aren't proficient.

Nevertheless, the yearly tuition is still beyond the means of many who would like to see their children go there. Pete's father, for example, never finished high school and works as a janitor for a small hotel. He wants his son to have the best education money can buy—but he doesn't have the money to buy much. Quest enrolled Pete in the parent-student work-study program. The school assigns Pete's dad evening and weekend janitorial and maintenance work under the watchful eye of the full-time school maintenance supervisor. Most of the non-teaching function of the school is provided this way. Eventually, Pete will do his part by supervising younger children as they watch the teaching videos, working with the cafeteria staff, and tutoring less-advanced students. Pete will not only get a Quest education, but a work reference as well. Pete will never have to worry about being classified as "unskilled labor."

Stephanie Baker's single mother wants her daughter to get a Quest education. Tuition, however, is beyond her means, and work-study is difficult because Stephanie's bedridden grandmother requires constant care. By providing the day school to three children with working mothers, Mrs. Baker pays for the rental of Quest video tapes and workbooks for Stephanie. Computer software is available too, but Stephanie's mother doesn't have a home computer. The children watch teaching videos, then use their workbooks to solve problems and test their understanding. Mrs. Baker answers their questions and helps them as much as she can. Every two weeks, the children are given a Quest test. Quest provides the children with recommendations for further studies. For example, one child had trouble with math and received a special series of videos and workbooks for his homework. As the children get older, they begin tutoring in their neighborhood to pay for the formal testing that colleges and employers frequently require.

The children Stephanie has tutored got most of their schooling from one of the cable television stations that carry programmed learning courses. For a monthly fee slightly higher than the entertainment channels, a family can order the educational programs geared to the ages of their children. Some parents have gotten each child his or her own television, and learning becomes an all-day affair at home. Workbooks and textbooks come with the cable subscription, complete with answer books to test questions. A number of correspondence courses are also available for subjects in which a professional's evaluation is desirable (e.g., essay writing).

Even less expensive are the TV-schooling channels supported by advertising. Many churches combine day care and education by providing space for volunteers to use. To keep the attention of the young people, the videos tend to be highly participatory. Children sing their alphabet to catchy jingles and march around the room chanting historical dates, names, and happenings. Madison Avenue techniques are used to produce stimulating programs so that the firms would pay top dollar to sponsor them. Some of this programming was pioneered before deregulation and was available in a few futurist locations.[31]

With all of the options available at costs ranging from substantial to trivial, few children are unschooled. The exceptions tend to be children of parents who despise education of any kind. Since family background is a significant factor in a child's scholastic achievement, many of these children would not have benefited by any kind of schooling. Before deregulation, these children would have disrupted the learning of others with drugs and violence, while learning little.

Now they do have a chance. The local Kiwanis and Rotary Clubs run newspaper advertisements asking concerned citizens to help them identify such children, hoping to get their parents' permission to get them special teaching assistance. With advertised educational TV channels widely available, few such children were located. People smart enough to want to learn are smart enough to tune the selector button to the channel that has what they want!

NON–AGGRESSION
IS THE EDUCATION OF CHOICE!

CHAPTER 11

SPRINGING THE POVERTY TRAP

When we use aggression to alleviate the poverty caused by aggression, we only make matters worse.

THE MARKETPLACE ECOSYSTEM AT WORK

Our country has a proud history. Less than 200 years after its founding, the United States was the richest nation on earth. Yet few who migrated here were wealthy; most people came to this country with little more than the clothes they were wearing. What made America the land of opportunity for penniless immigrants was something that could not be found in any other country at that time. People in the United States were relatively free, not to do as they pleased, but *free from aggression*. No minimum wage laws kept the disadvantaged worker from getting a start. Few licensing laws prevented people from providing services to willing customers. Education was available and affordable. It could be integrated into a working lifestyle. No wonder people were willing to leave their homes for a new culture and even a new language. In most other nations at that time, education and the creation of wealth were limited to the elite by aggression-through-government.

AGGRESSION DISRUPTS THE MARKETPLACE ECOSYSTEM

Today, of course, aggression once again keeps the disadvantaged from creating wealth for themselves and their loved ones. Minimum wage laws exclude unskilled workers from the job market, while increasing the prices they must pay for goods and services. Licensing laws squeeze small companies out of business. Sixty percent of all new jobs in the United

The government laws that have proven most devastating, for many blacks, are those that govern economic activity. The laws are not discriminatory in the sense that they are aimed specifically at blacks. But they are discriminatory in the sense that they deny full opportunity for the most disadvantaged Americans, among whom blacks are disproportionately represented.
—Walter Williams
black economist

Economic control is not merely control of a sector of human life that can be separated from the rest; it is the control of the means for all our ends.
—Ludwig von Mises
HUMAN ACTION

No matter how worthy the cause, it is robbery, theft, and injustice to confiscate the property of one person and give it to another to whom it does not belong.
—Walter Williams
Professor of Economics,
George Mason University

States are created by firms with fewer than 21 employees. These same businesses also provide 80% of all new minority positions.[1] Strangling the small businesses with aggression destroys jobs, especially for disadvantaged workers. As aggression increases, the large firms become monopolies and the price of services increases, further penalizing the poor.

If, in spite of all these setbacks, disadvantaged individuals manage to acquire something, they are the first to flounder in the alternating waves of inflation and deflation produced by the money monopoly. Moving to the poor side of town has grave consequences for the children of parents financially crippled by aggression, however. Unless the parents are willing and able to make heroic sacrifices, their children will be subjected to inner city–style public education. Less skilled than their parents, they are even more likely to be stopped—at gunpoint, if necessary—from creating wealth.

As we survey the plight of these unfortunates, we are usually unaware of the role we have played in creating their poverty. For example, we fail to notice that when minimum wages go up in a particular region of the country, welfare payments increase to the newly unemployed.[2] Without such awareness, we repeat our mistake of using aggression as we try to help the destitute. As a result, we used the aggression of taxation to support a massive "War on Poverty."

Two "wrongs" don't make a "right." Welfare, which is charity by aggression, ensnares the poor in a never ending cycle known as the poverty trap.

In the 1970s, welfare payments and other forms of aid available to poor families (e.g., food stamps, medical care, etc.) increased to such an extent that total benefits exceeded the median income of the average U.S. family! In 1975, working heads of households needed to make $20,000 to give their families benefits equivalent to what they could have on welfare. Only 25% of U.S. families earned this much![3] In 1979, the median family income was $1,500 less than the potential welfare benefits for a family of the same size.[4]

In the 1970s, two working parents had to make more than the minimum wage to match what they would receive on the dole.[4] A young working couple with children might find that their net income after child–care costs would be less than what they could receive on welfare. In these circumstances, accepting aid instead of working would seem like the smart thing to do.

Opting out of the work force at a young age has grave consequences later on, however. While a working person might start out with less than those on aid, experience would eventually result in raises and a higher standard of living. On welfare, however, little progress is made over time. Since most welfare benefits can be used only for food, medical care, and shelter, saving is almost impossible. When their working contemporaries are ready to buy their first house, those on welfare are still unable to afford a car.

The attraction of the short–term gain encourages many individuals to choose poverty for life. One study estimated that one–sixth of aid recipients could have worked but chose leisure and the other benefits of being supported by tax dollars instead.[5] An elaborate study involving almost 9,000 people documented the deleterious results of a guaranteed income. One group of subjects, who served as controls, received no benefits. An experimental group was told everyone would be given enough money to bring total individual income to a specified target amount. Those in the experimental group who worked would receive less money than those who didn't, so everyone would have the same income for three consecutive years.

When the control and experimental groups were compared, the results were unequivocal.

The fundamental fact in the lives of the poor in most parts of America today is that the wages of common labor are far below the benefits of AFDC, Medicaid, food stamps, public housing, public defenders, leisure time and all the other goods and services of the welfare state.
                    —George Gilder
                    WEALTH AND POVERTY

Young men who stayed unmarried throughout the experiment worked 43% less when income was guaranteed. These young men jeopardized their future earnings by getting less work experience than their peers. Wives in the experimental group cut their hours by 20%, and their husbands reduced their work week by 9%. If a female head of household lost her job, it took over a year for her to find a new one if she was receiving guaranteed income. Her counterpart in the control group found new employment in less than half the time.[6] Clearly, welfare payments decreased the incentive to work, especially for individuals with no family responsibilities.

Divorce rates went up by 36–84% for most couples in the experimental group. Evidently, part of what binds couples together is the economic benefits of a family unit. Guaranteed incomes made it easier to say good-bye. In one group, couples thought that their welfare payments would be stopped if they separated. As a result, divorce rates in that group were comparable to those of the controls.[7] Clearly, people adjusted their behavior to adapt to income guarantees.

The more that is given, the less the people will work for themselves and the less they work, the more their poverty will increase.
—Leo Tolstoy
author of
WAR AND PEACE

In 1980, I began to rehabilitate low-income housing in Michigan and observed this heart-wrenching situation repeated time and time again. My tenants were rarely disabled physically or mentally; most were able-bodied men and women with small children. These adults were quite capable of full-time employment. They seldom had trouble doing the arithmetic necessary to figure how much rent they owed, even if an erratic payment schedule made the calculation more difficult. Consequently, they easily figured out that women with several children were able to maintain a higher standard of living on welfare than women or men without dependents. More babies meant more benefits. Unskilled teenage women, eager to establish an independent household, found that having a child out of wedlock gave them sufficient income to do so.

In 1980, 82% of all black infants in the United States born to mothers aged 15 to 19 were illegitimate.[8] Paternal desertion is encouraged in many states because aid is unavailable to a woman if the father of her child lives with her.[9]

Industrious individuals who take jobs find their welfare benefits abruptly terminated and their net income lower than before. The welfare habit is difficult to break, partly because of the withdrawal period of lower income that accompanies an entry level job in the work place. Only the most determined recipients succeed in breaking out of the poverty trap.

Those who remain ensnared eventually come to believe that they are incapable of supporting themselves and their loved ones. Some simply lose their self-esteem or bitterly blame society for their plight. Sometimes they lose their sense of responsibility, not caring for their children or their home. Landlords refuse to rent to them, knowing that, on the average, their children are more likely to run wild and the apartment is less likely to be maintained. Children raised by parents with such attitudes have a lot of destructive conditioning to overcome.

The combination of welfare and other social services enhance the mother's role and obviate the man's. As a result, men tend to leave their children, whether before or after marriage. Crises that would be resolved in a normal family way break up a ghetto family. Perhaps not the first time or the fifth, but sooner or later the pressure of the subsidy state dissolves the roles of fatherhood, the disciplines of work, and the rules of marriage.
—George Gilder
WEALTH AND POVERTY

A LOSE-LOSE SITUATION

Just how have the minority poor adapted to the country's welfare system? In 1980, more 20- to 24-year-old black males were on welfare than the worst-case scenarios that had been based on the atmosphere of discrimination existing between 1954 and 1961. Black illegitimate births and single-parent homes were much higher than the most pessimistic predictions.[10] In the 1940s, less than 10% of all black babies were born out of wedlock; by 1982, more than 50% of them were illegitimate. The number living in poverty tripled from 1959 to 1982.[11] Easily accessible welfare payments had the same effect as guaranteed income. Individuals had less incentive than they did in earlier times to work and to maintain a family structure. Consequently, fewer did.

Black poverty was hardly a result of increasing discrimination. Blacks had unprecedented opportunities awaiting them in the work place. By 1980, the percentage of black workers employed in white-collar jobs, the percentage of blacks in college, and the black-to-white income ratio of full-time workers had exceeded optimistic projections based on the trend toward less discrimination established between 1961 and 1965.[10] Clearly, blacks who escaped the poverty trap could look forward to unprecedented gains. Unfortunately, the increased aggression of minimum wage, licensing laws, and welfare made that escape extremely difficult.

With the best intentions, we've hurt the poor instead of helping them. Our brotherly love has caused the disadvantaged to choose dependence over self-sufficiency, poverty over getting ahead, and severing family ties in times of stress over pulling together. As a result, by the late 1970s, 20% of all U.S. families depended upon government welfare for 96% of their income.[12] By 1980, more people were economically dependent on the government than in 1965,[13] when the War on Poverty programs began!

Like overprotective parents, we've stifled the development of self-reliance and self-esteem in our minority poor by trying to give them too much. No matter how much we might wish to save people from suffering through the low-paying entry-level job, it's simply not something we can do for them. In trying to protect them, we destroy their ability to protect themselves.

We pay handsomely to keep people poor. In 1982, enough of our taxes went toward social welfare programs to provide every poor family of four with an income of more than $46,000![14] Instead of the poor getting this amount, however, approximately 74 cents of every dollar went to the welfare industry![15]

Love is more than simply being open to experiencing the anguish of another person's suffering. It is the willingness to live with the helpless knowing that we can do nothing to save the other from his pain.
—Sheldon B. Kopp
IF YOU MEET THE BUDDHA ON THE ROAD, KILL HIM!

With so much welfare going to middle-class administrators, the hard-core needy are literally left out in the cold. Those truly incapable of producing significant wealth, especially those who are mentally disabled, may end up among the increasing numbers of homeless. In San Francisco, where I lived for a year, many of those unfortunates roamed the parks and cities scrounging for food and shelter.

The housing problem that generates homelessness has been linked to the aggression of rent control, zoning restrictions, building codes, and construction moratoriums, all of which limit the availability of inexpensive housing.[16] When construction is limited and landlords can charge only a minimal rent, they naturally rent to only the most affluent tenants, rather than the poor who might be late in their payments. Once again, aggression hurts those it is supposed to protect.

THE EASY WAY OUT

How can we take care of those truly in need without destroying the incentives and development of those who are truly able?

Many individuals are capable of creating wealth but are excluded from the job market by minimum wage and licensing laws. Much poverty can be alleviated by allowing people to create wealth at whatever level they can and "work their way up."

Guy Polhemus, a soup kitchen volunteer, realized that New York City's homeless might be able to create a little wealth for themselves by collecting beer and soda cans.[17] He started a non-profit organization, WE CAN, to redeem the cans and hired some of his earliest "customers" to help staff the fledgling business. Industrious collectors earn $25 to $30 a day by helping clean up the city's litter and reducing the garbage going into landfills. Some people have told Polhemus that scavenging cans was too degrading. Obviously, the homeless, who voluntarily participate, disagree.

...we could end up in an absurd situation where a third of the population produces goods and services, another third are social workers and the last third are welfare cases and pensioners.
—Jens Aage
Bjoerkeoe
Danish social worker

Cities with rent controls had, on average, two and a half times as many homeless people as cities without them.
—William Tucker
THE EXCLUDED
AMERICANS:
HOMELESSNESS AND
HOUSING POLICIES

It's me using my own mind to do something for me. It gives me pride. It's not like we are living off welfare or stealing.
—Jack Miller
a WE CAN customer

They *choose* to create what wealth they can. Polhemus was so impressed with their diligence that 12 of the homeless can collectors became WE CAN employees with full health benefits. Polhemus is starting new redemption centers to meet the demand. Now these employees will have a chance to work their way up into management.

Lupe Anguiano left the Department of Health, Education, and Welfare in frustration to create LET'S GET OFF WELFARE, which placed 42 San Antonio women into jobs. Six months later, the program had helped 500 women leave welfare for the work force. After one year, 88% were still employed. Anguiano is implementing her program in other cities too. She seeks funding from the corporate sector, because accepting government grants comes with so many regulations that not enough time is left to help the clients! Her training program costs less than $700 per person in 1973, while comparable public sector services ranged from $3,000 to $15,000.

In another case, 29-year-old Kimi Gray was approached by three teens who wanted to know how to get to college. Because she was a youth coordinator for the public housing project in which they resided, the teenagers thought she would know what to do. Kimi started a prep group, COLLEGE HERE WE COME, which met regularly. Twenty-five students drilled each other, practiced taking exams, and dreamed what seemed like a hopeless dream. Only two teens had ever left the housing development for college.

The enthusiasm of the determined students was catching, however, and soon the parents started a booster club to raise money through raffles, bake sales, and sundry other projects. Slowly but surely, the dream materialized. In August 1975, 17 youngsters left for out-of-town colleges amid the cheers and best wishes of the entire housing project.

COLLEGE HERE WE COME continues and boasts more than 600 students' success stories. Kimi Gray and other residents eventually convinced the city of Washington, D.C., to let them manage the public housing project where they live. Rent receipts went up by 60% and management costs went down by the same amount. Welfare and teenage pregnancy were cut in half, and crime fell by an incredible 75%.[19]

These success stories demonstrate that the poor and the homeless are capable of creating wealth. Our aggression destroys their opportunities. After crippling them financially, we offer to share the wealth we've created in the belief that they are helpless. Then we pat ourselves on the back for our generosity!

The best way to help the poor is to do away with the aggression that entraps them. For those who truly cannot support themselves and their loved ones, voluntary contributions of time and/or money would be more than adequate. For example, in 1984, individuals contributed $62 billion to charities. Eighty–five percent of the population makes some sort of donation, in spite of paying taxes for welfare. Almost half of all adults volunteer an average of 3 hours per week to charitable causes; the dollar value of this donated time is minimally estimated at $65 billion. The combined contributions of time and money by individuals to charitable causes exceeds the poverty budgets of federal, state, and local governments combined.[20]

The freedom from aggression that makes it possible to create great wealth also spurs Americans to generosity of spirit. Loving our neighbor comes more easily in a culture when we need not fear aggression from that neighbor! Loving our neighbor comes more readily when we are not accustomed to being aggressors ourselves.

Americans make really great sacrifices for the common good, and I have noticed a hundred cases in which, when help was needed, they hardly ever failed to give each other support.

—Alexis de Tocqueville
DEMOCRACY IN AMERICA

CHAPTER 12

BY THEIR FRUITS YOU SHALL KNOW THEM

It's just as well that our aggression creates poverty instead of wealth. Otherwise, we'd be eternally at war with each other!

Now that we have explored the impact of aggression–through–government on our wealth and well-being, what conclusions can we draw?

Aggression creates poverty and strife in our city, state, and nation just as it does in our one–on–one interactions in our neighborhoods. *The same means always create the same ends.*

Our desire to use aggression (first–strike force, theft, or fraud) to create a peaceful and prosperous world is like asking a triangle to be circular. Similarly, we'd be amused if someone wanted a barking cat.[1] "Cats don't bark!" we'd explain. "You can have a dog that barks or a cat that meows." Similarly, we can work toward peace and prosperity by honoring our neighbor's choice OR we can create poverty and strife with aggression. Aggression, individually or collectively through government, can never create prosperity and peace, because threatening first–strike force is *the* cause of war and the resulting waste. If no one strikes first, no conflict is possible.

Wealth is created by individuals, working alone or as part of a team. The size of the Wealth Pie does not depend primarily on natural resources, but on human creativity and productivity. When the marketplace ecosystem is free from individual and collective aggression, wealth grows and flourishes. The marketplace ecosystem is self–regulating: those who serve others best will reap the positive feedback of profit.

Aggression, perpetrated by individuals or through government, upsets the balance of the

The moral lesson we learn as children, becomes simple realism in adult life: ultimately the methods used to reach a goal do end up determining the outcome.
—Frances Moore
Lappe et al.
BETRAYING THE
NATIONAL INTEREST

All government intervention is "not merely ineffectual, but also pernicious and counterproductive." And that means all.
—Forbes
March 6, 1989

...the market system obliges individuals to be other–regarding....
—Michael Novak
WILL IT LIBERATE?

*I define evil, then, as
the exercise of political
power—that is, the
imposition of one's will
upon another by overt
or covert coercion—in
order to avoid...spiri-
tual growth.*
—M. Scott Peck
THE ROAD LESS
TRAVELED

marketplace ecosystem. Aggression-through-
government is an attempt to protect ourselves
from individual aggressors by doing unto them
before they do unto us. In fighting fire with
fire, we only increase the blaze. We abdicate
our responsibility for a peaceful resolution and
opt for war. Instead, we need to fight fire by
starving the flames. A better way to deal with
those who trespass against us is detailed in
Part III (*As We Forgive Those Who Trespass
Against Us: How We Create Strife in a World of
Harmony*).

THE COST OF AGGRESSION-THROUGH-GOVERNMENT

When we use aggression to deter aggression, we reap as we sow. Aggression causes
the Wealth Pie to shrink, and our piece gets
ever smaller. Countries with few regulations
and licensing laws enjoy an economic growth
rate *two and a half times* higher than countries
where aggression is more prevalent.[2] Since no
country today is completely free from
aggression, we would expect an even greater
economic growth (five times higher?) in its total
absence.

Taxation rates are frequently a reflection of
the level of aggression, since they are used to
enforce licensing laws and aggressive regulations. In the United States, economic growth
and employment decrease when federal taxes
increase.[3] Calculations suggest that *seven*
times as much growth in the real gross national product (GNP) might be expected in the
absence of taxation![4] Such an economic boom
would be beyond our wildest hopes! In Part III
(*As We Forgive Those Who Trespass Against
Us: How We Create Strife in a World of
Harmony*), we'll examine the feasibility of zero
taxation without sacrificing our defense
against aggressors, foreign or domestic.

These estimates suggest that we would
have five to seven *times* as much wealth as we
do now if we hadn't supported aggression-
through-government. This lost wealth is more

*When taxes are too
high, people go hun-
gry.*
—Lao-tsu
TAO TE CHING

than food and clothing. It includes forests and prairie lands devastated to keep a member of Congress in power and to line the pockets of special interests, bankruptcies of those living on the edge as boom–and–bust cycles alternate, and ghetto children who are too busy trying to stay alive in school to get an education. It includes life–saving drugs and anti–aging therapies that never come into being, as well as space explorations that might have been. The lost wealth means that the suffering we could have stopped must continue. Even the rich are poor compared to the wealth that the average person in a country without aggression–through–government would enjoy. That's quite a steep price to pay for failing to honor our neighbor's choice! Instead of trying so hard to control others, we'd be better off—and they'd be better off—if we'd let well enough alone!

Now we can understand why the United States is the wealthiest nation in the world. Its founders recognized the nature of aggression–through–government and attempted to limit it to an unprecedented extent. As a result, penniless immigrants flooded our shores to create the wealth they were forbidden to make in their homelands. The United States became the wealthiest nation on earth because it allowed the disadvantaged to create wealth for themselves and their loved ones. Countries that allow the disadvantaged to create wealth enjoy a more even distribution of income as well.[5]

When we allow people to create whatever wealth they can, *unemployment is optional.* Each person's service is worth *something.* When we allow individuals to work at whatever level they can, they receive exactly what they need to climb the Ladder of Affluence: training and experience to improve their skills in creating wealth.

Today, we create unemployment among the disadvantaged by kicking out the lower rungs on the Ladder of Affluence. Unable to

Government is not reason; it is not eloquence. It is force. And force like fire is a dangerous servant and a fearful master.
—George Washington
First President of the United States

I let go of all desire for the common good, and the good becomes as common as the grass.
—Lao-tsu
TAO TE CHING

get a foothold, the disadvantaged find themselves entangled in the poverty trap.

Contrast our founders' philosophy with that of the Soviet Union, who used aggression-through-government to control every aspect of a person's life, ostensibly for the common good. Since aggression was the means, poverty was the predictable result. One of three Soviet hospitals had no running water; indoor toilets serviced only 80% of the hospital beds![6] Life expectancy in the Soviet Union was ten years lower than ours and infant mortality two and one-half times higher.[7]

Of course, the United States and the Soviet Union have had vastly different histories, cultures, and geographies. The same cannot be said of East and West Germany before reunification, however. At the time the Berlin Wall was coming down, West Germans created two and a half times as much wealth as East Germans.[8] The difference is the degree of aggression-through-government. Whether agreed to by the majority or dictated by an elite minority, the impact is the same. If we continue to institute increasingly more aggression into our legal code, we can expect our prosperity to dwindle accordingly.

Your America is doing many things in the economic field which we found out caused us so much trouble. You are trying to control people's lives. And no country can do that part way. I tried it and failed. Nor can any country do it all the way either. I tried that, too, and it failed.
—Herman Goering
1946, Nazi minister

THE RICH GET RICHER—WITH *OUR* HELP!

The high cost of aggression makes it a tool of the rich. Only the well-to-do can afford to lobby, bribe, or threaten our elected representatives effectively. The luxuries of the wealthy might not be quite so opulent as they would be in a country that practiced non-aggression, but they will not experience the abject poverty to which aggression sentences the not-so-advantaged. As we'll find in subsequent chapters, *most poverty in the world today is caused by aggression, not ignorance.* The illusion that aggression-through-government benefits the poor at the expense of the rich is just that—an illusion. It is the wolf in sheep's clothing, the temptation in the Garden of

Eden, the spark from which the flames of war and poverty spring.

The more aggression we consent to, the more powerful the advantaged become. The Pyramid of Power grows as choice is taken from a multitude of individuals and given to a select few. Aggression discourages small businesses and favors conglomerates. Yet when the serpent tempts us, we are told that aggression is a tool to control the rich and powerful for the benefit of the many. When we listen, we reap as we sow: *in trying to control others, we find ourselves controlled.*

Taking responsibility for the way in which our choices create our world can be uncomfortable. Instead of depending on government to show us the way, we must recognize it as the instrument by which our choices are manifested.

In Chapter 1 (*The Golden Rule*), we saw how people who shocked others avoided this conclusion. By blaming the authority figure's directions or the victim's poor learning ability, the volunteers avoided taking responsibility for their actions. Because the authority figure represented himself as more knowledgeable, the volunteers deferred to him. The authority represented himself as a pillar of reasonableness. Similarly, those who wish to control us claim that the guns of government exist only for our protection. As such, aggression-through-government is represented as benevolence instead of violence, as love instead of war.

Those who wish to control us encourage our belief in a win-lose world where we must do unto others or have them do unto us. Once we accept this premise, we willingly defer to the authority figures who will attack those selfish others. When we recognize that we live in a win-win world, we no longer need to choose between the welfare of ourselves and others. Instead, we recognize that both rise and fall together. That is why it is in our own best interest to offer our neighbor love instead

Violence, even well-intentioned, invariably rebounds upon oneself.

—Lao-tsu
TAO TE CHING

The state spends much time and effort persuading the public that it is not really what it is and that the consequences of its actions are positive rather than negative.

—Hans-Hermann Hoppe
A THEORY OF SOCIALISM AND CAPITALISM

Don't be tricked into believing the choice is between sacrificing yourself to others or others to yourself...You wouldn't accept it if someone told you your only choice was between sadism and masochism, would you? The same principle applies here.

—Ayn Rand
author of THE VIRTUE OF SELFISHNESS

of war. Pointing the guns of government at our neighbor eventually results in the guns of government being leveled at us. *Honoring our neighbor's choice is the political manifestation of universal love.*

How wonderful it is that our world works this way! If striking first brought us a plentiful world, we would have to choose between either war and wealth or peace and starvation. A peaceful, prosperous world would be impossible. Instead, we can enjoy both harmony and abundance by honoring our neighbor's choice. Nature teaches us that aggression, even well-intentioned, boomerangs back to us. Truly, we live in a win–win world!

While our ancestors recognized this principle and tried to keep our country free from aggression–through–government, they did not know how to cope with *individuals* who defrauded others. We've seen that trying to deter individual aggression with collective aggression is a cure worse than the disease. In the next few chapters, we'll explore the alternative: the other piece of the puzzle!

True free enterprize is consistent with the nature of all humans.
—Ron Smothermon
TRANSFORMING #1

THE FRUITS OF HONORING OUR NEIGHBOR'S CHOICE!

PART III

AS WE FORGIVE THOSE WHO TRESPASS AGAINST US

HOW WE CREATE STRIFE IN A WORLD OF HARMONY

CHAPTER 13

THE OTHER PIECE OF THE PUZZLE

Justice does not consist of punishing the aggressor, but of making the victim whole.

So far, we've seen how our aggression, meant to protect us from selfish others, is a cure worse than the disease. Can we deter those who would aggress against us without becoming aggressors ourselves?

We know what we'd do if we accidentally put a baseball through our neighbor's window. We'd go to George and offer to fix it. If George had been cut by flying glass from the window, we'd pay his doctor bills. We might even offer George something to make up for lost time and trauma. George would be unlikely to hold a grudge against us if we "made things right" again.

If we didn't volunteer to pay for the window, George would probably be angry. If he had us arrested, we might spend a night in jail. George would still have a broken window to fix and perhaps doctor bills as well. In today's system, he'd pay taxes to cover the cost of apprehending, convicting, and imprisoning us. It's doubtful that George would feel very positive about dealing with us in the future.

The situation becomes even more unbalanced if we actually gained from our "crime." Had we stolen George's valuable coin collection instead of breaking his window, we might actually gain from the transaction, even if we spent a few days in jail. We might decide that crime pays handsomely and continue our aggressive behavior.

Apparently, many criminals are coming to the same conclusion. Of those imprisoned, one third will be convicted again within three years of their release.[1] Professional criminals average more than 100 crimes per year.[2] Only one prison term is served for every 164 felonies committed.[3] Approximately $25,000 per year is spent to keep someone in prison.[2] Victims are robbed twice: not only are they raped, mugged, murdered, or robbed, but they must pay to bring the criminals to justice as well!

Crime is on the rise. In 1960, two million felonies were reported in the United States. In 1988, almost 14 million had been committed,[4] although the population had increased by only 30%.[5] We are at war with each other, and large amounts of our wealth are consumed in fighting.

Perhaps we should not be surprised that outright aggression permeates our culture. As we saw in earlier chapters, we've condoned aggression of the majority against the minority. We've taught that a "good cause" can justify stealing George's wealth—at gunpoint, if necessary. Burglars, rapists, and murderers may rationalize that looking out for Number One is the best cause of all!

NON–AGGRESSION WINS THE GAME

The first step in putting an end to aggression is to stop teaching it by example. We should not be casting stones when we ourselves are guilty. Next, we must respond to aggression in a way that will deter aggression in the future. A well-known psychological game, the "iterative (repetitive) Prisoner's Dilemma," gives us insight into how our goal might be accomplished.

In the Prisoner's Dilemma, two individuals must decide, without prior communication, whether to deal honestly or fraudulently with one another. If they are both honest, each will benefit by receiving 3 points. If both are fraudulent, they receive only 1 point apiece. However, if each chooses differently, the cheater gets 5 points, while the honest victim gets nothing!

The point system reflects the cynical view of human nature that is prevalent in our political culture today. If selfish others intend to defraud us, we can only lose by being honest. If they are honest, we still gain more by cheating! Doing unto others before they do unto us seems to work quite well. This viewpoint is reflected in the aggressive laws of our nation, as described previously in Part II.

When players have to deal with each other repetitively, the situation changes dramatically. Instead of a single encounter, players enter a *relationship*. By remembering the way the other responded in each encounter, the players' next responses become predictable. If one player is always honest, it pays if the second is dishonest. If one player always cheats, an honest player will just be exploited.

Most people are not so rigid, however. They *adapt* to the other's response. If one player frequently cheats, honesty is abandoned. The lose-lose scenario (1 point apiece) becomes the most likely outcome. Must it be this way? Can we give feedback that encourages others to deal honestly with us and achieve the win-win scenario?

To answer this question, computers were programmed to play "Cooperation Games" instead of "War Games." Strategies of interaction were played against each other to give us insight into dealing with aggression.

The winning strategy was called TIT FOR TAT. In its first interaction with another strategy, it dealt honestly. After that, TIT FOR TAT reflected exactly what the "other" had done during the last interaction. If the other program had been honest, TIT FOR TAT was too. If the other program had defrauded, so did TIT FOR TAT. Other computer strategies quickly learned how TIT FOR TAT worked and began to deal honestly to create a win-win scenario.[6]

TIT FOR TAT practiced the first principle of non-aggression—and so did *every* program that scored in the top half of the games. TIT FOR TAT never was the *first* to defraud. When TIT FOR TAT encountered an aggressor, a program that defrauded *first*, it reflected exactly what the other gave it—nothing more, nothing less. When attacked, it defended. TIT FOR TAT did not try to deter aggression by becoming an aggressor itself. *TIT FOR TAT converted aggressors to non–aggressors by (1) setting a good example and (2) allowing aggressors to experience the fruits of their actions.*

TIT FOR TAT's strategy differs in several important aspects from our current thoughts about how to relate to our neighbors. First, as we've seen in the preceding chapters, we try, unsuccessfully, to deter aggression with aggression. *Just as in the computer games, aggression elicits retaliation, not cooperation.* If we are to mimic TIT FOR TAT's success, we must first practice non–aggression ourselves.

Second, we deter and rehabilitate aggressors when we allow them to experience the fruits of their actions. If we break George's window, we repair it. When we repair the damage we have done, we dissipate any hostility that may have arisen. We recreate the peace and wealth that we have destroyed. We right our wrongs.

Unfortunately, in our society, aggressors rarely experience the fruits of their actions by making their victims whole again. Less than one-third of convicted burglars are imprisoned.[7] Usually, they are not required to repair the damage they've done by paying their victim for the stolen property or the taxpayers for the costs of apprehension and trial. The punishment does not fit the crime. Criminals do not right their wrongs. Victims continue to be exploited; criminals learn that crime pays.

THE EASY WAY OUT

How could we implement TIT FOR TAT's strategy to deter aggression? Since 90% of all crimes involve theft or burglary,[8] let's first examine how such aggressors might experience the fruits of their actions by righting their wrongs.

Thieves would be billed by the court for the stolen property, the cost of apprehension and conviction, and any other losses resulting from their crime. Uninsured victims would receive payments, with interest, from the thief. If the victim was insured, the insurance company would pay the victim immediately and collect from the thief.

If the thief refused or was unable to make suitable payments, he or she might be put in a prison factory. They could earn money to pay their debts as well as the low costs of their minimum-security imprisonment. The harder the inmates worked, the sooner they would be released.

Obviously, imprisonment greatly increases the debt a thief would be required to pay. Most thieves would make regular payments to the victim or the victim's insurance company to avoid prison.

Most thieves would be quite capable of creating wealth in a society where jobs were not destroyed by minimum wage and licensing laws. In such a society, those who truly could not support themselves would be better cared for as well (see THE EASY WAY OUT in Chapter 11). Only individuals who refused to accept responsibility for their lives would likely end up in prison.

Taxpayers would no longer have to support those who did not agree to right their wrongs. Since food and other commodities would have to be purchased from the prison store, criminals who refused to work would have to rely on charity for sustenance. Prisoners would be motivated to take responsibility for their lives.

Inmates who refused to work would be unlikely to starve to death, however. Charitable individuals or groups could support prisoners if they felt circumstances warranted such compassion. Repentant young offenders facing a lifetime of payments for a single mistake might find charitable sponsors to shoulder part of their debt. Some uninsured victims might never be fully compensated. Partial payment, however, would be better

A thief must certainly make restitution, but if he has nothing, he must be sold to pay for his theft.
—THE HOLY BIBLE
Exodus 22:3

than nothing, which is what they usually receive today.

Our society currently views prison work as cruel and unusual punishment. Forcing victims to support both themselves and those who steal from them is even less humane!

When we try to protect aggressors from reaping as they have sown, we do them no favors. Until they have truly realized that aggression is a lose–lose game, ignoring their debt only enables them to continue their "addiction" to aggression. As the probability and severity of punishment rise, the incidence of crime goes down.[9]

The most successful substance abuse programs encourage people to take responsibility for their choices. If addicts break promises or behave destructively, they are allowed to experience the effects that they have caused. Without this "tough love," those who abuse never realize that to reap differently, they must sow differently. The best protection we can ever give others is not to shield them from reality, but to teach them how it works.

Are prisoners capable of creating wealth even when imprisoned? At the turn of the century, my great-grandfather's saddle tree factory provided employment for the inmates of the Missouri State Penitentiary. The prison was not only self-supporting, it made a small profit![10] The inmates grew their own food and manufactured brooms and men's clothing. The prison prided itself on the health of the prisoners, noting that epidemics were rare and the death rate "less than that of the average village."

In recent years, more than 70 companies have employed inmates in 16 states.[11] In Arizona, Best Western International uses prisoners to operate the hotel's telephone reservation system. Trans World Airlines hires young offenders in California to handle its telephone reservations. A private corporation, Prison Rehabilitative Industries & Diversified Enterprises (PRIDE) of Clearwater, Florida, manages 53 prison work programs. Wages are used to pay taxes, costs of imprisonment, restitution, and family support.[12] Some individuals on probation contribute to the cost of their supervision while working at regular jobs.[13] Before 1980, inmates of Maine State Prison manufactured arts and crafts, which were sold through the prison store. Individuals made as much as $30,000 per year. Some even found that their business was successful enough that crime no longer held its former attraction for them.[14] Obviously, prisoners are capable of creating considerable wealth for themselves and their victims. They can right their wrongs by experiencing the costs of their actions. They can learn to live differently. *Restitution through productive work is the most successful rehabilitation known.*[15]

In such an environment, inmates without work experience could gain some. Unskilled prisoners could participate in training programs to raise their hourly earnings if they agreed to pay for it as well. Instead of learning better ways to steal, they would learn alternatives to stealing. Those who learned to steal before they learned to create wealth would be given another option.

Today, it's difficult for young people to learn how to create wealth. When we destroy jobs with minimum wages and licensing laws, unemployment and criminal activity rise.[16] These findings should hardly surprise us. When aggression keeps the disadvantaged from creating wealth, stealing becomes a more attractive option, especially if the probability of being caught is low. When we destroy jobs with aggression, we increase the chances that we will be the victims of theft. Once again, we reap as we sow.

A Win-Win Scenario

When aggressors right their wrongs, everyone benefits. Victims are made whole again. Thus, they have more incentive to report crimes. Even the thieves benefit from this win-win scenario. Practicing wealth-creating skills should reduce future theft. When their victims are made whole, they have truly paid their debt.

The innocent would no longer be taxed—at gunpoint, if necessary—to imprison the guilty. Work prisons would be owned and operated by private firms with suitable expertise. Inmates could choose the facility that offered them the working conditions most conducive to the repayment of their debt. The ability of the prisoner to choose between competing institutions would provide incentive for the prisons to provide the most pleasant and productive conditions possible. If wardens beat or abuse inmates, the prison where they worked could be sued. Few prisoners would choose to go there. Business—and profits—would suffer. Each prison would reap as it sowed.

Contrast this self-regulation of the marketplace ecosystem with our current situation. Although 150 county governments and 39 states were charged with violating prison regulations in 1984, prisoners are unlikely to receive any compensation for their mistreatment.[17] The prisoners cannot transfer to a more humane institution.

Insisting that aggressors repay their victims could require the use of *retaliatory* force. Retaliatory force, by definition, is not *first strike* force, but a *response* to first strike force. Retaliatory force stops aggressors or makes sure they compensate their victims. Retaliatory force can become aggression if it goes beyond what is needed to accomplish these goals. Punishing aggressors makes us aggressors too. In the computer games, the strategies that punished by defrauding twice for every time that the other cheated did not do as well as TIT FOR TAT.

Turning the other cheek can discourage aggression when those who practice it are not aware of what they are really doing. Most people do not think of most government enforcement activity as aggression, because few dare to disobey. Just like a plantation of obedient slaves, everything looks peaceful on the surface. When the slaves try to choose for themselves instead of obeying their owner, out comes the whip. The situation is seen for what it really is.

India's Mahatma Gandhi understood this principle well. He and his followers engaged in non-violent civil disobedience, allowing themselves to be imprisoned, beaten, and even killed to demonstrate the true nature of an aggressive colonial government. The British, who did not wish to be thought of as aggressors, changed their ways.

Most individuals who harm others recognize the aggressive nature of their actions but believe that crime pays. When aggressors must right their wrongs, we take the profit out of crime.

Of course, aggressors can harm others in ways that cannot be totally undone. Monetary compensation to a person who has been raped or maimed, or to families whose loved ones have been killed, does not make things right again. In some cases, the victims, their family, or their insurance company might accept a monetary settlement as the best compensation available. The victims, their family, or their insurance company might insist that a repeat offender be imprisoned permanently so he or she could not strike again. In a self-supporting prison system, victims would not have to clothe and feed those who had harmed them as they do now.

...the one who struck the blow...must pay the injured man for the loss of his time and see that he is completely healed.
—THE HOLY BIBLE
Exodus 21:19

What Might Have Been

Instead of becoming aggressors themselves, Americans could have insisted that
aggressors right their wrongs. Many of the
problems outlined in Part II would never have
occurred. Instead of licensing laws, physicians
who deceived their patients about their training and experience or a pharmaceutical firm
that made false claims about drug testing
would have compensated those who were
harmed. However, individuals and businesses
would not be held liable for risks that the
consumer agreed to take. People who chose to
take a drug, even though the manufacturer
warned that its side effects were unpredictable, would be unlikely to collect in case of
injury. A person who hired a surgeon who
freely admitted that he had no training could
not successfully sue.

Frivolous lawsuits would be discouraged if
a false accuser had to repair the damage done
to an innocent defendant's reputation and
pocketbook. The trauma of false accusation
and waste of the defendant's time might be
judged worthy of compensation as well.

Bank owners and managers who promised
their customers that their money would be
available on demand could be held personally
liable for lost deposits. Few bankers would
wish to risk their life earnings by making risky
loans. Banks would likely insure themselves
and their decision makers against such liability. Insurance premiums would be high for
banks with careless management, thereby encouraging prudence. Wise consumers would
put their money in banks that carried such
insurance. If the banks failed, depositors
would not be taxed—as they are today—to
make their own deposits good!

Today, the Federal Deposit Insurance
Corporation (FDIC) charges all banks the same
rate. Well-managed banks subsidize poorly

managed ones—at gunpoint, if necessary. As a result, the careless banks continue to make risky loans. When these banks lose their double-or-nothing gamble, American taxpayers are forced—at gunpoint, if necessary—to pay taxes to make their own deposits good!

Crime just doesn't pay if aggressors must right their wrongs. One of the most important applications of this principle is the "pollution solution," described in the next chapter.

IF WE BREAK IT...

WE REMAKE IT!

CHAPTER 14

THE POLLUTION SOLUTION

Restoring what we have harmed is the best deterrent of all!

Righting our wrongs is the perfect solution to pollution. When dealing one-to-one, we practice this second principle of non–aggression naturally. If we accidentally dump trash on George's lawn, we clean it up. George is unlikely to hold a grudge if we fix what we have broken.

If we refuse to clean up our mess, George will probably allow us to experience the fruits of our actions in other ways. He may arrange to have the trash picked up and take us to court if we don't pay the bill. Perhaps he will dump trash on *our* lawn.

Unless we are willing to right our wrongs, we will forfeit harmonious relationships with our neighbors. We gain nothing by dumping trash in George's lawn if we are the ones who will have to clean it up. Therefore, we have no reason to pollute in the first place. Righting our wrongs is the best deterrent of all!

Unfortunately, the "pollution solution" is seldom used. If we listen to a conversation between our mayor and an industrial polluter, we find out why.

"Mr. Mayor, it's true we dump chemicals in the river, but that's a small price to pay for the many jobs we provide in your district. If we had to take these 'toxic wastes' as you call them and dispose of them 'properly,' it'd cost a lot of money. We'd have to lay off people or move our business to a more accommodating community. Either way, you'd be mighty unpopular. Your opponent won't be, though. She wants to see her constituents employed. That's more important to everyone than a few dead fish."

The mayor sighs in defeat. The chemicals are killing the fish. Local residents have complained, but they are unlikely to do anything about it. They might be able to convince a judge to stop the polluter, but the lawsuit would be expensive. The entire city would benefit from a clean river, but few citizens would voluntarily contribute to such a suit if the polluter would not be required to pay these clean-up costs. Since no one really owns the river, few are willing to pay to protect it. The company has a lot to lose if it can't use the river for dumping. The company will certainly back the mayor's opponent if he doesn't cooperate.

"I appreciate your perspective," the mayor explains to the polluter. "People's jobs *are* more important than a few fish." He hopes he has done the right thing. He can't help thinking that there must be a better way.

The mayor is right. There *is* a better way. The British have been using it for decades. Individuals were permitted to homestead many of the British waterways. When a polluter kills *their* fish, the owners have every incentive to take the polluter to court—and they do! The owners of Britain's rivers have successfully sued hundreds of polluters, individually and collectively, for the past century.[1] The owners are willing to pay the court costs to protect their valuable property. When we encourage homesteading, we put the environment in the hands of those who profit by caring for it. Ownership is rewarded by long-term planning. When private ownership is forbidden, our government "managers" profit only when they allow the environment to be exploited. Short-term planning is encouraged.

SOVEREIGN IMMUNITY CREATES LOVE CANAL

The Love Canal incident illustrates the different incentives of private ownership and public management. Until 1953, Hooker Electrochemical Company and several federal agencies dumped toxic wastes into a clay trench[2] under conditions that would probably meet Environmental Protection Agency (EPA) approval even today.[3] As the population of Niagara Falls grew, the local school board tried to persuade Hooker to sell this cheap, undeveloped land to the city for a new school. The company felt that it was unwise to build on such a site and refused to sell. The school board simply threatened to take it over with the guns of government through "eminent domain." Eminent domain allows a government agency to force a person—at gunpoint, if necessary—to give up his or her land if the project is "for the common good."

Hooker finally gave in to aggression-through-government. The school board bought the property for $1. Hooker brought the board members to the canal site to see the stored chemicals[2] in an effort to convince them to avoid building underground facilities of any kind.

In spite of these warnings, the city began construction of sanitary and storm sewers in 1957. In 1958, children playing in the area came into contact with the exposed chemicals and developed skin irritation. Hooker again warned the board to stop excavation and to cover the exposed area. The school board did not heed the warnings. By 1978 reports of chemical toxicity began surfacing. The EPA filed suit, not against the school board, but against Hooker Chemical! Taxpayers paid $30 million to relocate residents.[4] Thankfully, extensive testing of the residents found no significant long-term differences between their health and the health of the general population.[5,6]

The Love Canal incident is a classic case of the role of aggression in polluting our environment. The officers of Hooker Chemical took responsibility for their toxic waste by disposing of it carefully. They did not want to harm others. Hooker did not want to turn the property over to the school board for fear that the

new owners would not be as careful. The
company's fears were well–founded. The
school board was protected by sovereign
immunity, which holds government officials
blameless for whatever damage they cause.
Public officials are no different from you or
I—they work for incentives. Anyone who is
held responsible for mistakes or miscalcula-
tions will strive to avoid making them. The
school board members knew they would not
be personally liable for poisoning the public.
Instead, they were under pressure to find
cheap land for the school. If they excavated
Love Canal and nothing went wrong, they'd be
heroes; if the chemicals caused problems,
Hooker would take the heat. The board had
everything to gain and nothing to lose. How
different things would have been if school
board members could have been prosecuted
for the damage *they* had caused!

THE FOX IN THE HEN HOUSE

Sovereign immunity is probably responsible for more pollution in this country than any
other single cause. For example, in 1984, a
Utah court ruled that negligence in nuclear
testing was responsible for health problems in
10 out of 24 cases brought before the court.
The court of appeals, however, claimed that
sovereign immunity applied; therefore, the victims received nothing.[7] In 1988, the Department of Energy indicated that 17 weapons
plants were leaking radioactive and toxic
chemicals that would cost $100 billion and 50
years to clean up! The Departments of Energy
and Defense refused to comply with EPA
orders to do so.[8,9] Meanwhile, taxpayers are
expected to "Superfund" toxic waste cleanup.[6]

Sovereign immunity violates the second
principle of non–aggression. It allows government officials to do what individuals cannot.
We would not claim sovereign immunity if we
dumped trash on George's lawn nor could we
expect to enjoy a prosperous and peaceful

neighborhood. Somehow we think our country can be bountiful and harmonious even if our government officials can poison the property or body of our neighbors without having to undo the harm they have done. We go along with this sleight of hand because we think that *we* benefit when our government hurts others in seeking the common good. As usual, our aggression backfires.

Our lawmakers have extended the concept of sovereign immunity to include favored private monopolies. For example, in 1957, a study by the Atomic Energy Commission predicted that a major accident at a nuclear power plant could cause up to $7 billion in property damage and several thousand deaths. The marketplace ecosystem protected the consumer from such events naturally: no company would insure the nuclear installations, so power companies were hesitant to proceed. To encourage nuclear power, Congress passed laws to limit the liability of the power plants to $560 million. In the event of an accident, the insurance companies would have to pay only $60 million; the other $500 million would be paid through the further aggression of taxation![10] If the damage were more extensive, the victims would just have to suffer.

Sovereign immunity is a way of hiding the true cost of aggression–through–government. If our taxes reflected the cost of cleaning up pollution caused by the defense industry, we might not be so eager to give it free rein. If we had to compensate those whose loved ones died from nuclear testing, we might demand that such testing stop. If the price tag for insuring nuclear power plants were reflected in our electric bills, we might prefer alternative fuel. If we saw the true cost of our aggression—the raping of our planet—we might not choose to support it. Until we hold government officials for what they do, our environment will progressively deteriorate.

Likewise, private corporations are not always required to undo the damage they have done. As a result, the aggression of taxation is used to Superfund the cleanup.[6] If polluters don't restore the earth, we will be forced to.

CANCER FROM CHEMICALS?

We all want an environment safe from toxic chemicals that could cause cancer. Unfortunately for our peace of mind, half of all chemicals, both natural and synthetic, are carcinogenic when tested at high doses in animals. Plants make natural, carcinogenic insecticides to protect them from attack. Americans eat approximately 1,500 mg per day of these natural pesticides. The FDA estimates we consume 0.15 mg per day of the synthetics.[11]

Fortunately, these levels are well below established acceptable daily intakes.[12] Our liver is easily able to destroy small amounts of cancer-causing agents. When rats are given large quantities of potential carcinogens, this protective mechanism is overwhelmed. Many compounds that are quite safe may appear to be carcinogenic in such tests.

One such chemical, ethylene dibromide (EDB) was banned by the EPA in 1984. Although EDB can cause cancer when given to animals in large amounts, 50 years of human experience did not show increased cancer incidence among manufacturing personnel who are exposed to many thousand times more EDB than consumers over long periods. EDB had been used as a grain pesticide, preventing the growth of molds that produce aflatoxin, the most carcinogenic substance known. Naturally, farmers didn't want their grain contaminated with a potent cancer-causing substance, so they turned to the only other effective substitutes for EDB: a mixture of methyl bromide, phosphine, and carbon tetrachloride/carbon disulfide. Carbon tetrachloride and methyl bromide are both potent carcinogens in animals; phosphine and methyl

You can't eat a meal that doesn't have carcinogens....Human blood wouldn't pass the Toxic Substances Initiative if it got into a stream.
—Dr. Bruce Ames
inventor of
the Ames test
for carcinogenicity

bromide must be handled by specially skilled workers because they are so dangerous to work with.[13] By using the aggression of prohibitive licensing, the EPA left us to choose between moldy grain with highly toxic natural carcinogens or more dangerous mold-controlling pesticides!

One of these bans affected our overseas neighbors dramatically. By 1946, the insecticide DDT had been recognized as one of the most important disease-preventing agents known to humans. Used extensively in the tropics, it eradicated the insects that carried malaria, yellow fever, sleeping sickness, typhus, and encephalitis. Crop yields were increased as the larva that devoured them were destroyed. Human side effects from DDT were rare even though thousands of individuals had their skin and clothing dusted with 10% DDT powder or lived in dwellings that were sprayed repeatedly. Some individuals didn't use the pesticide as directed and applied vast quantities to land and water. Claims that the bird population was being harmed, that DDT remained too long in the environment, and that it might cause cancer led Sri Lanka (then Ceylon) to abandon its spraying in 1964. The incidence of malaria, down to 17 cases per year, rose to pre-DDT levels (2.5 million cases) by 1969 as a result.[14] More people died from withdrawing DDT than were harmed by it.

In some cases, banning additives and useful chemicals might actually increase our risk of dying from cancer. Pesticides make fresh fruits and vegetables more affordable, thereby increasing consumption, which is one of the best ways to fight cancer according to the National Research Council.[15] Even the EPA admits that cancer from pesticides is less likely than being killed in an auto accident.[16] Is banning pesticides more sensible than banning automobiles? Obviously, people must choose for themselves the extent to which they are willing to risk *their* lives—and honor the

DDT has had a tremendous impact on the health of the world....Few drugs can claim to have done so much for mankind in so short a period of time as DDT did.

—George Claus and
Karen Bolander
ECOLOGICAL SANITY

We should rename the EPA the Tobacco Protection Agency, because it focuses public attention away from the biggest risk of all to some of the very smallest.
—Rosalyn Yalow
Nobel Prize winner
Medicine

choices of their neighbors. Pesticides can be largely avoided by buying organic produce; automobile accidents can be avoided by walking instead of driving.

Pesticides are relatively harmless when compared to the natural carcinogens from tobacco smoke. These deadly carcinogens are believed to be responsible for 30% of all cancer deaths.[17] Lung cancer in the United States is on the rise; other types of cancers may actually be on the decline when the statistics are adjusted for the increasing age of the American public.[18] Convincing people not to smoke would seem to be the best way to lower the incidence of cancer in the United States. Instead, our EPA focuses on asbestos.

Although asbestos can promote lung cancer during manufacturing, it appears to be quite safe when placed in buildings and left undisturbed. When it is removed, however, the fibers break, releasing the asbestos. As a result, workers removing the asbestos at the mandate of the EPA are at risk. Because of release during removal, asbestos levels in schools and other public buildings are higher after removal.[19] Money that could have gone to educate people about the dangers of smoking is instead used to increase the risk of cancer from asbestos! If lives are endangered, sovereign immunity will protect the guilty.

Congress has great incentive to promote such programs, especially if the dangers will not be evident for many years. Imagine the conversation that takes place between your local congresswoman and a lobbyist from the asbestos removal companies.

"Ms. Congresswoman, if you don't vote for asbestos removal, we'll let your constituents know that you don't care about their safety. We'll give our support to your opponent in the next election. He cares about those schoolchildren who are exposed to all that asbestos."

"I'm concerned about those children too!" exclaims the congresswoman defensively. "That's why I'll vote against it. The scientific evidence shows that asbestos levels are higher after removal than before. The workers who remove the asbestos will be at greater risk as well."

"That may very well be," admits the lobbyist, "but you know politics. What are you going to do when your constituents ask what you've done to help protect them from pollution? You'll say you didn't need to do anything; they'll wonder why they should pay you to do nothing."

"I will have done something! I'll have voted against the environmental hazard of asbestos removal!" exclaimed the congresswoman.

"Voters will remember that when somebody starts suing the asbestos manufacturers because he or she got cancer. Even if that person is a crackpot, the publicity will give you a bad time. If people are harmed from asbestos removal, however, no one will blame you—you have sovereign immunity! If you wish to be re-elected, you must vote for this bill."

"I don't want to get re-elected if I have to kill people to do it!" the congresswoman says angrily.

"That's just as well," returns the lobbyist sadly, "because if you don't vote for this bill, you probably won't be reelected. We need conscientious people like you in the legislature. Sometimes compromise is necessary. Vote for this bill and keep up the good work that you were elected to do!"

Eventually the congresswoman will vote for the asbestos removal bill or lose her seat to someone more willing to do so. As voters, we control this situation. When we do not insist that polluters right their wrongs, they will continue to pollute.

THE EASY WAY OUT

Accidents do happen. If we inadvertently spilled acid on George's arm, we'd probably offer to pay for his hospital bills. We'd also make sure that whatever caused the accident

didn't happen again. If a company puts something in the air, water, or soil that makes
people ill, it needs to restore, as much as
possible, those it has harmed.

Today, some polluters simply claim bankruptcy. Victims are left to suffer, while the
polluters just start over. We could do things
differently. Those responsible for the decision
to pollute could compensate a victim through
time payments or could be sent to a work
prison if they did not voluntarily make
amends. Victims who were insured against
such injury would get immediate payment
from their insurance companies, which would,
in turn, collect from polluters.

Naturally, many companies would want to
insure themselves against poor decisions by
their corporate officers. The premium for such
insurance would probably depend on the
company's record for environmental pollution
as well as the reputation of the individual
manager. To protect its interests, the insurance company would examine its clients'
policies concerning pollution and suggest
changes that would lower their risk and their
premiums. Companies with the potential to
pollute would be effectively regulated by the
marketplace ecosystem, free from aggression.
The high cost of paying for cleanup simply
would be so great that few would dare to
pollute. No tax dollars would be required to
fund this effective program. The practice of
non-aggression is economical and effective.

If a particular food additive or pesticide
has adverse effects that didn't show up in
animal testing, publicity will enable consumers to boycott the product. In 1990, a news
program questioning the safety of Alar caused
a dramatic drop in apple sales virtually overnight.[15]

However, if such charges are false, those
who propagate them could be sued for fraud.
Manufacturers and farmers who had used Alar
lost hundreds of thousands of dollars when

consumers refused to buy Alar–treated apples. Evidence for the safety of Alar, including a study by the National Cancer Institute, was presumably ignored by those putting the "exposé" together.[15] Businesses need not fear irresponsible journalism if they too are required to right their wrongs.

Pesticide manufacturers, like pharmaceutical firms, know that killing the customer is bad for business. However, independent testing is always highly desirable. Consumers might wish to avoid foods grown with new pesticides until these chemicals had been given a seal of approval from a trusted evaluation center. Such testing agencies would be similar to those described for pharmaceuticals in Chapter 6 (*Protecting Ourselves to Death*).

Pollution or environmental damage often comes from a small number of vendors who can be easily confronted with the fruits of their actions. In some cases, however, almost everyone contributes to the pollution, such as automobile exhaust. How can we be protected from this type of pollution in a country practicing non–aggression?

Air pollution is a local problem. Rural areas dissipate car exhaust rapidly, while enclosed locations, such as the Los Angeles area, trap it. Concerned citizens in such places might take the local road companies to court, since pollution emanates from roads. Currently, governments control most of the roads and would claim sovereign immunity.

Without the aggression of taxation, all roads would be private. Since people would not be eager to face toll booths at every interconnection, road companies would undoubtedly devise a system of annual fees or electronic monitoring. For example, your annual license payment might give you access to all roads in your area. The road companies would divide your payment in proportion to the number of miles each firm maintained. Instead of annual payments, you might be given an electronic monitor that registered the number of miles you drive on each road. Every month you would be billed accordingly.

When residents of a particular locale sued the road companies, they would have to undo whatever damage they had done and prevent future pollution. They would raise their rates to compensate the victims. Since 10% of the cars cause 50% of the pollution because they are not regularly tuned,[20] rates might be lower for those who passed an emissions test. When polluters have to pay for the damage they do, most will decide against it. The few who continue to pollute will have to pay dearly for the privilege of doing so.

The solution to pollution is to require those who damage the property, body, or reputation of another to restore it. Making aggressors right their wrongs teaches that pollution doesn't pay.

For polluters to undo the damage they have done, they must first be caught and sentenced. As we learned earlier, criminals of all kinds are brought to justice infrequently in today's world. In the next few chapters, we'll learn why.

CHAPTER 15

DEALING IN DEATH

Using aggression to stop drug abuse kills more people than the drugs themselves!

If we honored our neighbor's choice, the people now enforcing the minimum wage and licensing laws would be available to go after the real criminals. In 1987, drug offenders made up 36% of the federal prison population.[1] As the War on Drugs escalates, more of our law enforcement dollar will be spent on drug-related crimes and less on rapists, murderers, and thieves. Is this the best way to deal with the drug problem?

AGGRESSION DIDN'T WORK THEN...

People who drink an alcoholic beverage in the privacy of their own homes are not using first-strike force, theft, or fraud against anyone else. Nor is a person smoking a joint or snorting cocaine, under the same conditions, guilty of anything more sinister than trying to feel good. We see no contradiction in arresting the cocaine user while we enjoy our favorite cocktail. Are we once again sanctioning aggression-through-government in an attempt to control the lives of others?

In the early 1900s, many people supported aggression-through-government to stop the consumption of alcoholic beverages. As we all know, Prohibition was tried, but it just didn't work. People still drank, but they had to settle for home-brews, which were not always safe. Some people even died from drinking them.[2] Since business people could no longer sell alcohol, organized crime did. Turf battles killed innocent bystanders, and law enforcement officials found they could make more money taking bribes than jailing the bootleggers. Aggression was ineffective—and expensive, both in terms of dollars and lives.

Vices are simply the errors which a man makes in search after his own happiness. In vices, the very essence of crime—that is, the design to injure the person or property of another—is wanting.
—Lysander Spooner, ???

The more prohibitions you have, the less virtuous people will be ....Try to make people moral, and you lay the groundwork for vice.
—Lao-tsu
TAO TE CHING

Prohibition ended in 1933 because the nation's most influential people, as well as the general public, acknowledged that it had failed. It had increased lawlessness and drinking and aggravated alcohol abuse.
—Thomas M. Coffey author of THE LONG THIRST—PROHIBITION IN AMERICA: 1920-1933

When Prohibition was repealed, people bought their alcohol from professional brewers instead of criminals. As a result, they stopped dying from bathtub gin. The turf fighting subsided, since there was no turf to fight about. The murder and assault rate that had skyrocketed during Prohibition fell steadily after its repeal.[3]

Today, Americans are switching from hard liquor to beer and wine.[4] Educating people about the deleterious effects of alcohol has proven more effective than force. Those concerned about alcohol abuse are educating and treating addicts rather than jailing them (e.g., Alcoholics Anonymous).

AGGRESSION ISN'T WORKING NOW!

An estimated 20% of adults age 20 to 40 years use illegal recreational drugs regularly.[5] The death toll from overdose was 7,000 in 1988[6] while 100,000 to 200,000 died from alcohol-related causes,[7] and 320,000 to 390,000 died from tobacco.[8] Tobacco is the hardest drug in terms of addictiveness.[9] Its popularity makes it the most serious drug-related threat to worldwide health. However, the biggest killer of all is overeating, believed to be responsible for 500,000 to 1,000,000 cardiovascular deaths each year.[10] Much effort and expense is being directed at a relatively minor problem, most of which comes from the aggression we are using to stop it!

For example, approximately 80% of the 7,000 deaths attributed to drug overdose would probably not have occurred if the recreational drugs had been marketed legally.[11] Legal drugs are tested for safety, while street drugs are sold even when they are highly toxic. They are frequently cut with other substances, such as quinine, caffeine, and amphetamines, which makes them even more dangerous. The user seldom knows how much drug is actually being administered, making overdose—and death—much more likely. Once again, prohibition puts more people at risk.

Street drugs are 100 times more expensive than their legal counterparts.[12] The safer oral route is shunned by drug users, because much more drug is needed to get the desired effects. Instead, users take the expensive drugs intravenously, sometimes producing fatally high blood levels. When users get in trouble, they delay seeking medical help for fear of arrest. The basketball player Len Bias had three seizures before his friends finally called the medics. By then, it was too late.[13]

If the estimate is correct that 80% of drug overdose deaths are needless, the true U.S. death toll caused by the inherent toxicity of recreational drugs would be closer to 1400 per year. In Amsterdam, where the drug user is not criminalized, there are only 60 drug-induced deaths per year, in a population 20 times smaller than that of the United States.[6] Thus, the estimate of an 80% overkill caused by drug prohibition appears to be very close.

In addition, prohibition causes some indirect deaths. Each year, approximately 3,500 drug users contract AIDS from sharing needles.[14] In Hong Kong, where needles can be bought without a prescription, AIDS is not spread by contaminated needles.[15]

Approximately 750 people are killed annually during black market turf fighting.[16] Each year 1,600 innocent individuals are killed while being robbed by users.[16] These robbery-related deaths would be unlikely if recreational substances could be sold legally, just as alcohol is. How many alcoholics need to steal to support their habit?

More than 11,000 people die each year because we succumb to the temptation to use aggression to control others. If we honored our neighbor's choice, fewer people would die each year, unless drug use increased eightfold. Given the current estimates of drug use, almost the entire U.S. population would have to take drugs for this level to be reached. The War on Drugs kill more people than the drugs themselves!

Who profits from these deaths? The money goes directly to the people in organized crime, just as it did during Prohibition. Our Central Intelligence Agency (CIA) sometimes protects and aids these people to get information or to pay for activities that Congress won't fund![17] Our eagerness to control our neighbors creates and sustains those with motives more sinister than just getting high!

Our own choices are compromised when we refuse to honor the choices of others. Recent changes in our laws allow the police to confiscate the property of *presumed* drug dealers before they are proven guilty.[18] In the *Pittsburgh Press*' 10-month study of such confiscations, 80% of the people subjected to seizure were never even charged with a crime![19] A vindictive neighbor could falsely accuse us of drug trafficking, and we could lose everything even though we were innocent. Our desire to control our neighbors gives them power over us. We create a world that sustains the Mafia, unauthorized CIA projects, punishment without a trial, and false accusations.

How much of the drug traffic do we stop after paying this enormous price? Estimates suggest that only 10% of the street drugs are interdicted before sale.[20] Clearly, our aggression hasn't solved the problem—it has simply created a more deadly one!

THE EASY WAY OUT

If aggression aggravates rather than solves the drug problem, there is no sense in continuing this "prohibitive" licensing. When marijuana was legalized in Alaska, consumption went down.[21] The Netherlands had a similar experience.[22] In Amsterdam, heroin addiction is half that of the U.S. rate, and crack is not widely available.[6] When we honor our neighbor's choice, he or she will often act differently than we would have predicted.

To get drugs out of our schools, we need to take aggression out of our legal code. The excessive profit that comes from prohibitive

If the government cannot stop people from using drugs in the prisons over which it has total control, why should Americans forfeit any of their traditional civil rights in the hope of reducing the drug problem?
—Inmate
Federal Correctional Institution, El Reno, Oklahoma
Time Magazine, October 16, 1989

licensing would not exist in the self-regulating marketplace ecosystem. Alcohol and cigarettes, which are illegal for minors, are less of a problem because they are less profitable.

If recreational drugs were legal, their medicinal properties could be more easily studied and employed. Today, red tape discourages physicians from giving marijuana to their patients, even though it can slow the progress of glaucoma, keep cancer patients from being nauseated by chemotherapy, and help treat multiple sclerosis.[23] Until it became illegal, marijuana was listed in the U.S. Pharmacopoeia for some of these purposes.[24]

Instead, our enforcement agents seized the marijuana plants of a retired postal worker suffering from cancer. Robert Brewser had used them to control the pain and nausea from his radiation therapy. The agents also took—without trial—the van his wife used to take him to the hospital for treatment![19] How much universal love do we show our neighbors when we support laws that make this possible?

Without the aggression of prohibitive licensing, scientists would study how they work and find out why people take them. The money now spent on aggression could be directed toward education and research. We would have a chance at really winning the war on drugs, just as we are now winning the war on alcohol, not by Prohibition, but by the only method that really works—convincing people that drug abuse is not in their best interest.

For the most part, drug abusers hurt only themselves. If they threaten to harm others, they should be held responsible for their actions.

Cravings for illegal recreational drugs may have both physiological and emotional components. Alcoholism is a disease. Dependence on drugs is a medical problem as well. People who are willing to sacrifice their health, wealth, and social standing for chemical highs require our help, not our condemnation,

Elvy Musikka...was arrested last month for possession of 4 marijuana plants. "I can't think of any crime that should be punished by blindness," Elvy said ....Doctors at Bascome Palmer Eye Clinic in Miami have said that without marijuana, her glaucoma is getting worse.
—On the Freedom Trail
May 1988

If even a small fraction of the money we now spend on trying to enforce drug prohibition were devoted to treatment and drug rehabilitation, in an atmosphere of compassion not punishment, the reduction in drug usage and in the harm done to users could be dramatic.
—Milton Friedman
Nobel Prize winner
Economics

The real question is why are millions of people so unhappy, so bored, so unfulfilled, that they are willing to drink, snort, inject or inhale any substance that might blot out reality and give them a bit of temporary relief.
—Ann Landers
syndicated columnist

especially when we may inadvertently contributed to their distress.

Aggression–through–government sets the stage for drug problems. When we discriminate against disadvantaged workers through minimum wage and licensing laws, we frustrate their economic goals. Getting high is certainly more attractive when other parts of one's life don't seem to be working. Selling drugs certainly seems like a lucrative career for a ghetto youth banned from legitimate paths of creating wealth. In addition to the other deleterious effects of licensing laws, they may well contribute to the drug problem.

Drug prohibition is counterproductive. We resist this conclusion, however, because we want to control other people's choices. Some people will indeed make what we consider to be poor choices for themselves. People who overeat, drink heavily, or engage in dangerous activities may prefer a shorter, more exciting, and intense life to a longer one with different rewards. They may prefer gratification over longevity. It is their life and their choice—if we would only honor it.

We cannot protect people from themselves. When we honor their choice of food, drink, drugs, or activities, we free our police to focus on individuals who would directly and purposefully harm us through force, theft, or fraud. When we stop trying to control others, we can more readily prevent aggressors from controlling us, as described in the following chapter.

CHAPTER 16

POLICING AGGRESSION

We can protect ourselves from aggression only by refusing to be aggressors ourselves.

In the past few chapters, we've seen how we create and encourage crime. First, disadvantaged workers are forbidden by law to create wealth through minimum wage and licensing laws. If they turn to theft, they find that they are not required to right their wrongs. Crime pays. When prohibitive licensing prevents legitimate businesses from selling recreational drugs, organized crime and youth gangs spring into action. The disadvantaged turn to theft once again to buy drugs that give them, for a time, a high that their reality does not. Polluters find it profitable to poison the environment when they are not required to undo the damage they have done. If we practiced non-aggression, we'd have much less crime to deal with.

We create crime and then blame our overworked police for not controlling it. Our local police are handicapped by being exclusive, subsidized government monopolies (Third Layer aggression). As always, the incentive structure of such monopolies results in high-cost, low-quality service with minimal innovation. As a result, we pay more money for less.

THE HIGH COST OF AGGRESSION

Reminderville, Ohio, and the surrounding township were aghast when the Summit County Sheriff's Department wanted to charge the community $180,000 per year for a 45-minute emergency response time and an occasional patrol. Corporate Security, a private police organization, offered to provide a 6-minute emergency response time and twice as many patrols for one-half of the cost![1] The community gained the benefits of contracting out—more service for less.

The private company saved its customers money with used cars and equipment.[2] The private police officers enforced the law, while clerical personnel took care of the "social-worker, caretaker, baby-sitter, errand-boy" activities that can amount to 80% of public police work.[3]

Oro Valley, Arizona, enjoyed similar savings when the town contracted out its police work to Rural/Metro in 1975. However, the Arizona Law Enforcement Officers' Advisory Council took the matter to court, arguing that an employee of a private company could not be a municipal police officer. The Council wanted the guns of government to give state troopers an exclusive monopoly on providing police service. Ironically, the public police wanted to use collective aggression against the very people they were supposed to protect from individual aggression!

The court expenses were too much for Rural/Metro. They withdrew from Oro Valley. In 1975, the city had paid $35,000 to Rural/Metro; by 1982, it needed $241,000 to subsidize the public police.[4] The police that were hired to protect the public used the guns of government to exploit them!

The Oro Valley community lost more than money, however. Rural/Metro could charge less and profit more by *preventing* crime instead of *fighting* it. Rural/Metro did things the public police had no incentive to do, such as checking homes twice a day when residents went out of town. These measures had cut burglary rates 95%![4]

The private police had to please their customers, or the community would hire a company that would. Rather than trying to offer to serve Oro Valley residents better, the public police used the guns of government against them. The blame cannot be laid at the feet of public police, however. Like most American communities, local voters had not honored their neighbor's choice when they established the public police as an exclusive, subsidized monopoly in the first place. In trying to control others, voters found themselves controlled.

DISCRIMINATION AGAINST THE DISAD-VANTAGED
Subsidizing the Rich

When a community such as Reminderville contracts with a private police company instead of hiring its own employees, local taxes are still used to pay for the service. Our enforcement agents take our money—at gunpoint, if necessary—to protect us from others who wish to take our money at gunpoint!

As usual, poor people are hurt the most by the aggression of taxation. The poor pay a large portion of their income for rent, which reflects the property taxes that support the local police. As a percentage of their income, the poor may pay more for police protection than their middle-income neighbors. Most crime occurs in low-income neighborhoods; nevertheless, the poor are largely ignored.

My mother and sister came out of a drug store one day to find their bikes had been stolen. They silently followed the thieves to a ghetto apartment, where my mother and sister could see their bikes just inside the open door. The police officer they called told the two women that the police just didn't go into that apartment complex because it was far too dangerous! He advised my mother and sister to get whatever money they could from their insurance company!

If my mother and sister couldn't get the police to rescue their bikes that were in plain sight, what chance would a person dwelling in that complex have of police support? If the poor could threaten to take their tax dollars elsewhere, they would at least have some leverage. Without having the option to vote with their dollars, poor people are largely ignored. When individuals have sued unresponsive police, the courts have ruled that "the police do not exist to provide personal protection to individual citizens."[5] The individuals who get the least protection of all are the poor. As a result, they are forced to provide their own, in addition to supporting a police force that favors other segments of the population over them. Only by giving poor people their economic vote back can we hope to achieve equality.

Leaving the Poor Defenseless

The poor pay taxes to subsidize a police force that discriminates against them. Left to their own resources, the poor patrol their own neighborhoods and rely on inexpensive handguns. Sophisticated alarm systems or trained dogs are beyond their economic reach. As if their plight were not bad enough, society attempts to disable the poor further by stopping them—at gunpoint, if necessary—from purchasing handguns.

The first such law, passed in 1870, was an attempt by Tennessee whites to disarm free blacks by prohibiting the sale of all but expensive military handguns.[6] Black people in America are three to six times as likely to be murdered as whites,[7] probably because blacks are more likely to live in low-income, high-crime areas. As a result, California's blacks kill more than twice as many people in self-defense as whites do.[8]

Defending oneself with a handgun makes sense: a victim who submits is twice as likely to be injured as a victim who resists with a gun. Defending oneself without a gun, however, results in injury more often than submission.[9] By the late 1970s, armed citizens were killing more criminals in self-defense than the police.[10]

Handgun ownership acts as a deterrent to crime. In October 1966, the Orlando police began a highly publicized program designed to train women in the use of firearms. The program was prompted by an increase in rape in the months preceding its implementation. The rape rate dropped from 34 incidents for every 100,000 inhabitants in 1966 to 4 incidents per 100,000 in 1967, even though the surrounding areas showed no drop at all. Burglary fell by 25%. No woman ever had to use her gun; the deterrent effect sufficed. Even five years later, Orlando's rape rate was 13% below the 1966 level, although the surrounding area was 308% higher.[11,12] In Albuquerque, New Mexico;[13] Highland Park, Michigan;[8] New Orleans, Louisiana;[8] and Detroit, Michigan,[8] crime rates, especially burglaries, plummeted when shopkeepers publicized their acquisition of handguns. When the city council of Kennesaw, Georgia, passed an ordinance requiring each household to keep a firearm, crime dropped 74% the following year.[14]

Surveys of convicted felons indicate that when the risk of confronting an armed victim increases, robberies are abandoned.[15] Among police officers, 90% believe that banning ownership of firearms would make ordinary citizens even more likely to be targets of armed violence.[16]

Criminals do respond to incentives.[17] When they think they will have their own actions reflected back to them, they choose cooperation instead of exploitation. The TIT FOR TAT strategy makes sure that crime doesn't pay.

Few criminals are affected by handgun bans anyway, since five-sixths of them don't purchase their guns legally.[18] Gun bans harm only the innocent.

Do handguns encourage domestic violence? After all, 81% of handgun victims are relatives or acquaintances of the killer.[19] However, two-thirds to four-fifths of the killers have prior arrest records, frequently for crimes of violence.[20] Thus, the average domestic killer is not a model citizen corrupted by gun possession, but a person continuing a life of violence.

A gun does not make one predisposed to kill any more than a functioning sex organ makes a man predisposed to rape. How one uses what one has determines its value. A gun can protect or kill. A man can violate or cherish. To castrate a man or disarm a person—at gunpoint, if necessary—is aggression.

Indeed, many of the domestic killings are acts of self-defense. One-half of murdered spouses are husbands of abused wives.[21] These women might be dead today if they had not had access to the family handgun. Guns give weaker victims equality with their attackers.

Women are quite capable of handling firearms. Some studies suggest that women learn how to handle guns more quickly than men![22]

New Zealand, Switzerland, and Israel have more gun ownership than the United States, yet in all these countries, homicides are less frequent.[23] On the other hand, the District of Columbia has the toughest antigun laws in the nation, yet it has become the murder capital of the United States.[24] Clearly, stopping people from owning guns—at gunpoint, if necessary—does not stop people from killing.

THE EASY WAY OUT

First, we encourage crime with our aggression in the form of minimum wage, licensing laws, drug laws, and prevention of homesteading. Aggressors find that crime pays when they do not have to right their wrongs. As a result, crime thrives. We become frustrated when our overworked police cannot cope with our creation. By making our police force an exclusive, subsidized government monopoly, we increase the cost and decrease the quality of protection, especially for the poor. By banning handguns, we disarm the disadvantaged.

As a result of our aggression, crime runs rampant. We lock ourselves inside our houses and take care when we walk through our world. We do not dare to give hitchhikers a ride for fear they will attack us. We live in the unfriendly world that we have created by our willingness to do unto others before they do unto us.

When we abandon our aggression, we will eliminate the crime we have encouraged. We will also set the stage for better protection against those who would trespass against us.

Eliminating the aggression of taxation would allow individuals or neighborhoods to hire the police service of their choice. If the private police didn't do the job they were hired to do, individuals could contract with someone else. Today, of course, consumers have no choice. They must subsidize police service without any guarantee of service.

Customers hiring private police might elect to make an annual payment that includes patrolling, apprehending criminals, or any other items mutually agreed upon. Since preventing burglaries and assaults would keep costs down and profits up, police officers would advise their clients of ways to prevent crime. Prevention might also include house checks when the client is out of town. A protection agency with a reputation for effective capture of criminals might deter criminals just by posting its logo on the insured's building.

The very poor could pay for police services by participating in neighborhood patrols organized by the neighborhood's protection agency. Today, in spite of paying taxes through their rent, the poor must patrol without compensation. In 1977, 55% of the citizen patrols were found in low-income neighborhoods, while only 35% and 10% were in middle- and high-income neighborhoods, respectively. Approximately 63% of the patrols were volunteers,[25] suggesting again that the poor pay both their taxes and their time for their inadequate protection. Without the aggression of handgun bans, the poor could be armed if they chose to be.

Police brutality, often directed at the lower classes, would also be curtailed. Private police would not only be liable if they failed to live up to their contract with their client, but they could also be held *personally* liable for any brutality toward those they apprehended. Law-abiding citizens would shun a firm with a reputation for viciousness and would effectively put such a company out of business.

Today, private police in more than 10,000 firms[26] outnumber public police two to one.[27] The private firms coordinate their activities with each other or with the public police, as appropriate. The well-to-do are voting with their dollars for more protection than the public police can provide. When we forsake aggression, those less fortunate will be able to afford adequate protection services as well.

Even when criminals are captured, they seldom go to prison. The courts are so crowded that plea bargaining is a regular practice.[28] The criminal gets a suspended sentence; the prosecutor tallies up another conviction. The victims have nothing to say about it—even though their taxes pay the prosecutor's salary.

Victims cannot even take criminal charges elsewhere if the prosecutor decides not to take their case. The prosecutor has an exclusive, subsidized government monopoly on bringing criminal charges.

Without this exclusive license, victims could hire the lawyers of their choice to prosecute—or could prosecute the case personally if they chose. Since a convicted criminal would have to pay the trial costs—in a work prison, if necessary—even a poor victim would be able to attract competent counsel on contingency. No taxes would have to be collected for justice to be served. No victims would have to pay for a prosecutor who would not help them.

Today, the guilty have everything to gain and nothing to lose by dragging out the court proceedings. If they had to pay all the costs associated with their conviction, however, they would not be so eager to appeal repeatedly. Instead, many would choose to settle with the victim out of court to avoid such costs. With fewer cases coming to trial, justice would be swifter than it is today.

If the disputing parties could not reach an agreement, they could hire a judge or arbitrator. In California and several other states, justice has been deregulated. Aggression to enforce an exclusive, subsidized government monopoly on judgeship has been abandoned. Anyone who is qualified for jury duty can render a legal judgment.[29] In addition to California's independent judges, companies such as Civicourt; Washington Arbitration Services, Inc.; Judicial Mediation, Inc.; Resolution, Inc.; and EnDispute, Inc., offer quick, inexpensive justice. Judicate, founded in Philadelphia, has been referred to as the "national private court," with offices in 45 states as of 1987.[30] The rapid and reasonably priced trials these private courts provide are obviously considered a good deal by both parties, since mutual agreement is required to take the case from the public courts to a private one.

Although most of the private courts currently deal with property disputes, there is no reason that litigants in a criminal case should not be able to choose their judges as well. With the criminal routinely paying for the costs of the trial, no taxes would be needed to support these courts.

Would such a system of multiple courts promote different codes of justice in different areas of the country? Probably not. Today, we have several layers of jurisdiction between city, county, state, and federal courts. Judgments, laws, and penalties differ from state to state, for example, without causing undue hardship.

History suggests that in the marketplace ecosystem, free from aggression, justice tends to be consistent. When the Western states were only territories, as many as four courts shared a jurisdiction. Those who observed such systems in action noted that "appeals were taken from one to the other, papers certified up or down and over, and recognized, criminals delivered and judgments accepted

from one court by another."[31] The judges had
the best motive in the world for making their
decisions clear and consistent—litigants would
not hire them if they didn't give clear, consistent judgments.

To improve our domestic security, all we
need to do is abandon aggression. If we were
successful in doing this, what would our
country be like?

CHAPTER 17

PUTTING IT ALL TOGETHER

The practice of non-aggression domestically creates a peaceful and prosperous nation.

How We Went Astray

The founders of our country knew the importance of honoring their neighbor's choice. They knew the secret of creating wealth was to avoid aggression-through-government. Our Constitution reflected the first principle of non-aggression—honoring our neighbor's choice—to a greater extent than any other nation of that time. Consequently, we became the wealthiest country in the world.

The second principle of non-aggression was not so well established, however. When individuals stole, defrauded, or attacked an innocent neighbor, they were not usually required to right their wrongs. The focus was on punishing the criminal without necessarily restoring the victim. When wrongs were not righted, crime paid, so it grew and flourished.

In frustration, Americans tried to fight fire with fire, but they only increased the size of the blaze. Those who lied about their medical credentials were not required to make their victims whole again. Instead, the guns of government were used to en*force* licensing laws for medical practitioners. Those who sold untested medicines while claiming they were safe paid fines to the government, but rarely compensated their victims fully. Trying to make up for a breadwinner's death might take a lifetime. Such a penalty would effectively deter those who would harm others.

Instead of requiring aggressors to experience the fruits of their actions, Americans tried to deter aggression by becoming aggressors themselves. Aggression-through-government was instituted in an attempt to deter aggression by individuals. As always, more aggression only made a bad situation worse. In the field of health care, medical practitioners became expensive and less available, innovation was stymied, and the introduction of new pharmaceuticals was delayed or prevented. Licensing laws in other areas had the same adverse affects.

The guns of government were used to prevent homesteading over vast areas of the country. The Pyramid of Power grew, giving control of our destinies to a powerful elite. Wealth creation slowed.

Naturally, the poor were most adversely affected as the Wealth Pie shrank. Aggression–through–government limited wealth–creating options of the poor. If they could not gain a foothold on the Ladder of Affluence, they more frequently turned to stealing or drug dealing. Still others surrendered themselves to the elusive pleasures of mind–altering drugs.

The justice system focused on enforcing aggression–through–government instead of defending against individual aggressors. Consequently, fewer thieves, murderers, and rapists were apprehended. Because taxpayers, not criminals, had to pay for the prisons, victims were robbed twice. Prisons became overcrowded and reduced sentences became common. Crime paid and so it flourished.

As crime grew, the police and court systems were unable to cope. As an exclusive, subsidized government monopoly, the justice 8system was less efficient and more costly than it otherwise would have been. When justice was slow, criminal activity became more profitable and widespread. Fear of others permeated our culture.

THE EASY WAY OUT

TIT FOR TAT showed us how to deter crime. First, we honor our neighbor's choice. Second, we allow aggressors to experience the consequences of their actions by requiring them to right their wrongs. When we teach aggression by becoming aggressors ourselves, we encourage crime. If we want a society free from crime, we must stop supporting the crime that we perpetrate through government.

Once we have rejected aggression, we make it easier for others to do so. When we allow the disadvantaged to create wealth for themselves, they don't need to steal. As the Wealth Pie grows, more is available to help the truly needy. Fewer people choose a life of crime when they can get ahead without it.

Those who do seek to exploit others would be brought to justice more rapidly in a country that practiced non-aggression. With more wealth available and fewer criminals to apprehend, capture would be more likely. When criminals pay the costs of their trial, capture, and imprisonment, justice would not be limited by the amount of money that the innocent were able to pay.

Righting our wrongs is less expensive than trying to control anyone who *might* harm us. We focus on the guilty few instead of the innocent many. Crime is effectively deterred when the probability of being caught and made to pay the full costs of one's crime is high.

Deterrents are especially important for polluters. When people know they will pay for the harm done to another's body or property, they are more careful.

When criminals fully compensate their victims, they have truly paid their debt. A restored victim is a victim no longer. Bygones can truly be bygones when the damage is fully undone. By practicing both aspects of non-aggression, we take responsibility for our choices and allow others to do the same. We treat all people as equals—equally free to choose and equally responsible for their choices.

HEALING OUR WORLD—AND OURSELVES!

When we attempt to force our choices on others, we are denying this reality. Not only

Center your country in the Tao and evil will have no power. Not that it isn't there, but you'll be able to step out of its way.

—Lao-tsu
TAO TE CHING

does this denial perpetrate poverty and strife, it is directly harmful to our physical well-being as well. Aggressive Type A personalities who are prone to heart attacks tend to blame others for their problems.[1] A Type A person in a political context might believe that selfish others are responsible for the world's woes. Type A's tend to view the world as a hostile place where "doing unto others before they do unto you" seems practical. As we've seen, our nation's laws reflect such attitudes. Could that be why heart disease is the Number 1 killer in the United States?[2]

Type C victim personalities are susceptible to cancer. They feel that they are helpless to acquire whatever they associate with happiness.[1] In a socioeconomic context, Type C people may believe themselves incapable of creating enough wealth to sustain themselves and their loved ones. They feel that they are victims of the system. Sometimes they might use this feeling of victimization as a justification for stealing and harming others.

These unhealthy attitudes fuel each other in a positive feedback, A/C Loop. Type A beliefs lead to the aggression of licensing laws, which prevent the disadvantaged from creating wealth for themselves and their loved ones. Type C people who can't reach the first rung of the Ladder of Affluence feel helpless to control their own destiny. Type A's then blame the plight of Type C individuals on the selfishness of others and propose the aggression of taxation to provide for these unfortunates. Charity by aggression ensnares more people in the Poverty Trap, reaffirming in the poor a Type C belief in their own helplessness. Could this be why cancer is our Number 2 killer[2] and why the poor are more susceptible to it?[3]

People who tend to live the longest ("Type S," for self-actualized) believe that their happiness (or unhappiness) results from their own choices.[1] Because Type S people do not blame selfish others for their plight, they focus on doing whatever they can to help themselves.

Since this attitude is most likely to result in accomplishing their goals, self-actualized people feel competent rather than helpless.

In a political context, Type S personalities honor their neighbor's choice, because they do not see selfish others as the cause of their woes. In a society where aggressors right their wrongs, victims are restored. Consequently, there is little reason to feel like a helpless victim. Non-aggression sets the stage for the evolution of the healthy Type S societal personality.

As long as we continue to be majorities and minorities, victims and aggressors, our society will be diseased—as individuals and as the body politic. When we practice non-aggression, we heal our world and ourselves.

A nation that practiced non-aggression would enjoy physical and economic health. Such a nation would be wealthier than any other. With an ethic of respect, tolerance, and righting any wrongs, prosperity and tranquillity would be the natural outcome. When we understand the *cause* of peace and plenty, we realize that these goals are well within our reach. When we stop trying to control others, we free ourselves from the bondage of war and poverty, disease and discontent!

And ye shall know the truth, and the truth shall set you free.
—THE HOLY BIBLE
John 8:32

Can a nation that practices non-aggression long survive in a world that does not? Once again, the computer games suggest that TIT FOR TAT (non-aggression) is highly likely to spread in a population of aggressors. Even a cluster of non-aggressors that make up only 5% of the population is able to accomplish this.[4] If the aggressors can't be converted, those people who practice non-aggression do so well with each other that they still come out ahead!

...mutual cooperation can emerge in a world of egoists without central control by starting with a cluster of individuals who rely on reciprocity.
—Robert Axelrod
THE EVOLUTION
OF COOPERATION

Aggressors end up teaching aggression. In the computer games, the best the aggressors can do after teaching aggression to those they interact with is one point each round. TIT FOR TAT practitioners, however, get three points apiece. To the extent that real life has similar payoffs, non-aggression is many times more profitable than aggression. Selfish others will be converted to non-aggression because it pays off on an individual level; altruists will practice non-aggression because it brings widespread peace and plenty. No matter how you look at it, non-aggression wins the game!

THE PRACTICE OF NON–AGGRESSION MAKES A WIN–WIN WORLD!

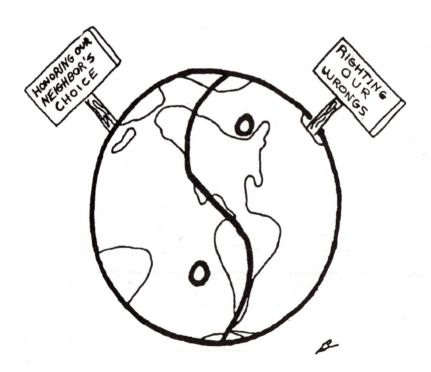

PART IV

LEAD US NOT INTO TEMPTATION

FOREIGN POLICY

CHAPTER 18

BEACON TO THE WORLD

The most effective way to help poorer nations is to practice non-aggression.

We are fortunate. We live in a nation founded by people who knew that aggression-through-government creates poverty and strife. Consequently, we have become the wealthiest nation on earth. How can we apply our new understanding to help the developing nations, where people still die regularly of starvation and disease?

CREATING POVERTY IN THE THIRD WORLD

Before we can help disadvantaged nations, we need to know what creates their poverty in the first place. In Chapter 2, we found that resource endowment had little bearing on a nation's wealth. Indeed, most developing nations have more strategic minerals than Japan, one of the wealthiest countries in the world. Lack of natural resources cannot account for the plight of the Third World.

Despite popular myths, rapid population growth and high population density are not major factors in Third World poverty either. Hong Kong and Singapore, with annual per capita GNPs in excess of $6,000 in 1985, had more than 10,000 people per square mile. In contrast, India and China, with fewer than 1,000 people per square mile, have per capita incomes of less than $400![1] Developing countries that enjoy the highest economic growth rate often have the highest population growth rates as well![2] Between 1775 and 1975, the United States had the biggest population explosion in history,[3] yet Americans now earn the highest wages in the world. Clearly, rapid population growth and high population density are no more responsible for poverty than inadequate resource endowment.

...economic studies have failed to demonstrate that population growth has bad effects.

—Jacqueline Kasun
THE WAR AGAINST POPULATION

Generation after generation, the poor have streamed to America and been lifted out of poverty. This "liberation theology" actually does liberate.

—Michael Novak
WILL IT LIBERATE?

...human development is frustrated in most Hispanic-American countries—and most Third World countries —by a way of seeing the world that impedes the achievement of political pluralism, social equality, and dynamic economic progress.
—Lawrence D. Harrison
UNDERDEVELOPMENT IS A STATE OF MIND: THE LATIN AMERICAN CASE

Let the Tao be present in your country and your country will be an example to all countries in the world.
—Lao-tsu
TAO TE CHING

Poverty in today's world is primarily due to aggression-through-government. When we look closely at Third World nations, we see this aggression everywhere. Jobs, and consequently the Wealth Pie, are constantly limited by it. In spite of all the examples given in the previous chapters, our country still enjoys more freedom—freedom from aggression—than most other nations. The level of aggression in underdeveloped countries is difficult for most Americans to even imagine.

For example, in Peru, it takes an average of 289 days to obtain a business license. It takes the equivalent of 32 times a Peruvian's monthly minimum living wage to open a small garment factory.[4] Small industrial firms spend approximately 70% of their profits to pay taxes and meet legal requirements.[5] A license to homestead state land takes an average of 83 months and the equivalent of 56 months of minimum wage pay.[6] Building a market "mall" legally can take 17 years.[7] A license for a new bus route takes approximately 53 months to arrange and is only rarely granted.[8] Under such restrictions, it is surprising that Peruvians create any wealth at all! The pattern is repeated, with some variation, in the poorer nations of the world.

Thus, the most effective way to help other countries is to export a repugnance for aggression-through-government. The best way to teach an idea is simply by living it and letting others observe the benefits. When our country was founded, it was the first Western country to reject monarchial rule in favor of a less-aggressive representative system. Today, a scant 200 years later, the few remaining Western monarchs are mere figureheads. Our system worked so well that it was emulated throughout the world. *We did little to produce this paradigm shift other than living our ideal.*

SUPPORTING DICTATORS

Today we reenforce the belief in aggression-through-government by practicing it in our dealing with our Third World neighbors. First, we tax our neighbors—at gunpoint, if necessary—to provide foreign aid. Most of this money goes for security assistance to under-developed nations.[9] To keep Third World governments friendly toward us instead of aligning with the Soviets, we've supported dictators such as Ferdinand Marcos (Philippines), Sergeant Samuel Doe (Liberia), Mobutu Seko (Zaire), and Zia ul-Haq (Pakistan), to name a few.[10] Much of this assistance was used to suppress the citizenry from protesting domestic policies of aggression. For example, almost three-fourths of U.S. aid to El Salvador during the early 1980s went to support the government's war against protesting civilians.[11] The Shah of Iran's cruel Savak and Idi Amin's "public safety unit" for internal security were trained with our help.[12] In Latin America in the 1970s, U.S. foreign aid was given to nations with the worst human rights violations.[13] Aid through aggression promotes aggression.

Third World citizens see their dictators kept in power by our aid—and hate us for it. Licensing laws, prohibition of homesteading, and other aggressive practices prevent the disadvantaged from creating wealth for themselves and their loved ones. This aggression is so pronounced in Third World countries that the rich have become immensely richer and the poor are barely surviving. This system is kept entrenched largely through our massive security assistance.

Most of this aid goes to loans and grants for the purchase of U.S.-made military equipment.[14] Security assistance becomes a subsidy from the U.S. taxpayer to the weapons manufacturers and dictators of the world. In the past, we've justified our aggression with the argument that we are keeping the Third World "free from communism." The next chapter shows that the opposite is true.

You can probably hear the representative from the weapons factory explaining to your local congresswoman. "Ms. Congresswoman,

Giving countries money that will be badly used is worse than not giving them any money at all.

—James Bovard
Cato Institute

When the U.S makes fear of the Soviet Union the...guide in policy decisions, it alienates Third World people.

—Frances Moore
Lappe et al.
BETRAYING THE
NATIONAL INTEREST

we charge top dollar for our weapons. Of course, our stockholders and our employees, who are your constituents, profit handsomely as a result. In fact, the local economy depends on us. If you don't vote for this aid package, we might have layoffs. People in these parts could get mighty angry come next election, and we couldn't blame them. In fact, we might even help them by throwing our financial support toward someone who stands up and fights for those who put them in office."

The congresswoman sighs and agrees to vote for the subsidy. After all, if she doesn't, the weapons manufacturers will back someone who will. Eventually the arms manufacturers will be successful, and the aid package will pass. Why should she sacrifice her career for something she can't stop? If the voters she represents care more about their paycheck than the exploitation of the Third World, why shouldn't she?

Tomorrow she will vote for range land subsidies in exchange for support on the foreign aid bill. Both sets of constituents will be happy, even though they are simply subsidizing each other's special interests and paying their congressional representatives very well to negotiate the deal. The voters in both districts end up with less than they would have if they had honored their neighbor's choice. The voters are reaping as they have sown.

PURCHASING POVERTY

Security assistance is just the beginning. Even humanitarian aid ends up subsidizing aggression. First, the aggression of taxation is used to subsidize U.S. agriculture, creating a surplus.[15] Next, taxes are used to buy up the surplus. The crops are shipped to foreign governments, which are given tax-subsidized loans to finance the food purchase. Sometimes the food is simply given away.[16] The governments dispose of the food as they see fit.

In the famine of the mid-1980s, Bangladesh sold "free" food at market price in urban areas and at one-fifth the market price to its military.[17] Somalia allocated 80% of food aid to its military and government employees.[18] During the famine in Ethiopia, the government sold donated food or diverted it away from the hungriest provinces as punishment to those areas for harboring rebels.[19] Haiti's Jean Claude Duvalier converted aid into personal gain.[20] When we remember that poverty and starvation in these countries are caused by the aggression of these same leaders, we should not be surprised that our aid becomes a tool for more aggression.

When concerned Third World governments do give away donated food or sell it cheaply to those in need, the results can be just as devastating. Local farmers are undersold and put out of business. As a result, fewer crops are planted the following year. To prevent such a disaster, angry Haitian farmers chased away helicopters bringing in U.S. rice in 1984.[21] Some farmers will turn to export crops and the uncertainty of the world market to avoid the problems caused by our largess. The country becomes dependent on imports to feed its populace.

Ironically, poor rural farmers—the ones we are supposed to be helping—are hurt the most by food aid. If the peasant farmers manage to survive our security assistance and food aid, however, our aggression causes still more problems.

...it's impossible to go through the powerful to reach the powerless.
—Frances Moore Lappe et al.
BETRAYING THE NATIONAL INTEREST

SUBSIDIZING ENVIRONMENTAL DAMAGE

U.S. citizens are taxed—at gunpoint, if necessary—to fund the World Bank. The Bank, in turn, lends Third World countries money for development projects that frequently promote environmental degradation. Forests were destroyed to build subsidized dams in Brazil and India and cattle ranches in Botswana.[22] Poorly managed irrigation projects have resulted in millions of hectares becoming flooded, waterlogged, and salinated.[23] Development through aggression results in projects controlled by those who wish to exploit rather than by those who wish to serve.

Why does our government keep giving such destructive aid in our name and with our tax dollars? Of every aid dollar, 82 cents is spent on American products.[24] Thus, the aid programs are really a transfer of wealth from the American taxpayer and the Third World poor to American-based multinational firms. Like any special interest group, these firms have a strong influence on our representatives, because they can commit large amounts of money to the campaign chests of those who serve them best.

Not understanding how wealth is created, many sincere heads of state agree to borrow money for such projects in the hope that prosperity will follow. World Bank projects usually create subsidized government monopolies. Because of the inevitable inefficiency and high cost, the project cannot generate enough new wealth to pay for itself. The country ends up with a debt to the World Bank that cannot be repaid.

...the World Bank has contributed as much to agricultural disaster in Ethiopia as the governments themselves.
—Yonas Deressa
President, Ethiopian Refugees Education and Relief Foundation

Sometimes, the World Bank steps in with more loans for agricultural development. In the early 1970s, Tanzania received more bank aid per capita than any other country. Much of this money was used to support the army's efforts to drive the peasants from their land to government villages or communes.[25] Generous loans to the governments of Vietnam,[26] Indonesia,[27] Ethiopia,[28] and Guatemala[29] funded similar resettlement programs in these countries. The communes were seldom productive.[30] Land taken from the peasants was awarded to political favorites. Once again, money taken by aggression from the U.S. taxpayer was used to support more aggression.

In Indonesia and Brazil, peasants who were robbed of their farms were often resettled on cleared rainforest land.[31] In some countries, the newly landless cleared the forests themselves in an attempt to create new farms. When the authorities caught up with them, the peasants simply moved on, clearing more rainforest as they went.

Governments claim the rainforests as their own, just as the U.S. government claims much of our western range land. The rainforests are populated by natives who create wealth by using the rainforests sustainably, just as the Native Americans once did on our Western Plains. Peruvian Amazon dwellers, for example, cultivate the rainforest profitably and sustainably by harvesting its fruit, rubber, and timber. They make up to three times as much as they would if they cleared the forest for cattle ranching.[32] Consequently, they have no incentive to destroy the forest that they have homesteaded.

Governments in developing countries, in their eagerness to repay the loans from the World Bank, use new loans to drive the natives off their homesteaded lands in much the same way as the U.S. government drove Native Americans onto reservations. The government rents the forest to loggers so that payments can be made to the World Bank. Since neither the loggers nor the politicians "own" the land and profit by caring for it, both groups have every incentive to exploit and no incentive to preserve or replant.

THE RICH GET RICHER—WITH OUR HELP!

You can probably hear the public relations woman from the World Bank asking your local congressman to support more taxes for her organization.

"You see, Mr. Congressman," she begins sweetly, "those loans are guaranteed by the U.S. taxpayer. If these Third World countries default, the United States will be plunged into a depression. It's much better that we lend a bit more and restructure their economy. With the resettlement programs, we can control what is planted on the farms and the villages. By focusing on export crops and clearing the rainforests for cattle grazing, we can ensure that we are repaid. In addition, the American consumer will enjoy cheaper coffee and cocoa prices when more farmland is devoted to export crops instead of food."

"But those poor peasants!" protests the congressman. "We're playing God with their lives and their land. What about the loss of the rainforests?" The congressman is clearly frustrated. He had supported World Bank funding in the first place in the hopes of helping the less fortunate. Because he doesn't understand that more aid through aggression will make the bad situation worse, he once again supports the World Bank's plan.

Even if the congressman had objected to throwing the taxpayers' money down the World Bank's "black hole," he would have gained little. The American-based, multinational firms that profited either from the rainforests or from the purchases made by the dictators have every incentive to generously fund his opponent in the next election if the congressman doesn't cooperate.

When I was in high school, I could not understand why Third World people called us "imperialists." Why would these ungrateful primitives try to bite the hand that feeds them? Now, of course, I understand. My tax dollars are used to exploit those who have so little in order to benefit dictators, multinational firms, and banks. Our desire to control our neighbors once again ripples outward, fueling the flames of poverty and strife. We reap as we sow—the money that goes into the pockets of the well-to-do comes, in the final analysis, from us by either inflation or taxation.

KICKING THEM WHEN THEY'RE DOWN

Against the background of aggression funded by their rich American neighbors, it's a wonder that the Third World nations create any wealth at all. When they do, we once again knock out the lower rungs on the Ladder of Affluence through the aggression of tariffs.

Tariffs are taxes paid by traders of foreign goods sold in the United States. The price that consumers pay is raised proportionately, so fewer goods are imported. If American citizens want to buy a product directly from a Third World vendor, bypassing the tariff, they'll be stopped—at gunpoint, if necessary. This form of aggression, which prevents Third World people from helping themselves, is used to protect American jobs. Like all forms of aggression, the outcome is very different from what was intended.

A LOSE-LOSE SITUATION

Tariffs actually harm the American worker. The extra money consumers would have saved by buying cheaper foreign clothing, for example, is not available to purchase other goods and services. For every job protected in the textile or apparel industry, at least one other American job is lost in another sector.[33]

Instead of creating new wealth, regulators who enforce the tariff law only stymie it. Thus, saving the job of one textile worker costs 3 to 12 times that person's annual earnings.[34] The consumer pays these additional costs. Tariffs and quotas increase prices for a family of four by an average of $2,000 per year,[35] which represents a hefty 32% of the purchasing power of families at the poverty level.[36] As with all aggression, tariffs only make poor workers poorer.

Tariffs harm Third World entrepreneurs as well. Essentially, the tariff is a license that those businesses are required to buy for every item sold. The tariff is passed on to the consumer through increased prices. Fewer consumers buy the tariffed item, discouraging trade. The underdeveloped countries advance more quickly when they trade,[37] because division of labor and specialization make

...according to the U.S. Department of Labor's own statistics, "protectionism" destroys eight jobs in the general economy for every one saved in a protected economy.

—Vincent Miller and
James Elwood
"Free Trade vs.
Protectionism"

wealth creation more efficient. When we discourage trade with tariffs, our aggression prevents Third World people from helping themselves.

Free from aggression, the marketplace ecosystem favors the entrepreneurs who serve their customers best. If a business enterprise in a poorer nation uses inexpensive labor to keep prices down, American consumers get more for their dollar. When Americans buy from the foreign vendor, they create jobs for the underprivileged. When Americans support the aggression of tariffs, they sacrifice the disadvantaged in a futile effort to help more-fortunate American workers who produce the same goods less efficiently.

It is no coincidence that some of America's most lethargic indus-tries—steel, footwear, rubber, textiles—are also among the most heavily protected.
—Thomas DiLorenzo
WHY FREE TRADE
WORKS

Just because other countries foolishly harm themselves with tariffs is no reason for us to do so. Japanese consumers, for example, pay up to ten times as much for their rice as they would without the tariffs imposed by their government.[38] When we follow Japan's pro-tectionist lead, we also pay more for less.

If other countries can produce certain items more economically, we benefit by turn-ing our efforts to businesses in which we excel. Yankee ingenuity is our forte. By focus-ing on innovation, we focus on developing a creative and intelligent populace. Our current protectionist position means more menial jobs for our populace and fewer white collar ones. When we buy goods manufactured with the cheap labor of Third World nations, we help them while helping ourselves.

THE EASY WAY OUT

If we truly wish to help Third World coun-tries to attain peace and plenty, our first goal is to set an example they can imitate. Once Edison showed us how to make a light bulb, it was relatively easy to follow his blueprint. Likewise, we can show the Third World na-tions the way to prosperity—if we are willing to practice non–aggression.

To set this example, we must abandon the aggression of tariffs and taxation that gives special interests and dictators control of the Third World people. When we abandon these forms of aggression, we will have set the stage for development in the Third World. If we continue our aggressive practices, we will create poverty and strife abroad just as surely as we are creating poverty and strife at home.

Instead of using our resources to make the poor nations poorer, we can volunteer our support. Those concerned about the rainforests can supply funds to native people who are defending their homesteading claims. The Malaysian village of Uma Bawang, for example, recently took its state government to court to legalize native homesteading rights.[39] Most native people are much more careful in managing their homeland than distant politicians are. When we encourage ownership of the environment, we increase the chances that Nature's bounty will be nurtured, protected, and preserved.

Some people object to individual ownership of rainforests for fear an unscrupulous, wealthy person might buy these sensitive environments and destroy them. The marketplace ecosystem regulates such individuals with the feedback of profit and loss. Daniel K. Ludwig, the richest man in the world in the 1970s, cut down 250,000 acres of rainforest for a tree farm. He lost billions of dollars because the new trees were not able to grow well there; naturally, he stopped cutting down rainforests.[40] Few individuals can afford to duplicate his mistake. Politicians, however, are more likely to continue such practices, because they do not lose money by destroying the rainforests; indeed, they profit by it.

When we stop supporting dictatorship, stop subsidizing environmental destruction, start encouraging recognition of homesteading claims, and start trading with Third World nations non-aggressively, we will contribute

...our greatest contributions to the cause of freedom and development overseas is not what we do over there, but what we do right here at home.
—Frances Moore
Lappe et al.
BETRAYING THE
NATIONAL INTEREST

*Genuine development
cannot be imported or
imposed; it can only be
achieved by a people
for themselves.*
—Frances Moore
Lappe et al.
BETRAYING THE
NATIONAL INTEREST

significantly to their progress. Ultimately, peace and plenty in these countries are a product of the hearts and minds of their people. Until they, individually and collectively, forsake aggression, Third World people will, like ourselves, reap its bitter fruits.

We hesitate to abandon our aggression overseas. We are fearful that somehow selfish others will take control if we don't. In our hearts, we still aren't sure that non-aggression works in the real world. Let's take a closer look at the Communist threat that affected our foreign policy over the past several decades to see if our fears are well founded.

CHAPTER 19

THE COMMUNIST THREAT IS ALL IN OUR MINDS

Using aggression domestically creates a foreign enemy here at home.

Since World War II, much of our foreign aid and military build-up has been to defuse the Communist influence. Has the Communist threat died with the breakup of the Union of Soviet Socialist Republics (USSR)? To answer this question, we must first understand what communism (also called socialism by some of its proponents) is.

AGGRESSION AS A WAY OF LIFE

Communists believe that individuals should give according to their ability and receive according to their needs. In this way, they hope to achieve an even distribution of wealth, so that no one will be in need. Communists see selfish others, who won't voluntarily share the wealth they have created, as the primary obstacle to their goal. The Communist solution is to force selfish others—at gunpoint, if necessary—to relinquish the wealth they have created. In choosing aggression as their means, Communists create poverty, strife, and inequality—the opposite of what they intend.

Many of us have experienced some form of the Communist ideal in our immediate families. Many parents do without so their children won't have to. Parents can keep the wealth they create for themselves, but they are likely to generously share with their children. No one points a gun at Moms and Dads to get them to comply. Parents *choose* to give out of love.

Communists believe that we should all be family to one another. If we won't voluntarily give to others until the available wealth is

It is wrong to demand that the individual subordinate himself to the collectivity or merge in it, because it is by its most advanced individuals that the collectivity progresses and they can really advance only if they are free ....The individual is indeed the key of the evolutionary movement.

—Sri Aurobindo
THE FUTURE EVOLUTION OF MAN

...violence is the cornerstone of socialism's existence as an institution.
—Hans–Herman Hoppe
A THEORY OF SOCIALISM AND CAPITALISM

evenly distributed, then we must be forced—at gunpoint, if necessary. Such tactics quickly destroy the love that is the source of such giving.

For example, we might help a family member in need, even if the need is frequent. If that family member insisted, with gun in hand, that we were going to help whether we wanted to or not, we'd probably feel less inclined to give anything at all. Instead, we'd probably hide what we have. Aggression inhibits spontaneous giving while encouraging resentment and hoarding.

Creating Strife

Traveling by train through Poland and East Germany in the early 1980s, I always knew which side of the border I was on by the temperament of the customs officials. Those from the so-called free nations were courteous and friendly; those from the Eastern Bloc seemed miserable and eager to take out their frustrations on the passengers. A society based on the belief that selfish others are to blame for the world's woes is a society in which others who have more are seen as enemies. One person's gain is seen as another's loss. A Communist society believes in a win–lose world.

Creating Poverty

Because of this win–lose belief, most of the wealth in Communist countries is taken from its creators—at gunpoint, if necessary—and is distributed by a handful of government officials. People who create more wealth than others seldom benefit by having more for themselves or their loved ones. Aggression has disrupted the marketplace ecosystem so much that the Wealth Pie is just a fraction of what it otherwise would be.

How much difference does aggression make in the size of the Wealth Pie? In the late 1980s, Soviets were allowed to keep the wealth they created by raising vegetables on their garden plots. Although these plots composed only about 2% of the agricultural lands in the Soviet Union, they produced 25% of the food![1] When Soviets kept the wealth they created, they produced almost 16 times more than when it was taken from them—at gunpoint, if necessary![2]

In 1913, under Czar Nicholas II, Russia was the world's largest food exporter. In 1989, it was the world's largest food importer.[3] Clearly, the creation of wealth in Russia has been dampened tremendously by communism, even compared with a czarist regime that could hardly be considered free from aggression.

A small Wealth Pie means fewer goods and services. In 1987, less than three-fourths of the Soviet housing had hot water; 15% of the population had no bathrooms.[4] Twenty percent of the urban residents breathed air that was dangerously polluted.[5] One out of three Soviet hospitals had no indoor toilets; some didn't even have running water.[3] Needles for intravenous injections were used over and over again, spreading hepatitis and AIDS.[3] Most hospitals had no elevators; the ill had to drag themselves up several flights of stairs.[6] While the life expectancy in Western nations has risen, that of the Soviet population has declined.[8] Alcoholism runs rampant as people try to forget their plight.[9] Poverty has been the bitter fruit of aggression.

Creating Class Distinctions

The Communist ethic championed a class-less society with an even distribution of wealth, but the aggression used to implement it in Communist countries actually produced the greatest extremes. Individuals who created goods and services that the government considered critical were rewarded with the best food and living conditions. Such people might have developed new military technology or excelled in athletic competition, for example. Under communism, the average Soviet waited

Soviet citizens have a worse diet than did Russians under Czar Nicholas II in 1913.

—Mortimer B. Zuckerman
editor-in-chief
U.S. News & World Report, 1989

Measured by the health of its people, the Soviet Union is no longer a developed nation.

—Nick Eberstadt
THE POVERTY OF COMMUNISM

in long lines at state stores for unwrapped and unattractive produce and occasional meat, while high-ranking party officials and political favorites ordered high-quality, well-packaged food in exclusive stores and restaurants that were off limits to the average Soviet.[10]

Medical care likewise depended on one's status. High-ranking party members and other citizens of status were able to get Western-style care in special hospitals.[11] In spite of the high-sounding rhetoric, top-level Communists enjoyed a lifestyle that the average Soviet had no chance of attaining, no matter how hard he or she was willing to work.

To understand how politicians dedicated to an even distribution of wealth could let this happen, put yourself in their shoes. Imagine that you are a concerned head of state who wants everyone in the country to enjoy the same standard of living. You have the guns of government at your disposal, so you start by forcing everyone—at gunpoint, if necessary—to work for the same wage.

Since doctors are paid the same no matter how many patients they see, the doctors work at a leisurely pace, and lines outside their offices grow. To counter this, you consider paying doctors according to how many patients they see. Since doctors respond to incentives like everyone else, they see as many people as possible, giving all patients cursory exams and sending them on their way. Soon the doctors are making more than the workers they treat. Using aggression as your means, you have created a privileged class!

Instead of paying the doctors per patient, you set a quota for each doctor and send someone to make sure that the doctor spends the allotted time with each patient. The monitors are paid the same regardless of what their reports on the doctors contain. Knowing this, doctors will undoubtedly suggest that the monitors look the other way while the physicians maintain a leisurely pace. In return, the doctor will put the monitor's family at the front of the line if they should need treatment. This "medical insurance" costs the monitors nothing, so they have every reason to accept it. If the doctor lets some patients bribe their way to the head of the line, some of this money might also be split with the monitor. You have created two privileged classes instead of one: the doctor and the monitor.

You could have a second monitor check on the first, but what prevents the new monitor from accepting bribes as well? The more layers of monitors you have, the less wealth is created, since monitors produce no new goods and services. More dissatisfaction arises.

You could ask the police to torture any monitor who takes bribes, but the monitors might very well bribe the police. Because monitors take bribes, they can probably offer the police a better deal than merely making the same as everyone else.

If you threatened to torture police who accepted bribes, you would incur the animosity of an armed elite skilled in violent action—not a good idea if you want a long life. To make your police unbribable, you must pay them more than anyone else. Once again, you must create class distinctions, with those who wield the guns of government at the top. Equality cannot be achieved through aggression.

The use of force to achieve equality will destroy freedom, and the force, introduced for good purposes, will end up in the hands of people who use it to promote their own interests.

—Milton Friedman Nobel Prize winner economics

Harming the Environment

The more that aggression thwarts the natural regulation of the marketplace ecosystem, the environment is devastated. In the United States, energy consumption is minimized so that profits will be maximized. As a result, the energy used in 1989 to produce a dollar's worth of goods was about half what it was in the late 1920s.[12]

In Communist countries, however, no one profits by conserving energy. People do not reap as they sow, because the wealth they create is taken from them—at gunpoint, if necessary. Manufacturing becomes wasteful.

As a result, the Communist economies use almost three times as much energy as the so-called free nations for every dollar of goods produced.[12]

In Communist countries, the only choices that are honored are those that the government officials make for the entire nation. If government control were the solution to pollution, the Eastern European countries would be pristine. Instead, pollution runs rampant to an extent seldom seen in the Western world. For example, in Copşa Mică, Romania, carbon spews nightly from a nearby tire factory, literally coating everything and everybody black.[13] In Leipzig, East Germany, more than 90% of the population suffers health problems because of the high level of sulfur dioxide.[14] Polish economists estimate that pollution destroys 10% to 15% of their nation's annual GNP.[15]

When man interferes with the Tao, the sky becomes filthy, the earth becomes depleted, the balance crumbles, creatures become extinct.
—Lao-tsu
TAO TE CHING

The Czechoslovakian Environment Ministry estimates that 5% to 7% of their country's annual wealth creation is similarly wasted.[15] Two-thirds of the forests may be dying, and half of the water is undrinkable.[16] One allergy specialist in the Bohemian city of Most blames pollution for lowering the life expectancy of the residents by 10 years, compared to the already low national average.[17]

The plight of Eastern Europe reminds us that aggression-through-government makes pollution worse, not better. When aggression prevents homesteading the waterways and owning the environment, individuals do not profit from protecting it.

The ecological situation in Czechoslovakia is, in a word, disastrous ....It's nothing short of catastrophe.
—Dr. Bedrich Moldan
Czechoslovakian Environmental Minister

Altruists who are willing to preserve the environment, even without the positive feedback of profit, find themselves thwarted by the guns of government as well. Sovereign immunity protects the government officials who choose pollution for the sake of political gain. Since selling out the environment is the only way the public officials can profit from it, they have little incentive to do otherwise.

Turning Adults into Children

The greatest tragedy of communism is not the poverty, sullenness, or even the environmental destruction it encourages. The devastation of the human spirit is communism's greatest casualty.

A medical colleague returning from Finland in the 1980s told me how Russian men would marry Finnish women so they could emigrate to Finland. Once there, however, the array of decisions that the average citizen makes concerning housing, shopping, etc., was just too much for many of them to bear. Overwhelmed by the task of taking responsibility for their life, the men went back to Russia where scarcity and aggression make choice a rarity. This destruction of the questing human spirit, of the confidence in one's ability to cope with the world, is the most devastating effect of the extreme aggression of communism.

Like overprotective parenting, aggression–through–government hinders normal human development. On the average, individuals, knowing their situation, strengths, and limitations, make the best choices for themselves. Even when they choose poorly, the lesson to be learned prepares them for better decisions later on. As each individual optimizes his or her own well-being without aggression, the whole society benefits. Looking out for Number 1 is nature's way of ensuring that we optimize the whole. If each cell maintains its health without harming the others, the body can hardly be diseased!

A little bit of communism is like a little bit of disease. Mixing aggression with non-aggression isn't a happy medium; it's the beginning of societal ill health—in more ways than one. As the United States embraced aggression, it started down the path to communism as well. The architects of communism knew this well. In 1847, Marx and Engels proposed ten steps to convert the Western nations to Communist countries without firing a shot.[18] Most of these ideas have been successfully

Our power does not know liberty or justice. It is established on the destruction of the individual will.
—Vladimir I. Lenin
Bolshevik
revolutionary leader

Socialism of any type leads to a total destruction of the human spirit....
—Alexander
Solzhenitsyn
Soviet dissident and
defector

Moderation in temper is always a virtue; but moderation in principle is always a vice.
—Thomas Paine
COMMON SENSE

implemented in our own country with little, if any, resistance!

Is It Happening Here?

One of the ten steps called for "centralization of credit in the hands of the state, by means of a national bank with state capital and an exclusive monopoly"—just like our own Federal Reserve!As described in Chapter 9, a central bank transfers the wealth of the average person to the well-to-do through inflation. Communism, like all aggression-through-government, is a tool of the rich. The next chapter explains how domestic aggression in the U.S. banking industry created our need for national defense by helping to establish the Communist threat overseas.

Another of the ten steps called for instituting "a heavy progressive or graduated income tax"—just like our own federal income tax! The next chapter (*National Defense*) shows how the aggression of income taxes, when combined with the aggression of central banking, foments war throughout the world.

Another step proposed by Marx and Engels was "abolition of all right of inheritance," which we come ever closer to as inheritance taxes increase. Taking wealth—at gunpoint, if necessary—that one person has created and given to another person is theft. Whether the wealth creator is alive or dead, the act and the impact are the same.

Another step was "free education for all children in public schools." Although our country still has many private schools in addition to the public ones, the content of both is dictated by aggression-through-government, to teach aggression.

Marx and Engels also recommended the "extension of factories and instruments of production owned by the state." In the past century, more and more services have become exclusive, subsidized government monopolies (e.g., garbage collection, water distribution,

Lenin is said to have declared that the best way to destroy the Capitalist system was to debauch the currency.
—John Maynard Keynes
THE ECONOMIC CONSEQUENCES OF THE PEACE

Give me four years to teach the children and the seed I have sown will never be uprooted.
—Vladimir I. Lenin
Bolshevik
revolutionary leader

mass transit, etc.). As a result, we pay twice as much for lower quality service!

Marx also called for the "centralization of the means of communications and transport in the hands of the state." Television and radio stations are licensed by the Federal Communications Commission. A station that does not pursue programming considered "in the public interest" is stopped—at gunpoint, if necessary—from further broadcast. In earlier chapters, we saw that licensing increased the cost of doing business, so that only the advantaged could obtain permission to create wealth in regulated professions. Not surprisingly, three-fourths of the stock of the three major television networks is controlled by a few large banks. Radio stations have an elite ownership as well.[19] Those who benefit from aggression-through-government have little incentive to tell the public that licensing is a tool of the rich!

The Interstate Commerce Commission regulates the licensing of truckers. Minorities are effectively excluded from the lucrative trucking business by the expense of obtaining one of a limited number of licenses.[20] The rich get richer.

Another of the ten steps calls for "confiscation of the property of all emigrants and rebels." As we learned in Chapter 15, our law enforcement agents can seize the wealth of anyone *suspected* of drug crimes *without a trial*! For many years, the Internal Revenue Service (IRS) has also been seizing the assets of taxpayers—*without a trial*—if the IRS thinks they *might* have underpaid their taxes![21] The wealth we have created can be taken from us—at gunpoint, if necessary—without a formal accusation or a chance to defend ourselves! Truly, we can no longer claim to be a free country. We have entrapped ourselves with aggression-through-government.

In addition, Marx and Engels called for "abolition of property in land and application

The control of the production of wealth is the control of human life itself.

—Hilaire Belloc
THE SERVILE STATE

The right of private property in land is forever abolished. All land owned by the Church, by private persons, by peasants, is taken away without compensation.

—Vladimir I. Lenin
November 8, 1917

of all rents of land to public purposes." In other words, land would not be privately owned. No homesteading would be permitted.

Our federal and local governments have title to 42% of the land mass of the United States.[22] Most of the remaining land is under government control as well. For example, today's homeowners can pay off their mortgages, but must still pay property taxes to the local government. If they stop payments, their property is taken from them. They are, in essence, renting their home from the local government. An owner can eventually pay off a mortgage and not have to make monthly payments; a renter must continue payments or be evicted.

When campaigning for the Kalamazoo City Commission in 1983, I met many older people who were moving from their homes because the property taxes were higher than their mortgage payments had been. Even though many of these people "owned" their homes "free and clear," they couldn't afford the escalating property taxes on a retiree's income! Having worked all their lives to pay off their homes, they found they could no longer keep them!

Even if these individuals had been able to afford to pay the "rent" of property taxes, some of them faced another threat. The city of Kalamazoo was considering an ambitious consolidation of the railway system. Businesses and residences that occupied an area proposed for development were targets for "eminent domain." Governments frequently evict—at gunpoint, if necessary—individuals from properties they "own" if the proposed project is considered for "the common good." Owners can do what they please with their property; renters hold it subject to the consent of their landlords. Eminent domain and property taxes have made a mockery of the American dream of home ownership. Individuals do not truly "own" their own property!

The American people will never knowingly adopt Socialism, but under the name of Liberalism, they will adopt every fragment of the Socialist program until one day America will be a Socialist nation without knowing how it happened.
—Norman Thomas
Socialist Party
Presidential
candidate

It is a known fact that the policies of the government today, whether Republican or Democratic are closer to the 1932 platform of the Communist Party than they are to either of their own party platforms in that critical year.
—Walter Trohan
Chicago Tribune
October 5, 1970

Eight of the ten steps designed to convert industrialized nations to communism have already been substantially implemented in our country! We have let communism in the back door because it wears the familiar face of our neighbors—and ourselves!

We've spent a lot of time, money, and effort fighting communism throughout the world because we didn't want it infesting our way of life. We didn't want someone to dictate to us how we were to live our lives. In trying to dictate to others, however, we walk the road toward communism of our own volition! Instead of being dominated by Soviet Communists, we dominate our neighbors and they dominate us! The real Communist threat begins with our belief that aggression serves us. It starts in our own minds and hearts.

Our missiles and bombs cannot save us if we refuse to honor our neighbor's choice. In the following chapter, we'll see how our aggression ripples outward to create enemies abroad.

The United States will eventually fly the Communist Red flag ....The American people will hoist it themselves.
—Nikita Khrushchev
Soviet premier
November 16, 1956

CHAPTER 20

NATIONAL DEFENSE

**The best defense against foreign aggression is
the practice of non-aggression domestically.**

In the previous chapter, we learned how
our desire to control our neighbors expands to
create the "foreign" threat of communism in
our own backyard. In this chapter, we'll explore how our domestic aggression establishes
enemies abroad as well.

CREATING COMMUNISM

Have you ever wondered how the former
Soviet Union, so unproductive that it could
barely feed its own people, managed to become
a military power second only to the United
States? Extensive research suggests that the
Soviet military-industrial complex is a creation of the Pyramid of Power we have built
here at home!

It was common knowledge earlier in this
century that U.S. banking interests helped
establish communism in Russia (Figure 20.1).
A 1911 cartoon from the *St. Louis Post Dis-
patch* by Robert Minor showed Karl Marx
welcomed to Wall Street by John D. Ryan
(National City Bank), and John D. Rockefeller
(Chase Bank and Standard Oil), as well as J.P.
Morgan and his partner George W. Perkins
(Guaranty Trust Co. and Equitable Life).
Andrew Carnegie and Teddy Roosevelt were
also featured. Why did America's wealthy
encourage a philosophy that portrayed them
as selfish others who should be forced—at
gunpoint, if necessary—to give up the wealth
they had accumulated?

These men were not stupid. They knew
that aggression-through-government always
favored the rich while fostering the illusion of
helping the poor. Many of them had profited
greatly from the aggression of licensing laws.

Figure 20.1 "DEE-LIGHTED!"

The bankers had done especially well, even before the Federal Reserve put the banks at the apex of the Pyramid of Power. Banks created more money than they would have in a marketplace ecosystem free from aggression. These extra dollars, subsidized by the American public primarily through inflation, were loaned or given to the Communists to aid them in their rise to power.[1]

In 1917, three factions were involved in the Russian revolution. Besides the Communists and those loyal to the czar, a small group championed the benefits of non-aggression.[2] Of the three groups, only the Communists favored the aggression of central banking. Not surprisingly, the banking and business elite gave substantial support to the Communists, the group most willing to reward their financiers with plunder gained through aggression.

As the Communists gained strength from Western support, they were able to defeat the czarists and the small group that advocated non-aggression. By allowing domestic aggression to create the money monopoly, Americans unwittingly laid the yoke of communism on the backs of the Russian people and saddled themselves with additional inflation and taxation.

The Communists repaid the loans from the banking interests with imperial gold coins taken from the czar's treasury.[3] By exporting large portions of farm produce as well, the Soviets were able to buy modern machinery.[4] As a result of exporting much of the food supply, starvation threatened the Russian populace in 1922. Herbert Hoover, then Secretary of Commerce, sent the Russians famine relief, subsidized by the U.S. taxpayer.[5] Without American aid through aggression, the Communist regime would probably have collapsed.

Instead, the Communists rewarded people who had helped them with licenses in the Soviet Union.[3] They took the privately-owned oil fields—at gunpoint, if necessary—and

...for the period 1917 to 1930 Western assistance in various forms was the single most important factor, first in the sheer survival of the Soviet regime and secondly in industrial progress to prerevolutionary levels.

—Antony Sutton
WESTERN TECHNOLOGY AND SOVIET ECONOMIC DEVELOPMENT

assigned them to their political favorites.[6] For example, Standard Oil was given control of the Russian oil fields that had prevented Rockefeller from keeping his worldwide monopoly on oil (Chapter 7: *Creating Monopolies That Control Us*).[7] By 1928, oil was the largest export, contributing almost 20% to Russia's foreign exchange.[8] By supporting communism, Rockefeller was able to escape the regulation of the marketplace ecosystem and do away with much of his international competition.

Chase National Bank helped the Soviets obtain a steady stream of credit.[9] The New York financial house of Kuhn, Loeb & Company financed the Soviet's First Five-Year Plan for economic development.[10] Without the massive creation of money made possible through the Federal Reserve System (Chapter 9: *Banking on Aggression*), these loans might not have been possible. The Communist regime was able to buy the technology their system could not produce, because Americans were willing to use aggression-through-government to control their neighbors.

In 1929, the Soviet government forced citizens—at gunpoint, if necessary—to turn their gold over to the government,[11] possibly to begin the necessary loan repayments. Did the Soviet government use these loans to feed and clothe its people? Hardly! Just as in the Third World today, the poor rural population was forcibly removed from their land and taken to collective farms. During Stalin's campaign in the 1930s, millions of people were killed.[11] The desire of Americans to control their neighbors rippled outward into other nations. The great wealth that Americans had created gave them incredible power to help or harm the rest of the world.

President Franklin D. Roosevelt supplemented the bank loans to the Soviets with taxpayer-financed assistance. He arranged secret military transfers with the Soviets, to help defeat Adolf Hitler. In addition, the Lend-Lease program transferred industrial and military supplies to the Soviets on easy credit terms from 1941 to 1946.[12] In 1944, Stalin noted that two-thirds of Soviet heavy industry had been built with U.S. help. Almost all the remaining one-third was imported from other Western nations.[13] Massive transfer of equipment and skilled personnel from the occupied territories to the Soviet Union supplied further technical expertise.[14] Our domestic aggression undertaken to protect the world from Hitler's dictatorship, created an equally vicious enemy that enslaved much of Eastern Europe.

Without U.S. assistance, Soviet technology would have remained so primitive that it is unlikely that they ever would have developed nuclear capabilities.[15] Without the bomb, the Cold War would never have been waged. Nuclear warheads could never have been shipped to Cuba. The United States need not have undertaken the massive military build-up that consumed its wealth.

Innovation and the creation of wealth are greatly stifled in aggressive Communist societies (Chapter 19: *The Communist Threat Is All In Our Minds*). Without U.S. aid, the Soviet Union could not have long survived. As evidence of this, consider that in 1960 the American government offered to release the Soviet Union from its Lend-Lease debt to the United States of $11 billion if the Soviets would pay $300 million of it. Although the Soviets reportedly had $9 billion in gold in their national treasury in 1960,[16] they refused. Without American-taxpayer assistance, the Soviets would have been bankrupt!

Even with such aid, however, the Soviet Union could hardly feed itself. The Soviet Wealth Pie was attenuated by massive aggression-through-government. American loans were used to assist the Soviets in financing food purchases after the poor 1972 harvest.[17] In Poland, such credits added over 10% to the national income in 1974![18] The ability of the United States to make massive contributions to the Eastern Bloc testifies to the incredible

...10,000 German scientists and technical specialists had been absorbed into Soviet industry by May 1947. There is no question that there were sizable Soviet equipment removals from occupied areas after World War II; a minimum value figure in excess of $10 billion in 1938 prices can be set for equipment thus removed.
—Antony Sutton
WESTERN TECHNOLOGY AND SOVIET ECONOMIC DEVELOPMENT

Our whole slave system depends on your economic assistance. When they bury us alive, please do not send them shovels and the most up-to-date earth-moving equipment.

—Alexander Solzhenitsyn
Soviet historian
Nobel Prize winner

wealth–creating ability of our marketplace ecosystem, which is less troubled by aggression than the Soviet one.

Although much of the Soviet aid was offered through private banks, the American taxpayer was usually at risk. Loans were usually guaranteed by the taxpayer–financed Export–Import Bank.[19] Even without such guarantees, U.S. taxpayers could be liable. Loans that are not repaid can bankrupt lending institutions. In such cases, taxpayers (not the bankers who took foolish chances with their depositors' money) are usually expected to make up the loss if the Federal Deposit Insurance Corporation (FDIC) cannot.

We expect our government to protect us from aggressors, whether they are individuals or other nations. The Soviet threat, however, was built largely through the guns of government that we hired to protect us! Communists won the Russian revolution with the help of bankers and industrialists who became enriched through exclusive licensing laws and further Soviet borrowing. Stalin's regime enslaved Eastern Europe with the extra money created through the exclusive, subsidized monopoly of the Federal Reserve. Lend–Lease, which probably contributed to the Soviet acquisition of nuclear technology, was paid for through the aggression of taxation. Finally, taxes were used to guarantee loans for food aid. At every turn, domestic aggression–through–government built and maintained the Soviet "enemy."

It's somewhat disheartening to discover that we were responsible for creating the superpower which we've feared for so many years. On the other hand, if our most formidable foe is only a paper tier dependent on us for its continued existence, maybe the world is not such a dangerous place after all!

TEACHING TERRORISM

Our domestic aggression may have contributed to other threats to our international

security as well. For example, when we follow
the history of developing nations, it is difficult
to find one where our Central Intelligence
Agency (CIA) has not left its mark. The U.S.
Senate's Church Committee documented 900
major, and several thousand minor, covert
operations undertaken by the CIA between
1960 and 1975.[20] The latest chapter in our
relations with Nicaragua exemplifies the way
in which our domestic aggression creates more
aggression overseas.

After the Sandanistas ousted the Somoza
dictatorship from Nicaragua, President Carter
gave them $75 million in foreign aid.[21] Shortly
thereafter, President Reagan declared that the
Sandanistas were exporting communism to El
Salvador with the ultimate intent of threatening our borders. Such fears seem unfounded.
The Sandanistas hardly appeared bloodthirsty;
they abolished the death penalty and limited
prison terms to 30 years.[22] Like all communist
countries the Sandanistas could not, without
help, create the wealth necessary to undertake
an invasion of the best–armed nation in the
world. Certainly Communist Cuba, barely 100
miles from our shores and subsidized by the
Soviets, had shown no inclination to invade us
after the nuclear warheads were removed in
the 1960s. Nevertheless, our government
spent more than $100 million in support of
the counterrevolutionary Contras before Congress forbade further expenditures in 1984.[23]

The civilian population failed to rally
significantly to the Contra cause. Instead, the
people voted 2 to 1 in 1984 to keep the Sandanistas in power in an election that international observers accepted as fair.[24] Most likely,
the average Nicaraguan did not think the
Sandanistas were any worse than the Somoza
dictatorship that preceded them. Because
many of the Contras had been associated with
the Somozan National Guard, an alliance
would have been easily forged between the
average citizen and the Contras if feelings
against the new government had run strong.[25]

For better or worse, as a nation, the Nicaraguans had made their choice.

Our CIA, however, did not honor this choice. Instead, they taught the Contras to terrorize the Nicaraguan population. When it surfaced, the CIA training manual, *Psychological Operations in Guerrilla Warfare*, became a great embarrassment to the Reagan administration.[26]

The Contras were encouraged to blow up bridges and attack health clinics, hospitals, and schools.[27] Widespread civilian killing, kidnapping, rape, torture, and mutilation by Contras were extensively documented.[28]

These terrorist tactics apparently had the desired effect. In 1990, the Nicaraguan population ousted the Sandanistas and voted for Violetta Chamorro who allegedly had up to $20 million in CIA campaign support.[29] Perhaps the Nicaraguans decided to accede to the demands of their Yankee neighbors in the hope of stopping the terrorism.

The Sandanista forces probably committed atrocities as well. Nevertheless, CIA intervention intensified the war of terrorism instead of letting it die a natural death. Without support from the United States or the Nicaraguan people, the Contras could not have continued and the civil strife would have ended.

This was not the first time our country had armed and trained terrorists. In the 1950s, the CIA recruited East German dissidents and trained them in bombing and damaging dams, bridges, trains, and other civilian facilities.[30] Could modern-day terrorists have learned their techniques from our own CIA or CIA-trained foreign operatives? When Americans are kidnapped, bombed, or tortured by terrorists, are we simply reaping as we have sown?

We don't need to fight fire with fire. We don't need to encourage torture and mayhem to topple Communist dictatorships. The former Soviet Union, favored with so much aid from the West, could not even feed its own people. Other aggressive governments will fare no better. With a few exceptions, all we need do is let them reap as they sow.

DRUGS FOR WAR

One ironic twist to our support of the Contras involved the War on Drugs. As Nancy Reagan toured the country asking our youth to say "No!" to drugs, the Contras supported themselves through profitable drug deals. Evidence suggests that these deals were facilitated by our own CIA.[31] One pilot even claimed he flew drugs directly into Homestead Air Force Base in Florida![32]

A wealth of evidence suggests that funding overseas covert operations with "protection money" from drug lords is not unusual.[33] The Drug Enforcement Agency (DEA) claims that the CIA has attempted to interfere with 27 prosecutions of drug dealers acting as CIA informants.[34] Our taxes went both to fight drug dealers and to protect them! When we use aggression as our means, we only end up fighting ourselves! When we start practicing non-aggression, we can stop spinning our wheels!

THE RICH GET RICHER

Our national government cannot protect us from such wasteful practices when we sanction aggression. Our national officeholders, just like our local ones, depend on special interest funding for their campaign chests. Local officials control the forests, grazing land, and other regional assets. Their electability is heavily influenced by the timber companies, cattle ranchers, and other local groups that can benefit from what these officials control.

Our national officials control the federal budget, funded by our tax dollars and deficit spending. Except for the separately funded social security program, our two biggest expenditures are defense (26% of federal outlays in 1989) and interest on the national debt (15% of outlays in 1989).[35] The primary special interest groups that profit the most from the

The justification for those actions was that we were living in a very hard, predatory, "cloak-and-dagger" world and that the only way to deal with a totalitarian enemy was to imitate him. The trouble with this theory was that while we live in a world of plot and counterplot, we also live in a world of cause and effect. Whatever the cause for the decision to legitimize and regularize deceit abroad, the inevitable effect was the practice of deceit at home.

—Norman Cousins
PATHOLOGY OF POWER

...We must guard against the acquisition of unwarranted influence by the...military-industrial complex.
—President Dwight D. Eisenhower January 1961

expansion of these items are the military-industrial complex and the money monopoly, respectively.

These groups have great incentive to see that candidates who support deficits and military build-up are elected. The War on Drugs contributes to U.S. deficits while providing huge drug profits to fund clandestine activities and arms sales abroad.

President George Bush, a former CIA director, was an ideal special-interest candidate. His office was reputed to have been the first informed when the Hasenfus plane crashed in Nicaragua and began the unraveling of the Iran-Contra affair during his vice-presidential years.[36] He ran up deficits faster than President Ronald Reagan, who himself set new records.[37] During Bush's term of office, U.S. troops landed in both Panama and Kuwait. Bush was committed to the War on Drugs as well.

We can hardly blame special interest groups for exploiting us when we have given them power by *our* attempts to control others. They only reflect our own actions back to us. We made the rules; we can hardly complain if we have been beaten at our own game. Once we forsake aggression, however, special interest power, whether due to ignorance, chance, or design,[38] simply dissolves. When we take responsibility for what we have created, we can consciously choose differently! We made the rules; we can change them!

A LOSE-LOSE SITUATION

The gains made by special interest groups are largely an illusion, however. To appreciate why this is so, we must first examine the impact that our curious national defense program has had on the world.

Let's start with Nicaragua. Since the Contras did not have popular support, it is unlikely that they would have had the ability to arm themselves and terrorize the countryside without U.S. assistance. A civil war after

Somosa's overthrow, if it happened at all, would have been much less devastating. Without our aggression, many of the 45,000 people who were killed might still be alive.[39] Much of the country's wealth might not have been destroyed by the war. Effort that could have created wealth was dedicated to defense instead. For ten years, the Nicaraguan Wealth Pie was attenuated much more than it would have been in the absence of aggression.

Other Third World nations have suffered similar fates. Civil strife in Korea, Vietnam, Cambodia, Laos, and Angola was instigated or prolonged by U.S. intervention.[40] Our hopes of helping the oppressed Third World people throw off their domestic oppressors turned sour because we did not know *The Easy Way Out* (see below). Instead, the Wealth Pie of many nations, already diminished by the aggression of their own domestic government, dwindled further. After being subjected to civil war and our aid by aggression (Chapter 18: *Beacon to the World*), it's a wonder the developing nations are still developing at all!

Our Wealth Pie also diminished as time, effort, and money were put into buying destruction rather than production. The Wealth Pie of the entire world is much smaller than it could have been.

Less wealth means our world has fewer goods and services. Would we have cures for cancer, AIDS, and Alzheimer's disease if we hadn't squandered our talents on aggression? Would we enjoy a 20-hour work week with 40-hour week benefits? Would we have extended our lifespan to encompass more than a century of healthful living? Would we have broken the barrier that the speed of light poses to interstellar travel? Would we live in a world where no one ever goes hungry? Would we have learned how to live in harmony with our environment and our own inner self?

By greatly slowing the global creation of wealth, even the special interests which seemingly profit from a world of strife, will lose. No

Every $1 billion of tax money the Pentagon spends on military purchases causes a loss of 18,000 jobs in the nation, compared with how consumers would have spent the money, a study said yesterday. Employment Research Associates of Lansing, Michigan, analyzed the effect of military spending on the U.S. economy using Defense Department and Bureau of Labor Statistics figures.
—United Press International
October 25, 1982

amount of money can buy wealth that has not been created. When they and their loved ones meet an early death due to an "incurable" disease, they pay the ultimate price of attenuating the world's Wealth Pie. Today's wealthy are poor compared to the wealth an average person would enjoy in a world of non-aggression. When special interests encourage aggression, they deprive themselves.

This impoverishment extends beyond the realm of physical wealth. I once had the opportunity to question a man who was intimately involved with the special interests that dominate our country's national defense policies. When asked what his goals were, he immediately responded, "Power and money!" Since this man was already quite wealthy and powerful, I eventually rephrased my question. "What would make you happy?" I queried.

Judge not lest ye be judged.
—THE HOLY BIBLE
Matthew 7:1

His answer was profound. He explained that he felt separated from the rest of humanity, as if he were apart and different from other people. He wanted that to change; he wanted to feel connected.

At the time, I didn't appreciate the implications of what he had said. After much reflection, it seems that this feeling of separation is a direct result of how we view those around us. If we tell ourselves that others are not as wise as we are, as unselfish, or as informed, if we *judge* their choices to be inferior to ours, we no longer consider them our equals. We set them apart from ourselves. If we follow this judgment by *forcing* our choices on them—at gunpoint, if necessary—the chasm between us grows. Aggression is the physical manifestation of our judgment of others. In this manner, a person who practices aggression regularly becomes separated from those he or she trespasses against. Those who create a reality where they, even with the best intentions, try to control the selfish others of the world may indeed find themselves looking down on the rest of humanity. At the apex of

For what shall it profit a man if he shall gain the world and lose his own soul?
—THE HOLY BIBLE
Mark 8:36

the Pyramid of Power, one is very much dis-
connected and alone.

I suspect humans require a sense of connectedness and community with the rest of
their kind to reach the heights of happiness
for which they were intended. When we use
aggression, we destroy connectedness and
community. When we use aggression, we
forfeit the happiness that we are ultimately
trying to achieve by controlling others.

Aggression is not in anyone's best interest.
Only when we realize this will we have peace
and plenty in both our inner and outer worlds.

Luckily, we do not need to wait until
others who practice aggression become enlightened. Special interest groups only fan the
flames of poverty and strife. Like the serpent
in the garden, special interests tempt us to
use the guns of government against our
neighbors to create the money monopoly and
levy taxes that pay for killing machines. When
we as a society say "No!" to aggression, we
render those who would control us impotent.

The power broker I spoke with acknowledged that the special interests would be foiled
if ordinary people ever realized what power
they possess. Indeed, special interest elite
spend much time and effort encouraging a
sense of helplessness among the American
public. We hold the key if we choose to use it.
We can be victimized by special interests only
when we try to victimize others. When we
refuse to do unto others, others cannot easily
do unto us!

THE EASY WAY OUT

Our national defense policy has a profound
effect on our world because of our great
wealth. Ironically, we achieved this power by
being, for a time, the least aggressive nation
on earth.

How can we reclaim our heritage of political non-aggression? If we want a world of
peace, the first sensible thing to do is to be

sure that our actions do not cause war. Otherwise, we will only be fighting ourselves. Conversely, when we abandon the domestic aggression that funds overseas dictators, teaches terrorism, and nurtures the Communist threat, we stop creating enemies!

Even without our country's aggression, however, it's unlikely that the world will be totally peaceful. How does a nation of non-aggressors fare in a world of aggressors?

Non-Aggression Wins the Game—Even in a World of "Meanies"

Once again, the computer games give us a pleasant surprise. Even a population of players as small as 5% do so well with each other using TIT FOR TAT that non-aggression is the most profitable strategy even if the rest of the population *always* aggresses![41] Even if other nations never followed our example, we would still come out ahead!

In the computer games, doing well meant getting points. In real life, the rewards of non-aggression are more tangible. Because non-aggression greatly increases the Wealth Pie, a lone nation practicing non-aggression would eventually be the wealthiest nation on earth. It would be technologically superior to other nations. Commercial aeronautical and space flight capability would be more advanced. Communications would be superior. Machinery would be more sophisticated. Nuclear energy would be better understood and applied. A country with such advanced technology would be a formidable foe. Indeed, at the turn of the century, the United States was evolving in exactly this way because it practiced non-aggression to a greater extent than most other nations.

One of the reasons a nation practicing non-aggression would be so prosperous is that its people could trade without the restriction of tariffs. International trade would flourish as it does in every duty-free zone.

Trading partners seldom need to resort to violence to work out their differences. They have every incentive to avoid fighting. On the other hand, stopping trade with the guns of government can provoke conflict. Indeed, some historians believe that a primary reason behind Japan's attack on Pearl Harbor was the embargo (prohibitive licensing) that prevented Americans from selling oil to Japan![42]

Without the aggression of embargoes and tariffs, a nation of non-aggressors would have few enemies. *If we practiced non-aggression, other nations would have little incentive to attack us!*

Protecting American Interests Abroad

While aggressor nations might be deterred from invading the borders of a non-aggressive nation, seizing American assets abroad would still be tempting. How would we, as a nation of non-aggressors, defend our interests abroad?

At times, our troops have been sent into a country when property of U.S. companies have been threatened by aggressors. The American citizenry has been forced— at gunpoint, if necessary—to subsidize the protection of profits when companies have taken the risk of locating in an unstable area.

If our neighbor George opened a convenience store in a high-crime area, we'd expect him to hire extra guards to protect it and pass these costs on to his customers by raising prices. No one would be forced at gunpoint to subsidize his business or his profit. We should expect American companies operating abroad to adopt the same non-aggressive approach.

Companies wishing to locate in another part of the world could hire their own protection agents or insure themselves against nationalization or confiscation. Insurance companies would charge higher premiums for businesses locating in unstable countries, just as they charge businesses more to insure them in high-crime areas. The marketplace

I spent 33 years...in active service...most of my time as a high-class muscle man for Big Business, for Wall Street, and the bankers. Thus I helped make Mexico, and especially Tampico, safe for American Oil interests in 1914. I helped make Haiti and Cuba a decent place for the National City Bank boys to collect revenue in. I helped in the raping of half-a-dozen Central American republics for the benefit of Wall Street ....I helped purify Nicaragua for the international banking house of Brown Brothers and Co. in 1909. I helped make Honduras "right" for American fruit companies in 1903.

—General Smedley Butler
Marine Corps Commandant

*Saddam is a Franken-
stein monster that the
West created.*
—Hans-Heino
Kopietz
English Middle East
analyst

ecosystem, free from aggression, encourages companies to locate in areas that practice non-aggression and to shun those that don't.

Toppling Modern-Day Hitlers

Sometimes our troops have gone into other countries to support one side or another in a civil war in the hopes of containing communism or saving the world from would-be Hitlers. Most often, we are only protecting ourselves from our own creations.

For example, Hitler, like the Soviet Union, was greatly empowered by the funding he received from German banks and the American elite.[44] Similarly, Saddam Hussein, the Iraqi strongman who invaded Kuwait, built his military machine through loans guaranteed by taxpayers of several Western nations, including our own.[45] Our domestic aggression help to create these invaders in the first place. *If we forsake aggression, we might have no Hitlers and Husseins to deal with at all!*

Even if our aggression no longer funds dictators, other banks and governments still could. We do not have the only central banks or weapons manufacturers. We are the most affluent, the most influential country in the world, but not the only one. Those who would dominate their countries require money and supplies for their military. Plundering peasants and destroying their means of wealth creation is a self-limiting supply system. Dictators cannot maintain their power without subsidies.

These subsidies usually come from the loans and gifts from Western nations, including the United States. Taxation and the inflation generated by the money creation of central banks makes these loans possible.

If a central bank inflated its nation's currency in a world where our country practiced non-aggression, citizens of the inflating nation would convert their currency into U.S. dollars to protect its value. They would not want their saving to be inflated away if they had another choice! As they made this conversion, they would be *deflating* the currency of their own nation. In a world where even one country practiced non-aggression, the central banks' ability to expand the money supply would be limited automatically! Subsidies to dictators would be limited as well! *If we practiced non-aggression, would-be world conquerors might not even be able to subdue their own people!*

Let's assume, however, that a head of state amassed enough power to invade another country. Today, a few government officials decide for everyone which side should be supported and to what extent. This support is taken—at gunpoint, if necessary—in the form of taxes, forced military service, or inflation. How would a nation of non-aggressors react?

Obviously, we would not all agree on exactly what should be done, any more than we would agree on what to do if we stumbled upon two people fighting each other in the street. Both combatants would claim to be the wronged party and cry for help. How would we know who is the aggressor?

Sometimes the answer to this all-important question is not always very clear, even when both sides stop fighting long enough to tell their story. Indeed, we seldom hear both sides of the story in an international crisis today. Our radio and television stations have licenses that can be revoked if they carry programs that aren't considered to be in the public interest.[46] Who determines what is in the public interest? Our government officials do, and they are frequently beholden to the special interests that profit from a nation at war. In a nation practicing non-aggression, both sides would be more likely to be heard.

Defusing Terrorism

If both sides of a conflict were welcome to present their side of the story and solicit support from Americans directly, terrorism against our people would dissolve. Terrorists

harm civilians in an attempt to change aggressive government policy.[47] If we had no
aggressive government policy, there would be
no incentive for terrorism! Dissidents could
solicit help directly from Americans. If the
dissidents weren't satisfied with the outcome,
terrorist action would only cost them the
support they did have. *If we practiced non-*
aggression, terrorism against our people would
serve no purpose!

Policing Aggression

In a non-aggressive society, people would
decide what to do about international conflicts
much as they do when witnessing a street
fight. After hearing both sides of the story,
some people might offer to arbitrate so the two
could settle their differences. Some people
might fight on one side; some might fight on
the other. Still others might not want to get
involved at all. We wouldn't dream of forcing
other bystanders—at gunpoint, if necessary—
to fight on the side we chose. We'd expend
more energy trying to force our neighbor to do
as we wish than we'd exert in vanquishing the
aggressor ourselves! In our neighborhoods, we
honor our neighbor's choice.

When it comes to an international dispute,
somehow we see the situation differently. We
want to stop aggression so badly that we are
willing to become aggressors ourselves to
achieve our goal. By using aggression as our
means, we only create ends we'd rather not
have. Think how differently Vietnam might
have been if we had honored our neighbor's
choice!

No More Vietnams

When the war started, many Americans
were proud to be "saving" South Vietnam.
However, as the fighting dragged on, senti-
ments changed. This shift was dramatized in
a recent movie, *Born on the Fourth of July*,
depicting Ron Kovic,[47] who enthusiastically

served in Vietnam and protested American involvement in Indochina when he returned.

In a non-aggressive society, those who no longer wished to contribute to a war effort could simply stop supporting it. Had we honored our neighbor's choice, Vietnam would almost certainly have ended sooner, saving many hundreds, even thousands, of lives. Instead, Americans were forced—at gunpoint, if necessary—to pay taxes to fund a war that few wanted. Young men were drafted into service—at gunpoint, if necessary. Our youth were forced to risk life and limb with monetary compensation well below the minimum wage. We could hardly hope to teach the virtues of freedom while enslaving our own youth!

Meanwhile, the money monopoly and military-industrial complex *profited* from the Vietnam War. The many paid through inflation and taxation, for the profits of the few. A recent movie, *JFK*, based on the research of Jim Garrison,[48] suggested that President Kennedy was assassinated because he did not support the Vietnam War which generated special interest profits. My own research suggests that we went to war in Vietnam for some purpose other than containing communism. I spoke with a high-ranking officer who commanded an aircraft carrier group sent to that region. He told me that the war could certainly have been won, but that the military was not permitted to take the necessary action.

When we honor our neighbors' choice, there will be no more Vietnams. If people vote against a war by not offering their time, money, or service, the issue is decided. Today, a few government officials decide whether a nation will go to war. As we've seen, these officials are beholden to special interest groups that profit from the fighting. As a result, they will choose war in situations where the average person would choose peace. TIT FOR TAT strategies clearly indicate that erring on the

Neither slavery or involuntary servitude... shall exist within the United States.
—U.S. Constitution
13th Amendment

We should have closed the harbor of Haiphong....we permitted them to import all the necessities of war....
—Admiral U.S.
Grant Sharp
Commander-in-Chief
of U.S. Naval
Operations in
Vietnam

252 Healing Our World

Suppose they gave a war, and no one came?
—Leslie Parrish-Bach actress, Vietnam War protestor, and Richard Bach's BRIDGE ACROSS FOREVER

...people want peace so much that one of these days governments had better get out of their way and let them have it.
—President Dwight D. Eisenhower, 1959

side of too little retaliation rather than too much teaches non-aggression best.[50] *When the decision of whether or not to go to war is left in the hands of each individual, the world will be a more peaceful place!*

We needn't worry that Americans would fail to come to the aid of a foreign nation beset by a vicious aggressor. Historically, Americans have shown their willingness to help those battling aggression. Large deficits and defense budgets have been accepted by the American populace when the cause is considered just. However, if we are willing to force our neighbors—at gunpoint, if necessary—to support such causes, *we* become like the enemy we are fighting. Our belief that we should force our view point on others is what Vietnams are made of.

Protecting the Home Front

Obviously, the best protection against foreign invasion is to create as few enemies as possible. As we've seen throughout this chapter, a nation practicing non-aggression is most likely to do just that. When we no longer fund aggressors through domestic aggression, when we listen to both sides of a dispute, when we support those fighting aggression, would-be world conquerors have trouble subduing their own people. *When we practice non-aggression, we stop would-be invaders before they begin!*

If a defense did become necessary, a nation practicing non-aggression would be likely to have the strongest one. As we learned in Part II (*Forgive Us Our Trespasses: How We Create Poverty in a World of Plenty*), non-aggression increases a country's wealth. Aggression, and defense against aggression, consume wealth rapidly. The wealthier a country is, the longer it can sustain its defense.

Our country currently has a strong nuclear deterrent that is primarily directed at the

former Soviet Union. Thankfully, most governments that possess nuclear technology have
little incentive to use it. Because we are the
wealthiest nation in the world, other countries
depend on our technology. Destroying us
would only make an attacking nation poorer
and could contaminate the entire globe with
radioactive fallout. Thus, a nuclear strike, if it
came at all, would most likely come as a
terrorist act. Against such strategies, we
currently have no defense. Indeed, our best
deterrent against a terrorist nuclear attack
would be to defuse the tensions that might
precipitate it by the practice of non-aggression.

Switzerland, a country historically dedicated to neutrality, has a strong defense against
armed invasion. Switzerland has a part-time
national government and no nuclear capability, yet sometime in the 1990s, it will have
bomb shelters for every man, woman, and
child. Every man is part of the army and is
required to keep his military weapon in his
home.[50] An invading army would literally have
to subdue every household to conquer that
nation. Indeed, in both World Wars, when the
Germans threatened to invade, the Swiss
simply dissuaded them by inviting key German officers to witness their preparedness!
The Germans had been considering a short-
cut through non-mountainous regions of the
tiny country. The Germans, however, decided
against invading "the little porcupine."[51]

A non-aggressive nation could easily and
affordably develop a Swiss-style defense,
without the aggression of taxation or the
universal draft that the Swiss use. People
fearing a nuclear strike could construct their
own shelters or participate in fund-raising for
community facilities. People concerned with
armed invasion could encourage the build-up
of community defense forces. Military Olympics might stimulate proficiency in defensive
skills among those who were inclined both

toward athletics and the civic pride associated with being part of a community militia. Some communities might support their local militia much as they support their local sports teams. Fees could be charged to watch the Olympics. Local businesses and clubs could engage in fund-raising to outfit the citizen army. These troops might also be hired by other nations or sent to aid them by Americans who supported their cause.

An armed citizenry is an important aspect of national defense that has been neglected in this country. Instead of discouraging firearms with licensing laws, we could encourage widespread proficiency with military hardware of all kinds. As we learned in Chapter 16 (*Policing Aggression*), we need not fear that an armed citizenry is a violent one. The belief in aggression, not the possession of firearms, is responsible for murder and mayhem. Proficiency in handling firearms among the general population, would deter foreign aggressors just as surely as it deters individual criminals. An armed populace forces an invader to conquer each household, making successful foreign takeover difficult, if not impossible.

Men are afraid that war might come because they know... that they have never rejected the doctrine which causes wars... the doctrine that it is right or practical or necessary for men to achieve their goals by means of physical force *(by* initiating *the use of force against other men) and that some sort of "good" can justify it.*
—Ayn Rand
Capitalism the
Unknown Ideal

Non-Aggression Is the Best Defense

In other sections of this book, historical examples of *The Easy Way Out* have been readily available. No nation with modern armaments has a national defense completely free from aggression. As a consequence, predicting exactly what such a defense would look like is, at best, speculative. Based on the other consequences of non-aggression detailed throughout this book, however, we can confidently expect such a defense to be less expensive and of higher quality than defense through aggression. More importantly, non-aggression provides us with the best deterrent of all, because it stops most would-be Husseins and Hitlers from ever coming to power.

Historically, we have felt that national defense is too important to put in the hands of ordinary, everyday people. However, if we are willing to force others—at gunpoint, if necessary—to provide time and money toward defense, don't *we* become the invaders? We are trying to protect our lives, liberty, and property from those who would choose differently for us. If in the process of defending ourselves, we turn on our neighbors and make their lives, liberty, and property forfeit, haven't we become what we most fear?

Only when we no longer sanction aggression, ours or anyone else's, will we excise the cancer that causes war. Nothing less will create a peaceful and prosperous world.

PART V

BUT DELIVER US FROM EVIL

Our Choices Make Our World

CHAPTER 21

A NEW AGE OR A NEW WORLD ORDER?

Once we understand how global peace and prosperity are created, we cannot be easily fooled.

We've seen that government, as we know it today, is not the benevolent protector we hoped it would be. Instead, it is a mechanism by which we direct the guns of government at our neighbors out of fear that they might choose differently than we would like them to. We reap as we sow. In trying to control others, we find ourselves controlled. In failing to honor our neighbor's choice, we create a world of poverty and strife.

Even when we defend ourselves against those who take aggressive action, we begin by becoming aggressors ourselves. With the guns of government, we tax our neighbors to establish exclusive, subsidized police and military monopolies. Like most monopolies, these protection agencies are more expensive and less effective than they would be in the absence of aggression. As we learned in Chapter 20 (*National Defense*), *actions undertaken for national security may have endangered us more than having no defense at all!*

As long as we employ the guns of government to force our neighbors to our will, aggression will be the instrument by which we enslave ourselves. This is as true of global government as it is of our local and national ones.

To many, unification through world government symbolizes the end of war. Unification can be achieved in one of two ways: by choice (non–aggression) or by force (aggression). The result we get is very different depending on the means we use to get there.

For example, the physical and emotional joining that occurs spontaneously between lovers differs considerably from the forcible unification of rape. Global unity, achieved or maintained by aggression instead of by honoring our neighbor's choice, is the antithesis of universal love as well.

Let's examine five areas that world government (sometimes referred to as the New World Order) would address to see if its consummation would be an act of love or rape.

CONTROLLING POPULATION GROWTH

As we learned in Chapter 2 (*Wealth Is Unlimited!*), population density has little impact on a country's wealth. Both Japan and West Germany are more populated than Mexico and East Germany, yet the former two countries are both much wealthier.[1] Famine results from restricting the creation of wealth by aggression–through–government (Chapters 18 (*Beacon to the World*) and 19 (*The Communist Threat Is All in Our Minds*), not from overpopulation. Nevertheless, prudent people know that the earth cannot sustain unlimited increases in population. Some believe the solution is to limit childbearing—at gunpoint, if necessary—through world government.

The "carrying capacity" of the earth depends on the type of society it sustains. The earth has a lower carrying capacity for hunting and gathering populations than for farming societies. Improved farming techniques regularly increase the yield per acre and the earth's carrying capacity along with it.[2]

Additional space in densely populated areas can be provided by multilevel buildings. Clearly, the carrying capacity of the earth changes with how we use the space that we have. The high standard of living enjoyed by the densely populated Japanese suggest that we are nowhere near reaching the earth's carrying capacity. Perhaps by the time we do reach it, colonizing other planets will provide another way of expanding.

In all likelihood, however, we will not need to worry about exceeding the earth's carrying capacity. As societies become wealthier, the number of births drops dramatically.[3] In the United States, we have come close to stabilizing our population, even though children are partially subsidized through income tax exemptions and encouraged by the structure of our welfare system.

The reasons people have more children in developing countries is not difficult to discern. In a rural economy, children contribute quite early to a family's financial well-being. Farming, especially in Third World countries, depends heavily on manual tasks simple enough for children to perform. If a world government were to limit the number of children a rural couple could have, they would lose a source of wealth-creating labor. As a family, they would be poorer and more likely to go hungry. A ban on children would probably create more famine, not less. As always, aggression-through-government is likely to aggravate the problem, not solve it.

In an industrialized economy such as ours, manual labor, especially child labor, creates little wealth relative to the work of experienced, skilled adults. As a result, children are a net drain on family resources for many more years than they are in rural economies. As nations become more affluent, people have the incentive to raise fewer children.

Thus, the most effective way to control population is to increase the Wealth Pie by doing away with the aggression-through-government that keeps the Third World poor. The most effective way to achieve zero population growth is to encourage the worldwide practice of non-aggression so that all people can climb the Ladder of Affluence.

PROTECTING THE ENVIRONMENT
Rainforests

As detailed in Chapter 18 (*Beacon to the World*), the clearing of the rainforests results from aggressive government policy. Third World governments fail to honor or defend the homesteading claims of the natives who inhabit them, especially when timber companies pay the heads of state for such oversights. The licensing laws and other restrictions on the creation of wealth imposed on the population (Chapter 18: *Beacon to the World*) drives people to exploit the rainforests as well. The same heads of state responsible for creating the rainforest problem will determine who represents their country in a world government just as these officials currently select who will attend the United Nations. Obviously, these representatives will defend the exploitation of the rainforest.

Special interest groups that profit from destroying the rainforests will lobby world government representatives in much the same way they lobby our domestic officials to cut down our national forests. The representatives do not personally profit from long-term planning for the rainforests, because they have no homesteading or ownership claim. By turning the rainforests over to special interest groups, however, these officials can be amply rewarded from the short-term profit the rainforests generate. World government representatives will have every incentive to turn their backs on the plight of the rainforests and their native inhabitants.

Representatives who are steadfast in their determination to preserve the rainforests will be pressured by other domestic special interest groups to sacrifice the rainforests to gain votes for their particular cause. A person willing to sacrifice domestic special interests for the global good will be replaced by a candidate able to maintain the lucrative special interest support. Special interests will influence the world government as they do in every country today.

As a result, world government will not protect the rainforests any better than national governments do. A policy that permits the destruction of the rainforests will do so on a global level, instead of a national one. We have only to observe how our national forests are sacrificed locally (Chapter 8: *Destroying the Environment*) to see what we can expect globally.

The way to protect the rainforests, as described in Chapter 18 (*Beacon to the World*), is to recognize the homesteading claims of the native inhabitants. Historically, governments have failed to do this. Instead, native people (including those indigenous to the United States), have been ruthlessly pushed aside so that special interests may be served.[4] More aggression-through-government will be part of the problem, not the solution.

Some people are uncomfortable with the idea of individuals or tribes owning part of the earth. Ownership conjures up the image of a selfish other withholding a part of Mother Earth from other fellow humans. A global "commons" sounds more inclusive, more sharing. These images, however, are sheer illusion, perhaps even perpetrated by the special interests that profit from such an outlook.

Because selfish owners want to profit as much as possible from their land, they have incentive to treat their property in a way that increases its value to *others*. The price that owners can get for the land depends on how *other* members of society value the care given to it. A selfish owner has incentive to heed the priorities of the whole.

What would prevent a special interest group from purchasing the rainforests? Nothing—as long as they were willing to pay the full costs of them. Today, the rainforests cost special interests only a convenient payoff to those who control these lands and do not benefit by long term management. The price of buying rainforest property from owners who can profit from long-term care would be much higher. Exploitation is no longer affordable.

Government officials who control the commons are as selfish as property owners. However, these officials profit only when they favor the special interests over the common good. If those controlling the rainforests nobly attempt to do otherwise, special interest groups probably will see that they lose their jobs. The interests of the few work *against* the interests of the many. With aggression, looking out for Number 1 goes against the welfare of the whole. Without aggression, the same drive becomes harnessed for the greater good. We truly live in a win–win world!

Endangered Species

On Land. Some conservationists see a global government as a way to enforce worldwide bans on hunting endangered species, such as elephants and rhinos. Such bans threaten first–strike force against those who try to create wealth by "harvesting" these unclaimed animals. The guns of government are used to prevent homesteading of wild herds in much the same way as they are used to prevent homesteading of land. Environmentalists support such bans in the belief that they preserve endangered species. In fact, just the opposite is true.

For example, elephant hunting has been banned in Kenya. In 1989, these animals numbered only 19,000, down from 65,000 in 1979.[5] On the other hand, in Zimbabwe, homesteading claims of natives to elephants on their land have been respected. Elephant products can be legally sold. Naturally, the natives protect their valuable elephants from poachers. The natives raise as many elephants as possible so they can sponsor safaris and sell elephant ivory, hide, and meat. As a result, the elephant population has increased from 30,000 to 43,000 over the past ten years. *People will protect the environment when they own it and profit from it.*

We never worry about cows and horses becoming extinct. They are plentiful because we own them and profit from their use. We have motivation to make sure they propagate. Ownership encourages effective stewardship of

People who do good things for the environment should benefit, and the people who harm the environment should pay the cost of the harm they cause.
—Richard Stroup
Political Economy Research Center, Bozeman, Montana

wildlife, just as it encourages protection of the land. Although it happens from time to time, few people are foolish enough to kill the goose that lays the golden egg.

On Sea. The same principle applies to marine life as well. In some states, homesteading of oyster beds is permitted. Private oyster beds are more prolific and profitable than public ones. The owners have incentive to invest money in caring for the beds and harvesting them sustainably.[6]

Unfortunately, the guns of government are used to prevent individuals and groups from homesteading parcels of ocean other than oyster beds. As a result, no one has incentive to fish sustainably. In the first half of this century, shrimp fishers along the Gulf coast attempted to homestead these areas as a group to prevent overfishing.[7] The government refused to recognize their claim.

Many other environmental benefits result from ocean ownership. If an oil tanker wanted permission to cross a fishery, owners likely would demand that the tanker carry adequate insurance or have safeguards against rupture. Insurance costs would be lower for ships with such safeguards, thus encouraging careful construction of tankers. As a result, oil spills would be less likely. Oil companies would be ready to deal with the few accidents that occurred since delay would increase the cost of righting the wrong.

Owners would also be more likely to invest in artificial reefs to bolster the fish population. Whalers could operate only with the permission of the owners, much as hunters must request permission to stalk deer on privately owned land. Ocean owners profit most by making sure that the valuable species in their region are not hunted to extinction. Migrating species could be protected by agreements between adjoining owners. Since some ocean plots might be quite expensive, corporations or conservation-oriented groups might purchase

*The world's 150 gov-
ernments have histori-
cally been enemies of
the environment.*
—Richard Stroup,
Political Economy
Research Center,
Bozeman, Montana

them. Conservationists could simply buy ocean lots favored by species they wish to protect, much as the Nature Conservancy and the Audubon Society purchase land today. If conservationists did not wish to buy ocean plots outright, they could pay owners for hunting rights and then not exercise them. Instead of lobbying government officials in the *hopes* of achieving effective legislation, they could buy protection of the environment directly!

World government would be unlikely to institute these reforms. Traditionally, governments have taken charge of the oceans much as they have done with the rainforests, disregarding the claims of those who have tended them. Instead, governments have turned these sensitive environments over to special interest groups. Since these groups do not actually *own* these areas, they cannot profit by giving them long-term care. If special interests groups had to purchase ocean plots or rainforests, instead of simply paying off government officials, destroying these environments would no longer be profitable. Only long-term planning would protect such an expensive investment.

CONTROLLING THE GREENHOUSE EFFECT

The media talk about the "greenhouse effect" as if it were established fact. Our meteorologists can hardly predict tomorrow's temperature accurately, yet somehow predictions of a few degrees of global warming over the next few decades is supposed to be possible! I don't need my Ph.D. in biophysics to know that this kind of logic just doesn't add up!

*I am certain that most
working climatologists
believe that there has
been no significant in-
crease in temperature
in the last 100 years.*
—William A.
Neirenberg
Scripps Institution
of Oceanography

Every week, I scan the prestigious *Science* magazine for the latest in the global warming debate. Scientists cannot seem to agree on whether or not global temperatures are rising unnaturally. Satellite data from 1979 to 1988 reveal no warming trend at all.[4] Surface measurements reveal an increase from 1880 to 1940, but little upward movement after 1940, the years of heaviest industrial activity (see Figure 21.1).[5]

Some scientists believe the increase in temperature earlier in this century was simply due to the urbanization of rural areas during that time. Urban areas tend to trap heat more than rural ones.[6] Temperature–sensing devices are usually located in cities and might reflect these fluctuations.

If, in spite of evidence to the contrary, we assume that the world is warming, what would cause it? The earth has gone through several Ice Ages and warming cycles without human help and might be doing so again. Indeed, some evidence suggests that the ozone level correlates better with sunspot activity than with human endeavors.[7]

Chlorofluorocarbons (CFCs), for example, were introduced in the second half of this century, while the largest temperature increases were seen before 1940.[5] CFCs do destroy ozone, but so do volcanoes. In 1976, for example, the eruption of the Alaskan Augustine Volcano produced 570 times as much chlorine as was put into the atmosphere by CFCs and other chlorine emissions in 1975![8] Consequently, banning CFCs would have minor impact on ozone levels. However, stopping the sale of CFCs—at gunpoint, if necessary—might have significant impacts on the health of the poor in developing nations.

The CFCs are used primarily as refrigerants. Current substitutes are more costly and less effective.[9] Worldwide refitting and shifting to these substitutes may cost as much as $100 billion within the next decade. Unable to afford new refrigerators, the poor, especially the Third World poor, may have to do without. Food spoilage with the accompanying threat of food poisoning is much more common in the tropical countries of the world and could become more frequent. Banning CFCs could very well kill long before a hole in the ozone ever could. That's a hefty price to pay for an inaccurate weather prediction.

Even a 5 percent decrease in the ozone layer, as calculated by the most pessimistic scenarios, would increase ultraviolet exposure only as much as moving sixty miles south—the same distance as from Palm Beach to Miami.
—S. Fred Singer, Professor of Environmental Sciences at University of Virginia

...probably more people would die from food poisoning as a consequence of inadequate refrigeration than would die from depleting ozone.
—Robert Watson NASA scientist, referring to the effects of a CFC ban

Figure 21.1 Global Temperatures Over the Past 100 Years

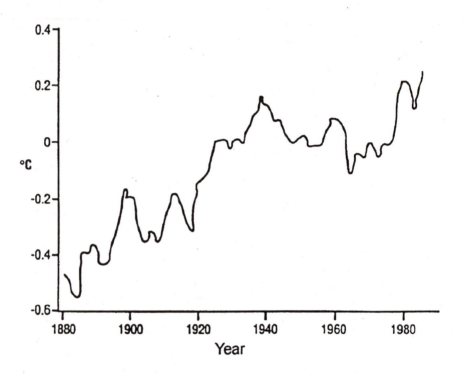

Note: Zero line shows the average temperature for the years 1951-1980.
SOURCE: D. James E. Hansen, NASA-Goddard Institute for Space
Studies.

Reprinted with permission of Consumers' Research Magazine.
1991 by Consumers' Research, Inc.

Such a sacrifice is likely to be unnecessary, even if we one day experience a greenhouse effect. Carbon dioxide is purported to account for about 49% of all greenhouse gases. An increase in carbon dioxide along with global temperatures will stimulate the growth of plants, both on land and sea. Some scientists believe that farmers would enjoy bumper food crops and warmer oceans would produce larger plankton populations.[10] Plants absorb carbon dioxide during photosynthesis, lowering the amount of carbon dioxide in the atmosphere. Global temperatures would probably be stabilized by Nature's self-regulating global ecosystem.

Should we ever face global warming, we may find it a pleasant surprise. A tropical earth would have more bountiful plant and animal life and require less fossil fuel for heating. Since the geological record suggests we may be due for an Ice Age,[11] inducing global warming might actually prevent a greater catastrophe!

Finally, the earth is such a large heat sink that any warming resulting from human activities would occur gradually over several decades, giving us plenty of time to react. Rising seas would inch forward year after year, providing ample time to build dikes and sea walls.[12] If a chemical were damaging others in any way, its price (in a non-aggressive society) would rise in order to compensate the victims. High prices would discourage use and encourage innovative substitutes without aggression.

A global government, patterned after the governments of today, would undoubtedly expect taxpayers, not the aggressor, to make the victims whole again. If people died needlessly because of a banned chemical, the representatives of a world government could claim sovereign immunity, as our own government did after poisoning people with fallout from nuclear testing. More aggression-through-government is not the solution to global warming, real or imagined.

ISSUING GLOBAL CURRENCY

A single, global currency sounds heavenly to world travelers who are constantly exchanging one type of money for another. However, these different currencies are an important part of the self-regulating marketplace ecosystem, even though the marketplace is hardly free from aggression. Each country's central bank has the power to inflate the currency as much as it wants, thereby increasing its profits. However, if other countries' central banks don't follow suit, this plan is foiled.

For example, if our Federal Reserve starts inflating our currency while the Japanese central bank does not, our dollar becomes worth less compared to the yen. Savvy investors bring their dollars into the banks and exchange them for the more valuable yen. The more the central bank tries to increase the money supply, the more people fearfully convert their dollars to something else. The banks can't profit if people won't take their dollars. The diverse currency in the marketplace ecosystem still regulates the central banks to some extent.

If everyone is forced—at gunpoint, if necessary—to use a single global currency, these checks and balances are destroyed. The central bank can manipulate the money supply at will. Through inflation, wealth would be transferred from those who had no property and savings to those who did. Alternating inflation with deflation would bankrupt those who failed to accurately predict the timing of the cycles and invest their resources accordingly (see Chapter 9: *Banking on Aggression*) for a review of this process). Those who control the money supply would get richer at the expense of the less fortunate.

The power at the apex of the Pyramid is so great that a global currency would allow those who control it to have more power than any ruling elite has ever known.

KEEPING THE PEACE

A global government would centralize military capability. Nations would turn their weaponry over to the international "peace keeping" force. When enough countries had joined, the global government could *force* the remaining nations into the pact in the name of global unity.

Once disarmed, nations could not go to war against each other. Peace would presumably ensue. In practice, the guns of world government would simply be pointed alternatively at majorities and minorities. Just as in our country, they would take turns being victims and aggressors. As always, aggression would favor the well-to-do. Special interest groups would once again triumph.

The banking interests would inflate the currency rapidly, redistributing wealth to those who are already well endowed. The earth's oceans and rainforests would remain in the custody of representatives who profit most by allowing special interests to exploit these resources. As usual, aggressors would not be required to compensate victims. Sovereign immunity would protect government officials when their actions harmed others. The world would grow ever poorer.

As we realized our mistake, we might try to assert our independence from the global government. We would then have to fight the combined weaponry of the entire world!

A worse fate might befall us, however. With no country permitted to try different ways of relating to others, there would be no example for us to imitate. With education controlled globally, the ideas of non-aggression might never be taught at all. We certainly didn't learn about it in *our* schools—in spite of our heritage as the first modern country to recognize the importance of the first principle of non-aggression, honoring our neighbor's choice. We might never realize that there could be a better way, a path to peace and plenty.

Government, in its last analysis, is organized force.
—President Woodrow Wilson

...once having joined the One-World Federated Government, no nation could secede or revolt...because with the Atom Bomb in its possession the Federal Government would blow that nation off the face of the earth.
—Cord Meyer, Jr. first president of the United World Federalists

...the need of a growing solidarity with our fellows and a growing collective soul in humanity is not in dispute. But the loss of the self in the State is not the thing these high ideals mean, nor is it the way to their fulfillment.
—Sri Aurobindo
SOCIAL AND POLITICAL THOUGHT

We shall have world government whether or not you like it—by conquest or consent.
—James Warburg
Senate Foreign
Relations Committee,
1950

If you want to be a great leader, you must learn to follow the Tao. Stop trying to control. Let go of fixed plans and concepts and the world will govern it-self.
—Lao-tsu
TAO TE CHING

We might remain in another Dark Age, so blind that we never realize that a win-win world is just within our grasp.

Earlier, we asked ourselves whether global government was the unity of love or rape. We've seen that a world government operating on aggression will not give us the unity we seek. Instead of a haven, it will be a trap. Instead of a blissful union, it will be *enforced* bondage. Instead of controlling selfish others, we will once more find ourselves controlled.

Only when we honor our neighbor's choice will we have true unity. We love others as ourselves when we treat their choices with the same respect we give our own.

When we practice non-aggression, we undo the damage we have done. When we right our wrongs, we have no reason to feel guilt or separation.

Together, these two principles make up the practice of non-aggression. Isn't this how we want others to do unto us? Isn't this the way we want the world to be?

CHAPTER 22

HOW TO GET THERE FROM HERE

If we each work on the piece of the puzzle that appeals to us most, the final picture will reflect the composite of our dreams.

TEACHING BY EXAMPLE

In a world steeped in aggression, non-aggression may seem like an unattainable ideal. Let's remember that a scant 200 years ago the world of monarchs mocked our founders, who claimed that a nation could thrive without a king. A short time later, all of Europe began following our example. History certainly demonstrated that the idealists had the more practical philosophy!

Notice that these nations did not have to be *forced* to adopt the American way. The young United States simply lived its ideals. At the time, our country was closer to practicing non-aggression than its contemporaries were. Americans, for the most part, honored their neighbor's choice. They did not, however, know the power of the other piece of the puzzle: righting wrongs to make victims whole once again. However, even partial non-aggression was so fruitful that other countries sought to imitate our nation.

CREATING THE VISION

Like our country's founders, we don't need to choose between the ideal and the practical. Since the means used dictate the ends attained, only non-aggression can give us a peaceful and prosperous world. Since aggression results in poverty and strife, it is neither ideal nor practical. Non-aggression will eventually become the norm because thankfully it is both ideal and practical.

Selfish others do not stand in our way. Indeed, non-aggression will infuse the earth precisely because each of us is a selfish other.

I wonder if we in the United States were to concentrate...on making ourselves the best possible society we can be, whether the nations of the world might once again, without any pressure except the influence of example, begin to emulate us.

—M. Scott Peck
THE DIFFERENT DRUM

Each of us seeks individual happiness with every thought, word, and deed. Just as in the computer games, we are learning that non-aggression (TIT FOR TAT) is a win–win strategy for everyone—even the special interest groups.

What joy to realize we needn't spend time and effort trying to control others at gunpoint to create a world of peace and plenty! What joy to realize that we live in a win–win world! We need not choose between our welfare and that of others; both are served by the practice of non-aggression. We need not choose between the individual and the common good; both benefit from non-aggression. We need not choose between the environment and our standard of living; both are balanced with non-aggression.

We may have created a world of war and poverty, but *because* it is our creation, we have the power to change it. When we are steadfast in our refusal to use aggression to control our neighbors, the power brokers and special interest groups lose their control over us. No longer will we put the guns of government at the disposal of the powerful. When we refuse to be tempted by the serpent, we cannot be thrown from the garden!

When we forsake aggression, we set the stage for cooperation and the innovative creation of wealth. Skilled workers cannot demand artificially high wages when ambitious, unskilled workers can negotiate training wages to learn their trades. Employers cannot exploit employees when the absence of licensing laws gives employees a chance to start a business of their own. Without monopoly by aggression, service providers must please customers or lose them to innovators who will put the customer first.

By creating wealth non-aggressively, employers and employees learn that when they take care of each other, there is more profit to share. Service providers learn that they reap profit for themselves by taking care of their

...the power system continues only as long as individuals *try to get something for nothing. The day when a majority of individuals declares or acts as if it wants nothing from government, declares that it will look after its own welfare and interests, then on that day the power elites are doomed.*
—Antony Sutton
author of THE BEST ENEMY MONEY CAN BUY

customers. As the Wealth Pie grows, so does the realization that by doing unto others, we do unto ourselves.

With a society of greater wealth and a-wareness, the few who cannot create enough wealth for themselves can be amply provided for. When we do not force others to be charitable, giving comes about naturally.

Some people in our society may still think that aggression serves them. They might manifest this belief by stealing, defrauding, raping, or killing their neighbors. The most compassionate act we can perform is to allow aggressors to reap as they sow, to experience the consequences of their actions, to right their wrongs. In this way, these individuals undo the harm they have done—to themselves as well as to others. We have no need to punish such individuals, only to heal them and those they have harmed.

If you have read this far, you probably share this vision, at least in part. Few people see things in exactly the same way. This is as it should be. As we work together, comparing interpretations and strategies, we will come closer to visualizing every aspect of our ultimate dream—a world of universal peace and plenty.

Clarity is the necessary first step to setting an example. The bad news is that war and poverty are caused largely by our drive to control our neighbors. The good news is that what we have done, we can undo. We are in control. Once our vision is clear, we can change *our* behavior to match it. We can honor our neighbor's choice by refusing to support laws that threaten first-strike force or fraud against others. We can encourage reforms that substitute restitution instead of punishment for aggressors.

...a next major step toward peace is the creation of an image of a future world of peace, an image that is widely credible and is ever-more-widely held.

—Richard Smoke and
Willis Harman
PATHS TO PEACE

RELATING TO CURRENT REALITY

Honoring our neighbor's choice means that we say "No!" to *licensing laws* and *regulations* that use first-strike force to prevent voluntary exchange between consumers and suppliers, employers and employees. Instead, we encourage *deregulation*.

Instead of maintaining *centralization* of power in the hands of the few through the guns of government, we promote *decentralization* of power by putting it into the hands of every individual. Instead of services provided by *regulated government monopolies*, we encourage *small businesses* that *compete* in the marketplace ecosystem *free from aggression* to serve the customer best.

We reject the idea of taking *taxes*—at gunpoint, if necessary—from our neighbors for *public* programs. We elect *private* sector services to lower costs, improve quality, and do away with *subsidies*. We encourage *private ownership* of land and sea to stop special interest groups from exploiting the *public domain*.

We reject imprisonment for those who hurt only themselves. For those who aggress against others, we substitute *restitution* for *punishment*. Through these reforms, we keep the marketplace ecosystem free from aggression *and* protect ourselves from those who would trespass against us.

CLARIFYING CONFLICT

We've learned that both parts of non-aggression—honoring our neighbor's choice and righting our wrongs—are necessary to create the peace and plenty we seek. Is it detrimental to honor our neighbor's choice *before* our system requires aggressors to right their wrongs?

The Health Care Crisis

The costs of medical care are skyrocketing because of the heavy regulation of the health care industry, including the licensing of physicians and pharmaceuticals. Should we consider using the aggression of taxation to subsidize national health insurance until deregulation?

Once again, using the guns of government to solve the problems created by aggression only makes matters worse. As we've learned, subsidies encourage waste. In countries with subsidized national health insurance, people demand care for minor ailments they used to tend to themselves. As a result, patients wait for critical care. In Newfoundland, a patient needing cardiac surgery waits an average of 43 weeks.[1] Affluent Canadians cross the border to our Cleveland Clinic;[2] the poor suffer. The waiting lists for all surgeries have doubled since 1967.[3] Canadians don't have better health care for less money, they just have less health care! This is not the solution we seek!

In Britain, the availability of health care may be even more limited. British doctors see five times as many patients as their American counterparts.[4] Thirty-five percent of kidney dialysis centers refuse to treat patients over 55 years of age![5] While the elderly are denied access to health care, the poor are neglected as well. Studies in Britain, Sweden, Canada, and New Zealand indicate that people with high social standing receive 2-6 times more health care than the less affluent.[6] National health programs even fail to deliver equal care!

These findings should hardly surprise us. More aggression cannot solve problems caused by aggression; it can only make matters worse. The Veterans' Administration hospitals are a good example of what national health care will bring. The recent movie, *Article 99*, depicted the poor care a person can expect under such a system.

Only non-aggression can turn the tide. When we deregulate medical care, as proposed in Chapters 5 (*Harming Our Health*) and 6 (*Protecting Ourselves to Death*), we will make health care costs affordable. Until then, we will have to pay the price for our aggression.

The Faltering Economy

We now recognize that our economic woes are due to the practice of aggression-through

Canada spends less of its GDP on health care not because we have found a way to produce health care at lower unit cost but because we have found a way to limit the total supply of services made available...we ration the supply, denying treatment to some and making others wait.
—Michael Walker
Executive Director of
the Fraser Institute
in Vancouver

Nationalized health is synonymous with delays, waiting lists, rationing, and high taxes.
—Christopher Lyon,
M.D.
ex-Englishman

government. Until we stop this aggression, poverty and unemployment will run rampant. Until we can raise the consciousness of our nation, should we offer tax-supported relief to the victims of aggression ?

As always, more aggression only makes the problems caused by aggression worse. If we raise taxes or increase deficits to help those harmed by aggression, we will only strangle the economy further. Many more people will become unemployed. Government-sponsored "aid" is a cure worse than the disease.

Non-aggression, however, works almost instantaneously to bring prosperity to all. When we take away the restrictions that keep the disadvantaged from working, poverty becomes optional. Government enforcement agents who were creating no new wealth can turn their skills into creating useful goods and services. As our national Wealth Pie grows, everyone's standard of living increases. Non-aggression makes us all winners!

Manifesting the Dream

If we are serious about achieving our dream of a peaceful and prosperous world, we must continue to question, learn, and grow. A number of mail order bookstores specialize in subjects related to political non-aggression.[7]

The proponents of political non-aggression can be found in virtually every country of the world. Since 1989, Leon Louw and Frances Ken-dall, two white South Africans, have been nominated three times for the Nobel peace prize. Their book, which suggests non-aggression for their troubled country,[8] is sold under the title After Apartheid in the United States.[9] A best seller in South Africa, its ideals were endorsed by blacks and whites alike. Only time will tell if its wisdom will be adopted.

Kendall and Louw found that the Swiss people are the best practitioners of the ideals of non-aggression. The Swiss national government's posts are part-time positions. Most decisions are made at the canton (state) level.

Swiss per capita income is the highest in the world,[10] showing that non-aggression pays.

How did the Swiss come to adopt a relatively non-aggressive constitution in an aggressive world? In the mid-1800s, they imitated our constitution—and stuck with it!

Louw and Kendall found that the ideals of non-aggression are easily shared in a group meeting at someone's home. The Advocates for Self-Government,[11] dedicated to spreading the practice of non-aggression, have similar programs here in the United States.

In San Francisco, the International Society for Individual Liberty[12] coordinates contacts among proponents of non-aggression worldwide. Along with Jan Sommerfelt Pettersen, the Society publishes the *Index on Liberty*[13] which lists groups active in the movement to promote non-aggression (also known as "libertarianism" or "classical liberalism").

Many countries boast a political party that advocates non-aggression. In the United States, the Libertarian Party[14] challenges our two-party system. Tonie Nathan, the 1972 Libertarian vice-presidential nominee, became the first woman to receive a vote from the Electoral College. In 1980, Libertarian candidate Ed Clark was on the ballot in all 50 states. Alaska has had three state representatives elected under the Libertarian label; New Hampshire elected four in 1992. In 1987, Big Water, Utah, elected an all-Libertarian city council and mayor. A former Republican congressional representative, Ron Paul, became the Libertarian presidential nominee in 1988. By 1990, more than 100 Libertarians had been elected to local office. Presidential candidate, Andre Marrou, had served earlier in the Alaskan State House as a Libertarian, making him more qualified than independent presidential hopeful Ross Perot. Nevertheless, Mr. Marrou and his running mate, Nancy Lord, were excluded from the televised debates, while millionaire Perot was invited. Perot advocated acceleration of aggression-

The basic premise of libertarianism is that each individual should be free to do as he or she pleases so long as he or she does not harm others.
—Internal Revenue Service

Legalize freedom—vote Libertarian!
—slogan of the Libertarian Party, U.S.A.

through–government. Did money and special interests determine whom American voters were exposed to?

Inside the Republican Party, the Republican Liberty Caucus[15] is attempting to promote non–aggression within the establishment. The Competitive Enterprise Institute,[16] based in Washington, D.C., lobbies Congress to keep the marketplace ecosystem free from aggression.

Throughout the country, a number of organizations publicize the benefits of non–aggression. The Reason Foundation[17] specializes in demonstrating how services that are now provided by government through aggression can be supplied better and less expensively in a marketplace ecosystem free from aggression. The Political Economy Research Center[18] pioneers the "New Resource Economics," the term given to the ecological application of non–aggression. The *Journal of Libertarian Studies*[19] provides a scholarly format for continued research. The National Center for Policy Analysis[20] issues extensive research papers on a wide variety of applications; the Pacific Research Institute for Public Policy Research publishes books involving timely topics as well.[21] The Heartland Institute[22] in the midwest focuses on regional issues.

In addition to research, the Manhattan Institute for Policy Research,[23] the Liberty Fund,[24] the Institute of Humane Studies,[25] the Foundation for Economic Education[26] and the Cato Institute[27] conduct conferences and seminars on non–aggression and human rights. Michigan's Mackinac Center[28] briefs high school debate teams on non–aggressive approaches to their annual topic.

Another Michigan institution, privately funded Hillsdale College,[29] practices non–aggression by refusing to take tax subsidies. It also sponsors conferences and publishes books on a marketplace ecosystem free from aggression. Hillsdale College will send you its newsletter, *Imprimis,* free at your request.

The Institute for Justice takes on legal cases of individuals or groups victimized by aggression-through-government.[30] Several of these cases have involved fighting the licensing laws that attempt to shut down small businesses employing the disadvantaged.

The Madison Group[31] networks with more than 60 organizations working toward a world of peace and plenty through non-aggression. A new group, the 21st Century Congress[32] networks with activists to integrate the spiritual aspects of community and individual sovereignty with the practice of non-aggression.

Freedom Now[33] is attempting to form a critical mass of non-aggressors in Fort Collins, Colorado. A high percentage of non-aggressors in a small community creates more cooperative interactions. Other such communities with more deliberate integration are being considered by other groups as well.

Non-aggression is an idea whose time has come. The above contacts represent a cross-section of people dedicated to creating a win-win world. In your efforts to bring about the healing of our world, you are not alone.

CHOOSING YOUR PATH

If you've read this far, you are undoubtedly interested in seeing at least some aspects of non-aggression implemented. Several ideas may seem more relevant to you than others. If you are wondering whether a lone individual like yourself can make a difference, please be assured that you can. Even the smallest contribution can be pivotal. My favorite story illustrating this point is about a blacksmith who failed to put the final nail in a horse's shoe. For lack of a nail, the horse lost his shoe and went lame. The rider, who was carrying critical news to his king, had to continue on foot. As a result, he reached his sovereign too late. Without this important information, the king lost the battle he was fighting and the kingdom fell to invaders. The humble blacksmith was pivotal to the safety of the kingdom.

Never doubt that a small group of committed, thoughtful citizens can change the world. Indeed, it's the only thing that ever has.

—Margaret Mead
American
anthropologist

Never doubt that your contribution is just as important. Remember that the family and friends who talk with you about the win–win world possible through non–aggression will in turn talk to others, who will share the good news. Like a chain reaction, your message of hope will spread throughout our country and the world, bearing fruit in the most unexpected ways. If you do nothing more than extol the virtues of non–aggression to those around you, you will have done much toward manifesting it!

Of course, you needn't stop there. The many groups cited above would welcome your participation. Are there any that excite you? Would you like to join a political campaign or speak on college campuses? Do you perceive a need for other strategies that you could initiate on your own or with others? Can you implement non–aggressive solutions in the midst of aggression–through–government, much like Guy Polheus and Kimi Gray did (Chapter 11: *Springing the Poverty Trap*)? All these things—and more—are needed to help others recognize that non–aggression is in everybody's best self–interest. We each have a part to play, a gift to the world that will one day be reflected back to us as better world.

Our world is a joint creation. We all have the power to affect those around us profoundly. Each of us through our own inner wisdom can identify the piece of the puzzle that we can lay in the mosaic. Every piece is needed to construct the whole; never doubt that what you can do, however small it may seem to you, is essential. I urge you to embrace whatever aspect of non–aggression seems most valuable to you and appropriate to your unique talents. Whether you work behind the scenes or in the limelight, rest assured that the world will take notice. Whatever way you feel moved to participate is a gift you give to yourself and others. Let me be the first to thank you for making the world a better place!

All truth passes through three stages. First, it is ridiculed. Secondly, it is violently opposed. Third, it is accepted as being self-evident. —Arthur Schopenhauer, German philosopher

REFERENCES

CHAPTER 1: THE GOLDEN RULE
1. Stanley Milgram, OBEDIENCE TO AUTHORITY (New York: Harper & Row, 1974), pp. 99–144.
2. Ibid., pp. 33–36.
3. Ibid., pp. 44–54, 73–88.
4. Ibid., pp. 27–31.

CHAPTER 2: WEALTH IS UNLIMITED!
1. Thomas Sowell, THE ECONOMICS AND POLITICS OF RACE: AN INTERNATIONAL PERSPECTIVE (New York: William Morrow and Company, Inc., 1983), p. 214.
2. Thomas R. Dye and Harmon Zeigler, "Socialism and Equality in Cross-National Perspective," *Political Science and Politics* **21**: 45–56, 1988.
3. Sowell, p. 211.

CHAPTER 3: DESTROYING JOBS
1. Keith B. Leffler, "Minimum Wages, Welfare, and Wealth Transfers to the Poor," *Journal of Law and Economics* **21**: 345–358, 1978.
2. Walter Williams, THE STATE AGAINST BLACKS (New York: New Press, McGraw-Hill, 1982), pp. 43–44.
3. Ibid., pp. 44–45; Leffler, p. 354; Matthew B. Kibbe, "The Minimum Wage: Washington's Perennial Myth," *Cato Policy Analysis No. 106*, pp. 7–9, 1988.
4. Kibbe, p. 5; S. Warne Robinson, "Minority Report," in REPORT OF THE MINIMUM WAGE STUDY COMMISSION, VOL. I (Washington, D.C.: U.S. Government Printing Office, 1981), p. 187.
5. Sowell, pp. 174–175.

CHAPTER 4: ELIMINATING SMALL BUSINESSES
1. Williams, pp. 92–94.
2. Ibid., pp. 90–97.
3. "New York's Frozen Taxis," *The Economist*, February 16, 1986, p. 27.
4. Williams, p. 78.
5. Ibid., pp. 78–79.
6. Charles Vidich, THE NEW YORK CAB DRIVER AND HIS FARE (Cambridge, Mass.: Schenkman Publishing Co., 1976), p. 146.
7. Williams, pp. 109–124.
8. Virginia Postrel, "Who's Behind the Child Care Crisis?" *Reason*, June 1989, pp. 20–27.
9. John Hood and John Merline, "What You Should Know About Day Care," *Consumers' Research*, August 1990, p. 25.
10. Ibid., p. 23.
11. Ibid., p. 26.
12. Howard Baetjer, "Beauty and the Beast," *Reason*, December 1988, pp. 28–31.
13. Joanne H. Pratt, "Legal Barriers to Home-Based Work," *National Center for Policy Analysis (NCPA) Policy Report No. 129*, September 1987, p. 31.
14. Ibid., p. 32.
15. Ibid., pp. 29–30.
16. Williams, pp. 68–69; Pratt, pp. 1, 22, 34; Simon Rottenberg, "The Economics of Occupational Licensing," in DISCRIMINATION, AFFIRMATIVE

ACTION, AND EQUAL OPPORTUNITY, W.E. Block and M.A. Walker, eds. (Vancouver, British Columbia: Fraser Institute, 1982), p. 4.

17. Dye and Zeigler, pp. 45–58.
18. Michael Novak, WILL IT LIBERATE? QUESTIONS ABOUT LIBERATION THEOLOGY (New York: Paulist Press, 1986), p. 91.

CHAPTER 5: HARMING OUR HEALTH

1. Sidney L. Carroll and Robert J. Gaston, "Occupational Restrictions and the Quality of Service Received: Some Evidence," *Southern Economic Journal* **47**: 959–976, 1981.
2. Ronald Hamoway, "The Early Development of Medical Licensing Laws in the United States, 1875–1900," *Journal of Libertarian Studies* **3**: 73–75, 1979.
3. Ibid., p. 98.
4. Elton Rayack, PROFESSIONAL POWER AND AMERICAN MEDICINE: THE ECONOMICS OF THE AMERICAN MEDICAL ASSOCIATION (Cleveland: The World Publishing Company, 1967), pp. 66–70.
5. Ibid., p. 79.
6. Hamoway, p. 103.
7. Rayack, p. 71.
8. Paul Starr, THE SOCIAL TRANSFORMATION OF AMERICAN MEDICINE (New York: Basic Books, Inc.), pp. 391–392.
9. Ibid., pp. 124–125.
10. Gene Roback, Diane Mead, and Lillian Randolph, PHYSICIAN CHARACTERISTICS AND DISTRIBUTION IN THE U.S. (Chicago: American Medical Association, 1986), p. 30.
11. Mark S. Blumberg, TRENDS AND PROJECTIONS OF PHYSICIANS IN THE UNITED STATES 1967–2002 (Berkeley, Calif.: Carnegie Commission on Higher Education, 1971), p. 9.
12. THE WORLD ALMANAC AND BOOK OF FACTS 1991 (New York: World Almanac, 1991), p. 836.
13. Bill No. AB3203, introduced by Assembly Member Speier, February 26, 1990, State of California.
14. "New Action by Council on Medical Education and Hospitals," *Journal of the American Medical Association* **105**: 1123, 1935.
15. Rayack, p. 6.
16. Rayack, pp. 7–10; John C. Goodman, THE REGULATION OF MEDICAL CARE: IS THE PRICE TOO HIGH? (San Francisco: Cato Institute, 1980), pp. 65–67.
17. Starr, p. 333.
18. Rayack, p. 255; Julius A. Roth, HEALTH PURIFIERS AND THEIR ENEMIES (New York: Prodist, 1976), pp. 60–67; Chester A. Wilk, CHIROPRACTIC SPEAKS OUT (Park Ridge, Ill.: Wilk Publishing Co., 1973), pp. 155–165.
19. *Wilk et al. v. American Medical Assoication et al.*, 76C3777, U.S. District Court, Northern District of Illinois, Eastern Division.
20. *Wilk et al.*, pp. 36–37.
21. *Wilk et al.*, pp. 155–158.
22. S. David Young, THE RULE OF EXPERTS (Washington D.C.: Cato Institute, 1987), p. 13.
23. Rayack, p. 113.
24. Mary J. Ruwart, Bob D. Rush, Karen F. Snyder, Ken M. Peters, Henry D. Appelman, and Keith S. Henley. "16,16 Dimethyl Prostaglandin E$_2$ Delays

Collagen Formation in Nutritional Injury in Rat Liver," *Hepatology* **8**: 61–64, 1988.

25. For a recent review of alcohol–nutrient interactions, see Charles S. Lieber, "Interaction of Alcohol with Other Drugs and Nutrients: Implication for the Therapy of Alcoholic Liver Disease," *Drugs* **40 (S3)**: 23–44, 1990.

26. Charles S. Lieber, Leonore M. DeCarli, and Emanuel Rubin. "Sequential Production of Fatty Liver, Hepatitis and Cirrhosis in Subhuman Primates Fed Ethanol with Adequate Diets," *Proceedings of the National Academy of Sciences* **72**: 437–441, 1975.

27. Charles S. Lieber, Leonore M. DeCarli, Ki M. Mak, Cho-Il Kim, and Maria A. Leo, "Attentuation of Alcohol-Induced Hepatic Fibrosis by Polyunsaturated Lecithin," *Hepatology* **12**: 1390–1398, 1990.

28. Barbara Barzansky, Division of Undergraduale Medical Education of the American Medical Association, personal communication, March 2, 1990.

29. Ewan Cameron and Linus Pauling, CANCER AND VITAMIN C (Menlo Park, Calif.: Linus Pauling Institute of Science and Medicine, 1979), pp. 133–134.

30. Office of Technology Assessment, ADDRESSING THE EFFICACY AND SAFETY OF MEDICAL TECHOLOGIES (Washington, D.C.: Congress of the United States, 1978), p. 7.

31. Michael B. Mock, "Lessons Learned from Randomized Trials of Coronary Bypass Surgery: Viewpoint of the Cardilogist," *Cardiology* **73**: 196–203, 1986.

32. Leonard Tabachnik, "Licensing in the Legal and Medical Professions, 1820–1860: A Historical Case Study," in PROFESSION FOR THE PEOPLE: THE POLITICS OF SKILL, J. Gerstl and G. Jacobs, eds. (New York: Halsted Press Division, John Wiley and Sons, 1976), pp. 25–42.

33. Harris S. Cohen, "Regulatory Politics and American Medicine," *American Behavioral Scientist* **19**: 122–136, 1975.

34. Julian L. Simon and Herman Kahn, eds., THE RESOURCEFUL EARTH: A RESPONSE TO GLOBAL 2000 (New York: Basil Blackwell, Inc., 1984), p. 51.

35. Rayack, pp. 72–78; Susan Reverby and David Rosner, HEALTH CARE IN AMERICAN (Philadelphia: Temple University Press, 1979), pp. 188–200.

36. Alex Maurizi, "Occupational Licensing and the Public Interest," *Journal of Political Economy* **82**: 399–413, 1974.

37. Goodman, pp. 22–25.

38. Ibid., p. 36.

39. Ibid., p. 42.

40. Ibid, pp. 30–31.

41. Starr, p. 117; Reverby, p. 194.

42. Gerald Charles, David H. Stimson, Michael D. Maurier, and John C. Good, Jr., "Physician's Assistants and Clinical Algorithms in Health Care Delivery: A Case Study," *Annals of Internal Medicine* **81**: 733–739, 1974; John W. Runyan, Jr., "The Memphis Chronic Disease Program: Comparisons in Outcome and the Nurse's Extended Role," *Journal of the American Medical Association* **231**: 264–267, 1975; Anthony L. Komaroff, W.L. Black, Margaret Flatley, Robert H. Knopp, Barney Reiffen, and Herbert Sherman, "Protocols for Physician Assistants: Management of Diabetes and Hypertension," *New England Journal of Medicine* **290**: 307–312, 1974.

43. Evan Charney and Harriet Kitzman, "The Child–Health Nurse (Pediatric Nurse Practioner) in Private Practice," *New England Journal of Medicine*

285: 1353-1358, 1971.

44. Walter O. Spitzer, David L. Sackett, John C. Sibley, Robin S. Roberts, Michael Gent, Dorothy J. Kergin, Brenda C. Hackett, and Anthony Olynich, "The Burlington Randomized Trial of the Nurse Practitioner," *New England Journal of Medicine* **290**: 251-256, 1974.

CHAPTER 6: PROTECTING OURSELVES TO DEATH

1.   William Booth, "An Underground Drug for AIDS," *Science* **241**: 1279-1281, 1988.
2.   Ryuji Ueno and Sachiko Kuno, "Dextran Sulphate, a Potent Anti-HIV Agent in Vitro Having Synergism with Zidovudine," LANCET **I(3)**: 1379, 1987.
3.   Philip M. Boffey, "F.D.A. Expands Earlier Stand by Allowing Mailing of Drugs," *Wall Street Journal*, July 25, 1988.
4.   John M. Fromson, "Perspectives in Pharmacokinetics," *Journal of Pharmacokinetics and Biopharmaceutics* **17**: 510, 1989.
5.   Kenneth I. Kaitin, Barbara W. Richard, and Louis Lasagna, "Trends in Drug Development: The 1985-86 New Drug Approvals," *Journal of Clinical Pharmacology* **27**: 542-548, 1987.
6.   Ibid., pp. 90-91; Charles O. Jackson, FOOD AND DRUG LEGISLATION IN THE NEW DEAL (Princeton: Princeton University Press, 1970), p. 20; Harry F. Dowling, "The American Medical Association's Policy on Drugs in Recent Decades," in SAFEGUARDING THE PUBLIC: HISTORICAL ASPECTS OF MEDICINAL DRUG CONTROL, John B. Blake, ed. (Baltimore: Johns Hopkins University Press, 1968), pp. 123-124; James G. Burrow, "The Prescription-Drug Policies of the American Medical Association in the Progressive Era," in SAFEGUARDING THE PUBLIC: HISTORICAL ASPECTS OF MEDICINAL DRUG CONTROL, John B. Blake, ed. (Baltimore: Johns Hopkins University Press, 1968), pp. 113-115; Glenn Sonnedecker, "Contribution of the Pharmaceutical Profession Toward Controlling the Quality of Drugs in the Nineteenth Century," in SAFEGUARDING THE PUBLIC: HISTORICAL ASPECTS OF MEDICINAL DRUG CONTROL, John B. Blake, ed. (Baltimore: John Hopkins Press, 1968), pp. 105-106.
7.   Stephen Wilson, FOOD AND DRUG REGULATION (Washington, D.C.: American Council on Public Affairs, 1942), pp. 22-23.
8.   Jackson, pp. 17-22.
9.   Wilson, p. 27.
10. Edward C. Lambert, MODERN MEDICAL MISTAKES (Bloomington: Indiana University Press, 1978), pp. 70-71.
11. Ibid., pp. 71-72.
12. Ibid., pp. 78-80.
13. Ibid., pp. 73-75.
14. Wilson, p. 102.
15. Young, p. 16.
16. Dowling, p. 124; William M. Wardell and Louis Lasagna, REGULATION AND DRUG DEVELOPMENT (Washington, D.C.: American Enterprise Institute for Public Policy Research, 1975), p. 13.
17. David Leo Weimer, "Safe and Available Drugs," in INSTEAD OF REGULATION, Robert W. Poole, Jr., ed. (Lexington, Mass.: Lexington Books, 1982), p. 243.
18. *Journal of the American Medical Association* **109**: 1531, 1937.

19. Weimer, pp. 243–244.
20. James L. Schardein, DRUGS AS TETROGENS (Cleveland, Ohio: CRC Press, 1976), p. 5.
21. L. Meyler, ed., SIDE EFFECTS OF DRUGS (New York: Elsevier, 1966), Vol.V, pp. 43–44.
22. Sam Kazman, "The FDA's Deadly Approval Process," *Consumers' Research*, April 1991, p. 31.
23. Weimer, pp. 245–246.
24. Sam Peltzman, REGULATION OF PHARMACEUTICAL INNOVATION (Washington, D.C.: American Enterprise Institute for Public Policy Research, 1974), pp. 44–45.
25. William M. Wardell, "Introduction of New Therapeutic Drugs in the United States and Great Britain: An International Comparison," *Clinical Pharmacology & Therapeutics* **14**: 773–790, 1973.
26. Peltzman, pp. 13–18; Wardell and Lasagna, pp. 57–59.
27. Arthur D. Little, Inc., COST-EFFECTIVENESS OF PHARMACEUTICALS #7: BETA-BLOCKER REDUCTION OF MORTALITY AND REINFARCTION RATE IN SURVIVORS OF MYOCARDIAL INFARCTION: A COST-BENEFIT STUDY. (Washington, D.C.: Pharmaceutical Manufacturers Association, 1984), p. I-5.
28. Louis Lasagna, "Congress, the FDA, and New Drug Development: Before and After 1962," *Perspectives in Biology and Medicine* **32**: 322–343, 1989; William M. Wardell, "Rx: More Regulation or Better Therapies?" *Regulation* **3**: 30, 1979.
29. Mary J. Ruwart, Bob D. Rush, Nanette M. Friedle, Jerzy Stachura, and Andi Tarnawski, "16,16–Dimethyl–PGE$_2$ Protection Against α–Napthylisothiocyanate–Induced Experimental Cholangitis in Rat," *Hepatology* **4**: 658–660, 1984; Bob D. Rush, Margaret V. Merritt, M. Kaluzny, Timothy Van Schoick, Marshall N. Brunden, and Mary J. Ruwart, "Studies on the Mechanism of the Protective Action of 16,16–Dimethyl PGE$_2$ in Carbon Tetrachloride–Induced Acute Hepatic Injury in the Rat," *Prostaglandins* **32**: 439–455, 1986; Bob D. Rush, Karen F. Wilkinson, Nanette M. Nichols, Ricardo Ochoa, Marshall N. Brunden, and Mary J. Ruwart, "Hepatic Protection by 16,16–Dimethyl Prostaglandin E$_2$ (DMPG) Against Acute Aflatoxim–B$_1$–Induced Injury in the Rat," *Prostaglandins* **37**: 683–693, 1989.
30. Durk Pearson and Sandy Shaw, LIFE EXTENSION: A PRACTICAL SCIENTIFIC APPROACH (New York: Warner Books, Inc., 1982), p. 274.
31. Richard T. Robertson et al., "Aspirin: Teratogenic Evaluation in the Dog," *Tetrology* **20**: 313–320, 1979; William M. Layton, "An Analysis of Teratogenic Testing Procedures," in CONGENITAL DEFECTS, D.T. Janerich, R.G. Skalko, and I.H. Porter, eds. (New York: Academic Press, 1974), pp. 205–217.
32. William M. Wardell, "Regulatory Assessment Models Reassessed," in REGULATION, ECONOMICS, AND PHARMACEUTICAL INNOVATION, Joseph D. Cooper, ed. (Washington, D. C.: American University, 1976), p. 245.
33. Peltzman, p. 70.
34. G. Frederick Roll, "Of Politics and Drug Regulation," *Publications Series PS-7701* (Rochester, N.Y.: Center for the Study of Drug Development, 1977), p. 20.
35. Weimer, pp. 265–266.

CHAPTER 7: CREATING MONOPOLIES THAT CONTROL US

1. Mark J. Green, "Uncle Sam, the Monopoly Man," in THE MONOPOLY MAKERS: RALPH NADER'S STUDY GROUP REPORT ON REGULATION AND COMPETITION, Mark J. Green, ed. (New York: Grossman Publishers, 1973), p. 1.
2. Dominick T. Armentano, ANTITRUST POLICY: THE CASE FOR REPEAL (Washington, D.C.: Cato Institute, 1986), p. 24; Burton W. Folsom, Jr., ENTREPRENEURS VS. THE STATE: A NEW LOOK AT THE RISE OF BIG BUSINESS IN AMERICA, 1840–1920 (Reston, Va.: Young America's Foundation, 1987), pp. 83–84.
3. Folsum, pp. 93–94; Ferdinand Lundberg, THE ROCKEFELLER SYNDROME (Secaucus, N.J.: Lyle Stuart Inc., 1975), p. 132.
4. Folsom, p. 91.
5. David Freeman Hawke, JOHN D.: THE FOUNDING FATHER OF THE ROCKEFELLERS (New York: Harper & Row, 1980), p. 167.
6. Folsom, pp. 89–90.
7. Allan Nevins, STUDY IN POWER: JOHN D. ROCKEFELLER, VOL. I, (New York: Charles Scribner's Sons, 1953), pp. 277–279, 555–556, 671–672.
8. Hawke, p. 175.
9. Ida M. Tarbell, THE HISTORY OF THE STANDARD OIL COMPANY, VOL. II (New York: Macmillan, 1925), pp. 196–198.
10. Hawke, p. 177.
11. Folsom, p. 90.
12. Milton Copulos, "Natural Gas Controls Are No Bargain," *Consumers' Research*, March 1983, p. 17.
13. Nevins, Vol. I, pp. 256, 296–297.
14. Jules Abels, THE ROCKEFELLER BILLIONS (New York: Macmillian, 1965), pp. 208–209.
15. Armentano, p. 25.
16. Peter Samuel, "Telecommunications: After the Bell Break-Up," in UNNATURAL MONOPOLIES: THE CASE FOR DEREGULATING PUBLIC UTILITIES, Robert W. Poole, ed. (Lexington, Ky.: D.C. Heath and Company, 1985), pp. 180–181.
17. John R. Meyer, Robert W. Wilson, Alan Baughcum, Ellen Burton, and Louis Caouette, THE ECONOMICS OF COMPETITION IN THE TELECOMMUNICATIONS INDUSTRY (Cambridge, Mass.: Oelgeschlager, Gunn & Hain, 1980), p. 31.
18. Ida Walters, "Freedom for Communications," in INSTEAD OF REGULATION: ALTERNATIVES TO FEDERAL REGULATORY AGENCIES, Robert W. Poole, ed. (Lexington, Ky.: D.C. Heath and Company, 1982), pp. 117–118.
19. Ibid., p. 118.
20. Ibid., pp. 120–123.
21. Ibid., pp. 122.
22. Meyer et al., p. 30.
23. Meyer et al., p. 29.
24. Walters, pp. 120–124.
25. Parker Payson, "Why Your Phone Bills Keep Going Up," *Consumers' Research*, June 1989, p. 12.
26. Ibid., p. 10.
27. Ibid., p. 11.
28. Ibid., pp. 12, 14.
29. Jerome Ellig, "Consumers on Hold," *Reason*, July 1989, pp. 36–37.
30. Payson, p. 13.
31. Walter J. Primeaux, Jr., "Total Deregulation of Electric Utilities: A Viable

Policy Choice," in UNNATURAL MONOPOLIES: THE CASE FOR DEREGULATORY PUBLIC UTILITIES, op. cit., pp. 121-146; Walter J. Primeaux, Jr., DIRECT ELECTRIC UTILITY COMPETITION: THE NATURAL MONOPOLY MYTH (New York: Praeger, 1985), pp. 37-41; Walter J. Primeaux, Jr., "Competition Between Electric Utilities," in ELECTRIC POWER: DEREGULATION AND THE PUBLIC INTEREST, John C. Moorhouse, ed. (San Francisco: Pacific Research Institute for Public Policy for Public Policy, 1986), pp. 395-423.

32. William Rathje, "Rubbish," *Atlantic Monthly*, December 1989, pp. 99-109.

33. Nancy Oliver, "Why Your Service Is So Primitive," *Consumers' Research*, June 1989, pp. 14-15.

34. Robert Stobaugh and Daniel Yergin, eds., ENERGY FUTURE (New York: Random House, 1979), pp. 159-160; Yale Brozen, "Making Crisis, Not Energy," *Regulation*, March-April 1980, pp. 11-14.

35. Kenneth R. Sheets and Robert F. Black "Generating Cash from Trash," *U.S. News & World Report*, August 22, 1988, pp. 38-40.

CHAPTER 8: DESTROYING THE ENVIRONMENT

1. Thomas E. Borcherding, "The Sources of Growth in Public Expenditures in the U.S.: 1902-1970," BUDGETS AND BUREAUCRATS: THE SOURCES OF GOVERNMENT GROWTH, Thomas E. Borcherding, ed. (Durham, N.C.: Duke University Press, 1977), p. 62; James T. Bennett and Manuel H. Johnson, BETTER GOVERNMENT AT HALF THE PRICE (Ottawa, Ill.: Green Hill, 1981).

2. National Center for Policy Analysis, "Privatization in the U.S.: Cities and Counties," *NCPA Policy Report No. 116*, June 1985, p. 17.

3. Philip Fixler, Jr., Robert W. Poole, Jr., Lynn Scarlett, and William D. Eggers, "Privitization 1990" (Santa Monica, Calif.: Reason Foundation, 1990), p. 8; Randall Fitzgerald, WHEN GOVERNMENT GOES PRIVATE: SUCCESS-FUL ALTERNATIVES TO PUBLIC SERVICES, (New York: Universe Books, 1988), pp. 158-163.

4. Robert Poole, Jr., CUTTING BACK CITY HALL (New York: Universe Books, 1980), pp. 62-78.

5. Ibid., pp. 79-87.

6. Poole, pp. 152-154; Fitzgerald, pp. 177-181.

7. Lynn Scarlett, "From Silent Waste to Recycling," *Privitization Watch*, July 1989, pp. 3-4.

8. Lynn Scarlett, "Managing America's Garbage: Alternatives and Solutions," *Policy Study No. 115*, Reason Foundation, September 1989.

9. Janet Marinelli, "Composting: From Backyards to Big Time," *Garbage*, July/August 1990, pp. 44-51.

10. Randall R. Rucker and Price V. Fishback, "The Federal Reclamation Program: An Anlaysis of Rent-Seeking Behavior," in WATER RIGHTS, Terry L. Anderson, ed. (San Francisco: Pacific Institute for Public Policy Research, 1983), pp. 62-63.

11. Terry L. Anderson and Donald R. Leal, FREE MARKET ENVIRONMENTALISM: A PROPERTY RIGHTS APPROACH (San Francisco: Pacific Research Institute for Public Policy Research, 1990), pp. 55-56.

12. John Baden, "Destroying the Environment: Government Mismanagement of Our Natural Resources" (Dallas, Tex.: National Center for Policy Analysis, 1986), pp. 20-21.

13. Baden, p. 38.

14. Ronald M. Latimer, "Chained to the Bottom," in BUREAUCRACY VS. ENVIRON-
     MENT, John Baden and Richard L. Stroup, eds. (Ann Arbor, Mich.:
     University of Michigan Press, 1981), p. 156.

15. Baden, p. 18.

16. Gary D. Libecap, LOCKING UP THE RANGE (San Francisco: Pacific Research
     Institute for Public Policy Reserach, 1981), p. 27.

17. Ibid., p. 46.

18. Ibid., p. 76.

19. Peter Kirby and William Arthur, OUR NATIONAL FORESTS: LANDS IN PERIL
     (Washington, D.C.: The Wilderness Society and the Sierra Club, 1985),
     p. 4.

20. Baden, p. 10.

21. Thomas Barlow, Gloria E. Helfand, Trent W. Orr, and Thomas B. Stoel, Jr.,
     GIVING AWAY THE NATIONAL FORESTS (New York: Natural Resources Defense
     Council, 1980), Appendix 1.

22. Baden, p. 14.

23. Katherine Barton and Whit Fosburgh, AUDUBON WILDLIFE REPORT 1986 (New
     York: The National Audubon Society, 1986), p. 129.

24. Terry L. Anderson and Donald R. Leal, "Rekindling the Privitization Fires:
     Political Lands Revisited," *Federal Privitization Project, Issue Paper No. 108*
     (Santa Monica, Calif.: Reason Foundation, 1989), p. 12.

25. "Special Report: The Public Benefits of Private Conservation," *Environmental
     Quality: 15th Annual Report of the Council on Enviromental Quality Together
     with the President's Message to Congress,* (Washington, D.C.: U.S.
     Government Printing Office, 1984), pp. 387–394.

26. Ibid., pp. 394–398.

27. Tom McNamee, "Yellowstone's Missing Element," *Audubon* **88**: 12, 1986.

28. Alston Chase, PLAYING GOD IN YELLOWSTONE: THE DESTRUCTION OF AMERICA'S
     FIRST NATIONAL PARK (New York: Atlantic Monthly Press), pp.123–124.

29. Chase, pp. 12, 28, 29.

30. Chase, pp. 155, 173.

31. Tom Blood, "Men, Elk, and Wolves," in THE YELLOWSTONE PRIMER: LAND AND
     RESOURCE MANAGEMENT IN THE GREATER YELLOWSTONE ECOSYSTEM, John A.
     Baden and Donald Leal, eds. (San Francisco: Pacific Research Institute for
     Public Policy, 1990), p. 109.

32. "Special Report: The Public Benefits of Private Conservation,"
     p. 368.

33. Richard L. Stroup and John A. Baden, NATURAL RESOURCES: BUREAUCRATIC
     MYTHS AND ENVRIONMENTAL MANAGEMENT (San Francisco: Pacific Institute for
     Public Policy Research, 1983), pp. 49–50.

34. Anderson and Leal, pp. 51–52.

35. Peter Young, "Privitization Around the Globe: Lessons for the Reagan
     Administration," *NCPA Policy Report No. 120* (Dallas, Tex.: National Center
     for Policy Analysis, 1986), pp. 1–23.

36. John Crutcher, "Free Enterprise Delivers the Mail," *Consumers' Research*,
     September 1990, pp. 34–35.

37. William C. Dunkelberg and John Skorburg, "How Rising Tax Burdens Can
     Produce Recession," *Policy Analysis No. 148*, February 21, 1991.

38. Warren T. Brookes, THE ECONOMY IN MIND (New York: Universe Books,

1982), pp. 187–195; Gerald W. Scully, "How State and Local Taxes Affect Economic Growth," *NCPA Policy Report No. 106* (Dallas, Tex.: National Center for Policy Analysis, 1991).

39. U.S. Department of Commerce, STATISTICAL ABSTRACT OF THE UNITED STATES, 1990 (Washington, D.C.: U.S. Government Printing Office, 1990), p. 311.

CHAPTER 9: BANKING ON AGGRESSION

1. Lawrence H. White, FREE BANKING IN BRITAIN: THEORY, EXPERIENCE AND DEBATE, 1800–1845 (New York: Cambridge University Press, 1984), pp. 23–49; Charles A. Conant, A HISTORY OF MODERN BANKS OF ISSUE (New York: Augustus M. Kelley, 1969), pp. 142–170.

2. White, p. 41.

3. Scottish deposits as a percentage of Great Britain's were 26% in 1880 and on the decline; see S.G. Checkland, SCOTTISH BANKING: A HISTORY, 1695–1973 (Glasgow: Collins, 1975), p. 750. Without any correction for percentage deposits, the English were 48 x 2 = 96 times as likely to lose money. Since the English had four times as much money on deposit (probably less in 1841, the height of Scottish banking prominence), they were 96/4 = 24 times as likely to lose their deposits when corrected for total holdings.

4. C.A. Phillips, T.F. McManus, and R.W. Nelson, BANKING AND THE BUSINESS CYCLE: A STUDY OF THE GREAT DEPRESSION IN THE UNITED STATES (New York: Arno Press and *The New York Times*, 1972), pp. 23, 25, 79, 82–84.

5. Ibid., p. 25.

6. Ibid., p. 30.

7. Ibid., p. 82.

8. Ibid., p. 84.

9. Ibid., p. 81.

10. Ron Paul and Lewis Lehrman, THE CASE FOR GOLD (Washington, D.C.: Cato Institute, 1982), p. 125.

11. Richard E. Band, *Personal Finance* 15: 182, 1988. Band cites data from Merrill Lynch and the Federal Reserve Board showing a precipitous drop in "M2," a measure of the money supply just before the October 1987 crash.

12. Phillips et al., p. 167.

13. Paul and Lehrman, pp. 126–128; Milton Friedman and Anna Jacobson Schwartz, A MONETARY HISTORY OF THE UNITED STATES, 1867–1960 (Princeton, N.J.: Princeton University Press, 1963), p. 332.

14. Paul and Lehrman, p. 129.

15. Bert Ely, "The Big Bust: The 1930-33 Banking Collapse—Its Causes, Its Lessons," in THE FINANCIAL SERVICES REVOLUTION: POLICY DIRECTIONS FOR THE FUTURE, C. England and T. Huertas, eds. (Boston: Luwer Academic Publishers, 1988), pp. 55–56.

16. Conant, pp. 448–479.

17. George A. Selgin, THE THEORY OF FREE BANKING: MONEY SUPPLY UNDER COMPETITIVE NOTE ISSUE (Totowa, N.J.: Rowman & Littlefield, 1988), pp. 11–12.

18. A. Ralph Epperson, THE UNSEEN HAND (Tuscon: Publius Press, 1985); Larry Abraham, CALL IT CONSPIRACY (Seattle: Double A Publications, 1971); Gary Allen, SAY "NO!" TO THE NEW WORLD ORDER (Seal Beach, Calif.: Concord Press, 1987); Gary Allen and Larry Abraham, NONE DARE CALL IT CONSPIRA-

CY (Rossmoor, Calif.: Concord Press, 1972); G. Edward Griffin, A SURVIVAL COURSE ON MONEY (Westlake Village, Calif.: American Media, 1985).

19. James R. Adams, THE BIG FIX (New York: John Wiley & Sons, Inc., 1991), pp. 289–290.
20. THE WORLD ALMANAC AND BOOK OF FACTS, 1991, p. 104.
21. Robert V. Remini, ANDREW JACKSON AND THE COURSE OF AMERICAN DEMOCRACY, VOL. III (New York: Harper & Row, 1984), pp. 105–113.
22. Adams, p. viii.

CHAPTER 10: LEARNING LESSONS OUR SCHOOLS CAN'T TEACH

1. Samuel L. Blumenfeld, IS PUBLIC EDUCATION NECESSARY? (Boise, Idaho: The Paradigm Co., 1985), p. 4.
2. National Commission of Excellence in Education, A NATION AT RISK: THE IMPERATIVE FOR EDUCATIONAL REFORM (Washington, D.C.: U.S. Government Printing Office, 1983).
3. David T. Kearns and Denis P. Doyle, WINNING THE BRAIN RACE: A BOLD PLAN TO MAKE OUR SCHOOLS COMPETITIVE (San Francisco: Institute for Contemporary Studies, 1988), p. 15.
4. Fitzgerald, p. 141.
5. Gregory Byrne, "U.S. Students Flunk Math, Science," *Science* **243**: 729, 1989.
6. Myron Lieberman, "Market Solutions to the Education Crisis," *Cato Policy Analysis, No. 75*, (Washington, D.C.: Cato Institute, 1986), p. 2.
7. Fitzgerald, p. 141; Robert W. Poole, Jr., CUTTING BACK CITY HALL (New York: Universe Books, 1980), p. 184; Herbert J. Walberg, "Should Schools Compete?" *Heartland Perspective ISSN #0889-7999*, September 29, 1987, p. 3.
8. Fitzgerald, p. 147.
9. Blumenfeld 1985, pp. 68, 126; Samuel L. Blumenfled, "Why the Schools Went Public," *Reason*, March 1979, p. 19.
10. Stanley K. Schultz, THE CULTURE FACTORY: BOSTON PUBLIC SCHOOLS, 1789–1860 (New York: Oxford University Press, 1973), pp. 32–33.
11. Blumenfeld, 1985, p. 42.
12. Schultz, p. 25.
13. Carl F. Kaestle, THE EVOLUTION OF AN URBAN SCHOOL SYSTEM: NEW YORK CITY, 1750-1850 (Cambridge, Mass.: Harvard University Press, 1973), p. 89.
14. Tyler Cowen, THE THEORY OF MARKET FAILURE (Fairfax, Va.: George Mason University Press, 1988), pp. 374–377.
15. Joel Spring, "The Evolving Political Structure of American Schooling," in THE PUBLIC SCHOOL MONOPOLY, R.B. Everhart, ed. (San Francisco: Pacific Institute for Public Policy Research, 1982), pp. 89–92.
16. Blumenfeld 1985, p. 92; Schultz, p. 25.
17. Sowell, p. 198.
18. Poole, pp. 175–176.
19. Thomas W. Vitullo-Martin, "The Impact of Taxation Policy on Public and Private Schools," in THE PUBLIC SCHOOL MONOPOLY, R.B. Everhart, ed. (Cambridge, Mass.: Ballinger Publishing Co., 1982), p. 444.
20. Fitzgerald, pp. 143–144; Poole, pp. 184–186.

21. Vitullo-Martin, pp. 445–458.
22. Thomas Sowell, EDUCATION: ASSUMPTIONS VERSUS HISTORY (Stanford, Calif.: Hoover Institution Press, 1986), p. 103.
23. Kearns and Doyle, p. 17; Fitzgerald, p. 142.
24. Fitzgerald, p. 147.
25. Ibid., pp. 142–143.
26. Carolyn Lochhead, "A Lesson from Private Practitioners," *Insight*, December 24, 1990, pp. 34–36.
27. John M. Hood, "Miracle on 109th Street," *Reason*, May 1989, pp. 20–25.
28. Norma Tan, "The Cambridge Controlled Choice Program: Improving Educational Equity and Integration," *Education Policy Paper No. 4*, (New York: Manhattan Institute Center for Educational Innovation, 1990).
29. Carol Innerst, "Minorities Overwhelmingly Favor Public School Choice," *Insight*, August 24, 1990, p. A-3.
30. Lewis J. Perelman, "Closing Education's Technology Gap," *Briefing Paper No. 111* (Indianapolis, Ind.: Hudson Institute, 1989).
31. Dave Meleney, "Private TV Channel Catches on in 4,000 High Schools," *Privatization Watch*, No.164, August 1990, p. 6.

CHAPTER 11: SPRINGING THE WELFARE TRAP

1. National Commission of Jobs and Small Business, MAKING AMERICA WORK AGAIN: JOBS, SMALL BUSINESS, AND THE INTERNATIONAL CHALLENGE (Washington, D.C.: The National Commission on Jobs and Small Business, 1987), p. 13.
2. Leffler, pp. 345–358.
3. "Welfare and Poverty," *NCPA Policy Report No. 107* (Dallas, Tex.: National Center for Policy Analysis, 1983), pp. 4–5.
4. Charles D. Hobbs, THE WELFARE INDUSTRY (Washington, D.C.: Heritage Foundation, 1978), pp. 83–84.
5. Lowell Gallaway and Richard Vedder, "Paying People to Be Poor," *Policy Report No. 121* (Dallas, Tex.: National Center for Policy Analysis, 1986).
6. Charles Murray, LOSING GROUND: AMERICAN SOCIAL POLICY 1950-1980 (New York: Basic Books, Inc., 1984), pp. 148–153.
7. Ibid., p. 152.
8. Ibid., p. 127.
9. Vee Burke, "Cash and Non-Cash Benefits for Persons with Limited Income: Eligibility Rules, Recipient, and Expenditure Data, FY 1982-1984," *Congressional Research Source Report No. 85-194 EPW, September 30, 1985*, p. 52 as cited in John C. Goodman and Michael D. Stroup, "Privatizing the Welfare State," *NCPA Policy Report No. 123* (Dallas, Tex.: National Center for Policy Analysis, 1986), p. 23.
10. Murray, pp. 135–142.
11. "Welfare and Poverty," p. 3.
12. Edgar K. Browning and Jacqueline M. Browning, PUBLIC FINANCE AND THE PRICE SYSTEM (New York: Macmillan Publishing Co.,1979), p. 204, Tables 7 and 8.
13. Murray, p. 127.
14. "Welfare and Poverty," p. 1.
15. Robert L. Woodson, "Breaking the Poverty Cycle: Private Sector Alternatives

to the Welfare State," (Harrisburg, Penn.: The Commonwealth Foundation for Public Policy Alternatives, 1988), p. 63.

16. William Tucker, THE EXCLUDED AMERICANS: HOMELESSNESS AND HOUSING POLICIES (Washington, D.C.: Regnery Gateway, 1990).

17. "Guy Polhemus," *Noetic Sciences Review*, Summer 1989, p. 32.

18. Fitzgerald, pp. 127–129.

19. Fitzgerald, pp. 33–35

20. Goodman and Stroup, pp. 17–18.

CHAPTER 12: BY THEIR FRUITS YOU SHALL KNOW THEM

1. Milton Friedman, "Barking Cats," *Newsweek*, February 19, 1973, pp. 70.

2. Gerald W. Scully, "The Institutional Framework and Economic Development," *Journal of Political Economy* **96**: 658–662, 1988.

3. Dunkelberg and Skorburg, p. 7.

4. Ibid., p. 6. A 5% real GNP growth is associated with a federal tax burden of 18%. Every 1% in tax decrease leads to a 1.8% increase in economic growth. If this relationship is linear, then a 0% tax rate would be associated with a 32% increase in real GNP, for a total of 37%. This is more than seven times the 5% rate of GNP growth observed at a federal tax burden of 18%.

5. Dye and Zeigler, pp. 45–58.

6. Mortimer B. Zuckerman, "Russian Roulette," *U.S. News & World Report*, November 20, 1989, p. 100.

7. Yuri N. Matlsev, "The Soviet Medical Nightmare," *The Free Market*, August 1990, pp. 1, 3.

8. Douglas Stanglin, Clemens P. Work, and Monroe W. Karmin, "Reinventing Europe," *U.S. News & World Report*, November 27, 1989, p. 43.

CHAPTER 13: THE OTHER PIECE OF THE PUZZLE

1. Joan Petersilia, Susan Turner, and Joyce Peterson, PRISON VERSUS PROBATION, (Santa Monica, Calif.: Rand Corporation, 1986), p. v.

2. *Wall Street Journal*, March 21, 1989.

3. Morgan Reynolds, "Crime Pays: But So Does Imprisonment," *NCPA Policy Report No. 149* (Dallas, Tex.: National Center for Policy Analysis, 1990), p. 9.

4. Ibid, A–1.

5. U.S. Department of Commerce, p. 7.

6. Robert Axelrod, THE EVOLUTION OF COOPERATION (New York: Basic Books, Inc., 1981), pp. 27–54.

7. Reynolds, p. 6.

8. Morgan O. Reynolds, CRIME BY CHOICE: AN ECONOMIC ANALYSIS (Dallas, Tex.: Fisher Institute), 1984, p. 68.

9. For a good review of the literature in this area, see Bruce L. Benson, THE ENTERPRISE OF LAW: JUSTICE WITHOUT THE STATE (San Francisco: Pacific Research Institute for Public Policy for Public Policy, 1990), pp. 253–268.

10. J.W. Johnston, ed., "The Missouri State Penitentiary," ILLUSTRATED SKETCHBOOK OF JEFFERSON CITY AND COLE COUNTRY (Jefferson City, Mo.: Missouri Illustrated Sketchbook Co., 1900), pp. 250–251.

11. James K. Stewart, letter to *Wall Street Journal*, July 26, 1989.

12. Thomas A. Roe, "A Guide to Prison Privatization," *Heritage Foundation Backgrounder No. 650*, May 24, 1988, pp. 3-4.
13. Ted Gest, "Why More Criminals Are Doing Time Beyond Bars," *U.S. News & World Report*, February 26, 1990, pp. 23-24.
14. Jeffrey Shedd, "Making Goods Behind Bars," *Reason*, March 1982, pp. 23-32.
15. Randy E. Barnett, "Restitution: A New Paradigm of Criminal Justice," *Ethics* **87**: 293, 1977.
16. Belton M. Fleisher, THE ECONOMICS OF DELINQUENCY (Chicago: Quadrangel Books, 1966), pp. 68-85.
17. Philip E. Fixler, Jr., "Can Privatization Solve the Prison Crisis?" *Fiscal Watchdog*, April 1984, p. 1.

CHAPTER 14: THE POLLUTION SOLUTION

1. Jane S. Shaw and Richard L. Stroup, "Gone Fishin'," *Reason*, August/September 1988, pp. 34-37.
2. Eric Zuesse, "Love Canal: The Truth Seeps Out," *Reason*, February 1981, pp. 16-33.
3. Ralph Blumenthan, "Fight to Curb 'Love Canals'," *New York Times*, June 30, 1980, pp. B-1, B-11.
4. Elizabeth M. Whelan, TOXIC TERROR (Ottawa, Ill.: Jameson Books, 1985), pp. 94-98.
5. Ibid., pp. 102-105.
6. Fred Smith, Jr., "Superfund: A Hazardous Waste of Taxpayer Money," *Human Events*, August 2, 1986, pp. 10-12, 19.
7. "Court Rules U.S. Not Liable in Deaths from Atom Tests," *San Francisco Examiner*, January 11, 1988, p. A-1.
8. "The Biggest Cleanup in History," *Nucleus*, Winter 1989, p. 5.
9. "Regulate Thyself," *Dollars & Sense*, July/August 1988, p. 16.
10. Jim Lewis, "Nuclear Power Generation: Cut the Cord!" *National Gazette*, September 1987, p. 1.
11. Bruce Ames, "Too Much Fuss about Pesticides," *Consumers' Research*, April 1990, pp. 32-34.
12. "Pesticide Residues in Our Food," *Consumers' Research*, June 1990, pp. 33-34.
13. Whelan, pp. 120-125.
14. Ibid., pp. 68-74.
15. Warren T. Brookes, "How the EPA Launched the Hysteria about Alar," *The Detroit News*, February 25, 1990, pp. 9-11.
16. "Not All Risks Are Equal," *The Detroit News*, February 26, 1990, p. 3.
17. Richard Doll and Richard Peto, "Proportions of Cancer Deaths Attributed to Various Factors," *Journal of the National Cancer Institute* **66**: 1194, 1981.
18. A.E. Harper, "Nutrition and Health in the Changing Environment," in THE RESOURCEFUL EARTH: A RESPONSE TO 'GLOBAL 2000,' J.L. Simon and H. Kahn, eds. (New York: Basil Blackwell, Inc., 1984), pp. 511-515.
19. "Assessing the Asbestos Risk," *Consumers' Research*, July 1990, pp. 10-13.
20. "Rethinking the Clean Air Act Amendments," *Policy Backgrounder No. 107*,

National Center for Policy Analysis, October 16, 1990, p. 9.

CHAPTER 15: DEALING IN DEATH

1. Peter Kerr, "War on Drugs Puts Strain on Prisons, U.S. Officials Say," *New York Times*, September 25, 1987, p. 1.
2. Dorothy M. Brown, "Bootlegging," in THE ENCYLCOPEDIA AMERICANA INTERNATIONAL EDITION (Danbury, Conn.: Americana Corporation, 1980), Vol. 4, p. 263.
3. David E. Kyvig, REPEALING NATIONAL PROHIBITION (Chicago: University of Chicago Press, 1979), p. 27. Henry Lee, HOW DRY WE WERE: PROHIBITION REVISITED (London: Prentice-Hall, 1963), p. 8. U.S. Bureau of the Census, HISTORICAL STATISTICS OF THE UNITED STATES, COLONIAL TIMES TO 1970, Part 1 (Washington, D.C.: U.S. Government Printing Office, 1975), p. 441, as cited in James Ostrowski, "Thinking About Drug Legalization," *Cato Institute Policy Analysis No. 121* (Washington, D.C.: Cato Institute, May 25, 1989), p. 1.
4. Ethan Nadelman, "Prohibition in the United States: Costs, Consequences, and Alternatives," *Science* **245**: 945, 1989.
5. Ostrowski, p. 8.
6. Robert Lewis, "Dutch View Addicts as Patients, Not Criminals," *Kalamazoo Gazette*, September 24, 1989, p. A-6.
7. The lower figure comes from *The Detroit News*, May 18, 1988, p. 14A; the higher figure is from Ostrowski, p. 47, footnote "b," which describes the Fifth Special Report to the U.S. Congress on Alcoholism and Health from the Secretary of Health and Human Services.
8. The lower figure comes from *The Detroit News*, May 18, 1988, p. 14-A; the higher figure is from Ostrowski, p. 47, footnote "a," "Reducing the Health Consequences of Smoking: 25 Years of Progress," Surgeon General's Report (1989).
9. Durk Pearson and Sandy Shaw, "The Hardest Drug," in *Life Extension Newsletter* **1**: 55, 1988.
10. Ostrowski's reference #140: personal communication from Dr. Regan Bradford of the National Heart, Lung, and Blood Institute in which he said he believes that 90% of the one million cardiovascular deaths in the United States each year could be prevented by low-fat diets.
11. Ostrowski, p. 14.
12. Ostrowski, p. 11; Pearson and Shaw 1982, p. 715.
13. Ostrowski, p. 23.
14. Ostrowski, p. 14. The estimate made from sources cited in Ostrowski, reference 47, is closer to 9,000 (i.e., 18% of the 50,000 deaths expected in 1991 from those infected now). Ostrowski's estimate is conservative at 3,500.
15. Nicholas D. Kristof, "Hong Kong Program: Addicts Without Aids," *New York Times*, June 17, 1987, p. 1.
16. Ostrowski, p. 15, table 1.
17. "A Spreading Drug Epidemic," *The Washington Spectator*, August 1, 1988, pp. 1-3; Jonathan Marshall, "Drugs and United States Foreign Policy," in DEALING WITH DRUGS, R. Hamowy, ed. (San Francisco: Pacific Research Institute for Public Policy for Public Policy, 1987), pp. 164-174.

18. Jarret B. Wollstein, "Calculated Hysteria: The War on Drugs," *Individual Liberty*, Summer 1989, p. 4; Stefan B. Herpel, "United States v. One Assortment of 89 Firearms," *Reason*, May 1990, pp. 33–36.
19. Andrew Schneider and Mary Pat Flaherty, "Drug Law Leaves Trail of Innocents: In 80% of Seizures, No Charges," *Pittsburgh Press*, August 11, 1991, pp. 1, 13.
20. "Drugs and Foreign Policy," *The Detroit News*, May 17, 1988, p. 10A.
21. Ostrowski, p. 3.
22. Ethan Nadelman, "Help Victims," *Reason*, October 1988, pp. 27–28.
23. Nadelman, "Prohibition in the United States: Costs, Consequences, and Alternatives," p. 942; Lester Grinspoon and James B. Bakalar, "Medical Uses of Illicit Drugs," in DEALING WITH DRUGS, R. Hamowy, ed. (San Francisco: Pacific Research Institute for Public Policy for Public Policy, 1987), pp. 183–220.
24. *Detroit News*, May 16, 1988, p. 11A.

CHAPTER 16: POLICING AGGRESSION

1. Theodore Gage, "Cops Inc.," *Reason*, November 1982, p. 23.
2. Bruce L. Benson, THE ENTERPRISE OF LAW: JUSTICE WITHOUT THE STATE (San Francisco: Pacific Research Institute for Public Policy for Public Policy, 1990), p. 185.
3. Abraham Blumberg, CRIMINAL JUSTICE (Chicago: Quadrangle Books, 1970), p. 185.
4. Gage, p. 26.
5. Don B. Kates, "Guns, Murder, and the Constitution: A Realistic Assessment of Gun Control," (San Francisco: Pacific Research Institute for Public Policy for Public Policy, 1990), pp. 19–21.
6. David B. Kopel, "Trust the People: The Case Against Gun Control," *Policy Analysis No. 109* (Washington, D.C.: Cato Institute, 1988), p. 31.
7. Ted Gest and Scott Minerbrook, "What Should Be Done," *U.S. News & World Report*, August 22, 1988, p. 54.
8. Gary Kleck and David Bordua, "The Factual Foundation for Certain Key Assumptions of Gun Control," *Law and Policy Quarterly* 5: 271–298, 1983.
9. Philip J. Cook, "The Relationship Between Victim Resistance and Injury in Noncommercial Robbery, *Journal of Legal Studies* 15: 405–406, 1986.
10. Mary Lorenz Dietz, KILLING FOR PROFIT: THE SOCIAL ORGANIZATION OF FELONY HOMICIDE (Chicago: Nelson-Hall, 1983), Table A.1, pp. 202–203.
11. Gary Kleck, "Policy Lessons from Recent Gun Control Research," *Journal of Law and Contemporary Problems* 49: 35–47, 1986.
12. Alan Krug, "The Relationship Between Firearms Ownership and Crime: A Statistical Analysis," reprinted in *Congressional Record*, 99th Cong., 2nd Sess., January 30, 1968, p. 1496, n. 7.
13. Carol Ruth Silver and Donald B. Kates, Jr., "Self-Defense, Handgun Ownership, and the Independence of Women in a Violent, Sexist Society," in RESTRICTING HANDGUNS: THE LIBERAL SKEPTICS SPEAK OUT, Donald B. Kates, ed. (Croton-on-Hudson, N.Y.: North River Press, 1979), p. 152.
14. "Town to Celebrate Mandatory Arms," *New York Times*, April 11, 1987, p. 6.
15. Bruce L. Benson, "Guns for Protection, and Other Private Sector Responses

to the Government's Failure to Control Crime," *Journal of Libertarian Studies* **8**: 92–95, 1986.

16.   Gerald Arenberg, "Do the Police Support Gun Control?" (Bellevue, Wash.: Second Amendment Foundation, n.d.), p. 10.

17.   For a good review of the literature in this area, see Bruce L. Benson, THE ENTERPRISE OF LAW: JUSTICE WITHOUT THE STATE (San Francisco: Pacific Research Institute for Public Policy for Public Policy, 1990), pp. 253–268.

18.   James Wright and Peter Rossi, ARMED AND CONSIDERED DANGEROUS: A SURVEY OF FELONS AND THEIR FIREARMS (New York: Aldine, 1986), p. 185.

19.   Kopel, p. 7.

20.   Ibid., p. 6.

21.   Kates, Jr., p. 25.

22.   Ibid., pp. 29–30.

23.   Ibid., pp. 37–38, 40–43.

24.   "Fifty-One and Counting," *Spotlight*, February 13, 1989, p. 2.

25.   Benson 1990, p. 208.

26.   Ibid., p. 293.

27.   Ibid., p. 4.

28.   Ibid., pp. 137–140.

29.   Gary Pruitt, "California's Rent-a-Judge Justice," *Journal of Contemporary Studies* **5**: 49–57, 1982.

30.   Benson, p. 223–224.

31.   J.H. Beadle, WESTERN WILDS AND THE MEN WHO REDEEM THEM (Cincinnati, Ohio: Jones Brothers, 1878), p. 477.

CHAPTER 17: PUTTING IT ALL TOGETHER

1.   Hans J. Eysenck, "Personality, Stress, and Cancer: Prediction and Prophylaxis," *British Journal of Medical Psychology* **61**: 57–75, 1988.

2.   THE WORLD ALMANAC AND BOOK OF FACTS, 1991, p. 836.

3.   John M. Merrill, "Access to High-Tech Health Care. Ethics." *Cancer* **67 (S6)**: 1750, 1991; Marilyn Frank-Stromborg, "Changing Demographics in the United States. Implications for Health Professionals," *Cancer* **67 (S6)**: 1777, 1991.

4.   Axelrod, pp. 55–69.

CHAPTER 18: BEACON TO THE WORLD

1.   Jacqueline Kasun, THE WAR AGAINST POPULATION (San Francisco: Ignatius Press, 1988), p. 52.

2.   Colin Clark, POPULATION GROWTH: THE ADVANTAGES (Santa Ana, Calif.: R.L. Sassone, 1972), p. 84.

3.   Michael Novak, WILL IT LIBERATE? QUESTIONS ABOUT LIBERATION THEOLOGY (New York: Paulist Press, 1986), p. 89.

4.   Hernando de Soto, THE OTHER PATH: THE INVISIBLE REVOLUTION IN THE THIRD WORLD (New York: Harper & Row, 1989), p. 134.

5.   Ibid., p. 148.

6.   Ibid., pp. 139, 142.

7.   Ibid., p. 144.

8.   Ibid., pp. 144, 146.

9.   Frances Moore Lappe, Rachel Schurman, and Kevin Danaher, BETRAYING

THE NATIONAL INTEREST: HOW U.S. FOREIGN AID THREATENS GLOBAL SECURITY BY UNDERMINING THE POLITICAL AND ECONOMIC STABILITY OF THE THIRD WORLD (New York: Grove Press, 1987), p. 9.

10. Ibid., pp. 19–25.
11. Ibid., p. 40.
12. Holly Burkhalter and Alita Paine, "Our Overseas Cops," *The Nation*, September 14, 1985, p. 197.
13. Lars Schoultz, "U.S. Foreign Policy and Human Rights Violations in Latin America: A Comparative Analysis of Foreign Aid Distributions," *Comparative Politics* **13**: 162, 1981.
14. Lappe et al., p. 35.
15. For a good review, see Clifton B. Luttrell, THE HIGH COST OF FARM WELFARE, (Washington, D.C.: Cato Institute, 1989).
16. Lappe et al., pp. 84–85.
17. Ibid., p. 85.
18. Ibid., p. 103.
19. David Osterfeld, "The Tragedy of Foreign 'Aid'," *The Pragmatist*, June 1988, p. 6.
20. "Duvalier Accused of Graft on Food," *The New York Times*, March 18, 1986, p. 18.
21. Lappe et al., pp. 89–90.
22. James Bovard, "The World Bank vs. the World's Poor," *Cato Policy Analysis No. 92*, September 28, 1987, pp. 23–24.
23. Ibid., p. 24.
24. Ibid., p. 25.
25. Agence Frace-Presse, "Tanzania Resettlement Described as 'Cruel'," *Washington Post*, May 1, 1976, p. B8.
26. Shirley Scheibla, "Asian Sinking Fund: The World Bank Is Helping to Finance Vietnam," *Barron's*, September 3, 1979, p. 7.
27. Bovard, p. 4.
28. Ibid., p. 5.
29. Lappe et al., p. 101.
30. Bovard 1987, p. 22; James Bovard, "The World Bank: What They're Doing with Your Money Is a Crime," *Reason*, April 1989, pp. 26–31.
31. Bovard 1987, p. 22.
32. Washington Correspondent, "A Back Door into the Amazon," *Economist*, February 11, 1989. p. 39.
33. Linda C. Hunter, "U.S. Trade Protection: Effects on the Industrial and Regional Composition of Employment," *Federal Reserve Bank of Dallas Economic Review*, January 1990, p. 4.
34. William Cline, THE FUTURE OF WORLD TRADE IN TEXTILES AND APPAREL (Washington, D.C.: The Institute for International Economics, 1987), p. 194.
35. John W. Merline, "Trade Protection: The Consumer Pays," *Consumers' Research*, August 1989, p. 16.
36. Ibid., p. 17.
37. R.R. Kaufman, Daniel S. Giller, and Harry I. Chernotsky, "Preliminary Test of the Theory of Dependency," *Comparative Politics* **7**: 304, 1975.
38. Thomas J. DiLorenzo, "The Political Economics of Protection," *The Freeman* **38**: 269–275, 1988.

39. Andre Carothers, "Defenders of the Forest," *Greenpeace*, July/August 1990, p. 12.

40. "Great Moments in Forest Management," *Econ Update*, April 1989, pp. 10–11.

CHAPTER 19: THE COMMUNIST THREAT IS ALL IN OUR MINDS

1. Susan Dentzer, Jeff Trimble, and Bruce B. Auster, "The Soviet Economy in Shambles," *U.S. News & World Report*, November 20, 1989, p. 36.

2. Since 25% of the agricultural output was produced on 2% of cultivated land in private hands, 12.5% of Soviet food came from every 1% of the land that was privately farmed. Since 75% of the food came from the remaining 98% of available farmland, state–sponsored farming produced 0.77% of the Soviet food supply for every 1% of land cultivated. Thus, private farming is more than 16 times as productive as collective farming (i.e., 12.5/0.77 = 16.23).

3. Mortimer B. Zuckerman, "Russian Roulette," *U.S. News & World Report*, November 20, 1989, p. 100.

4. Dentzer et al., pp. 25–26.

5. Ibid., p. 26.

6. Yuri N. Maltsev, "The Soviet Medical Nightmare," *The Free Market* (Burlingame, Calif.: Ludwig von Mises Institute), August 1990, p. 4.

7. David K. Willis, KLASS: HOW RUSSIANS REALLY LIVE (New York: St. Martin's Press, 1985), p. 183.

8. Nick Eberstadt, THE POVERTY OF COMMUNISM (New Brunswick, N.J.: Transaction Books, 1988), p. 12.

9. Ibid., p. 14.

10. Willis, pp. 2–3, 28–32.

11. Ibid., pp. 188–193.

12. Mikhail S. Bernstam, THE WEALTH OF NATIONS AND THE ENVIRONMENT, (London: Institute of Economic Affairs, 1991), as cited in "Progressive Environmentalism: A Pro–Human, Pro–Science, Pro–Free-Enterprise Agenda for Change," (Dallas, Tex.: *National Center for Policy Analysis*, 1991), pp. 11–14.

13. Jon Thompson, "East Europe's Dark Dawn," *National Geographic*, June 1991, pp. 64–69.

14. Jeremy Cherfas, "East Germany Struggles to Clean Its Air and Water," *Science* **248**: 295.

15. Hilary F. French, "Eastern Europe's Clean Break with the Past," *World Watch*, March/April 1991, p. 23.

16. Rob Waters, "A New Dawn in Bohemia?" *Sierra*, May/June 1990, p. 35.

17. Ibid., p. 164.

18. Karl Marx and Friedrich Engels, BASIC WRITINGS ON POLITICS AND PHILOSOPHY (Garden City, N.Y.: Doubleday & Co., Inc., 1959), pp. 28–29.

19. Michael Parenti, INVENTING REALITY: THE POLITICS OF THE MASS MEDIA (New York: St. Martin's Press, 1986), p. 27.

20. Williams, pp. 109–123.

21. George Hansen, HOW THE IRS SEIZES YOUR DOLLARS AND HOW TO FIGHT BACK (New York: Simon and Schuster, 1981), pp. 20–31.

22. John Baden, "Destroying the Environment: Government Mismanagement

of Our Natural Resources" (Dallas, Tex.: National Center for Policy Analysis, 1986), pp. 20–21.

CHAPTER 20: NATIONAL DEFENSE

1. Antony C. Sutton, WALL STREET AND THE BOLSHEVIK REVOLUTION (New Rochelle, N.Y.: Arlington House Publishers, 1974), pp. 170–172; Epperson, p. 111.
2. Voline (V.M. Eikhenbanum), THE UNKNOWN REVOLUTION (Detroit: Black & Red, 1974), pp. 173–179.
3. Sutton 1974, pp. 59–161.
4. Benjamin M. Weissman, HERBERT HOOVER AND FAMINE RELIEF TO SOVIET RUSSIA, 1921–1923 (Stanford, Calif.: Hoover Institution Press, 1974), pp. 141–144.
5. Ibid., p. 144.
6. Antony C. Sutton, WESTERN TECHNOLOGY AND SOVIET ECONOMIC DEVELOPMENT, 1917–1930, VOL. I (Stanford, Calif.: Hoover Institution on War, Revolution, and Peace, 1968), p. 42.
7. Ibid., p. 44.
8. Ibid., pp. 21–23.
9. Sutton 1968, pp. 90, 207–209, 226, 262, 277–278, 289–291; Antony C. Sutton, WESTERN TECHNOLOGY AND SOVIET ECONOMIC DEVELOPMENT 1930–1945 VOL. II (Stanford, Calif.: Hoover Institution Press, 1971), pp. 71–72.
10. Sutton 1971, p. 17.
11. Epperson, p. 111.
12. Antony C. Sutton, WESTERN TECHNOLOGY AND SOVIET ECONOMIC DEVELOPMENT, 1945–1965, VOL. III (Stanford, Calif.: Hoover Institution Press, 1973), pp. 3–14.
13. Larry Abrahams, CALL IT CONSPIRACY (Seattle: Double A Publications, 1971), p. 112.
14. Sutton 1973, pp. 15–38.
15. Epperson, pp. 330–332.
16. U.S. Senate, 88th Cong., 1st Sess., "Hearings Before the Committee on Banking and Currency: Government Guarantees of Credit to Communist Countries" (Washington, D.C.: U.S. Government Printing Office, 1963), pp. 45, 47.
17. Alexander Wolynski, WESTERN ECONOMIC AID TO THE USSR (London: Institute for the Study of Conflict, 1976), p. 8.
18. Ibid., p. 9.
19. Ibid., p. 6.
20. U.S. Senate, 94th Cong., 1st Sess., "Hearings Before the Select Committee to Study Government Operations with Respect to Intelligence Activities," Vols. I–VII, 1975.
21. Shirley Christian, NICARAGUA: REVOLUTION IN THE FAMILY (New York: Random House, 1986), pp. 167–168.
22. Reed Brody, CONTRA TERROR IN NICARAGUA. REPORT OF A FACT-FINDING MISSION: SEPTEMBER 1984–JANUARY 1985 (Boston, Mass.: South End Press, 1985), p. 11.
23. Jonathan Marshall, Peter Dale Scott, and Jane Hunter, THE IRAN CONTRA CONNECTION: SECRET TEAMS AND COVERT OPERATIONS IN THE REAGAN ERA

(Boston, Mass.: South End Press, 1987), pp. 10–11.

24. Brody, p. 16.
25. Ibid., pp. 131–152.
26. Leslie Cockburn, OUT OF CONTROL: THE STORY OF THE REAGAN ADMINISTRATION'S SECRET WAR IN NICARAGUA, THE ILLEGAL ARMS PIPELINE, AND THE CONTRA DRUG CONNECTION (New York: The Atlantic Monthly Press, 1987), p. 7.
27. Brody, p. 10.
28. Ibid., pp. 28–124.
29. John Stockwell, THE PRAETORIAN GUARD: THE U.S. ROLE IN THE NEW WORLD ORDER (Boston, Mass.: South End Press, 1991), p. 69.
30. William Blum, THE CIA: A FORGOTTEN HISTORY (New Jersey, Zed Books, Inc.,1986), pp. 64–65.
31. Cockburn, pp. 152–188.
32. Ibid., pp. 182–184.
33. "A Spreading Drug Epidemic," *The Washington Spectator*, August 1, 1988, pp. 1–3; Jonathan Marshall, "Drugs and United States Foreign Policy," in DEALING WITH DRUGS, R. Hamowy, ed. (San Francisco: Pacific Research Institute for Public Policy, 1987), pp. 164–174.
34. Stockwell, p. 118.
35. Robert A. Mosbacher, Thomas J. Murrin, Michael R. Darby, and Barbara Everett Bryant, STATISTICAL ABSTRACT OF THE UNITED STATES 1990 (Washington, D.C.: Department of Commerce, 1990), pp. 310–311.
36. Stockwell, pp. 22–23.
37. David Hage, Terri Thompson, and Sara Collins, "The Recipe for Fiscal Disaster," *U.S. News & World Report*, January 20, 1992, pp. 28–30.
38. See note 18, Chapter 9.
39. Stockwell, p. 65.
40. Blum, pp. 44–55, 133–161, 284–291.
41. Axelrod, p. 131.
42. Epperson, p. 279.
43. Antony Sutton, WALL STREET AND THE RISE OF HITLER (Seal Beach, Calif.: '76 Press, 1976).
44. Rachel Flick, "How We Appeased a Tyrant," *Reader's Digest*, January 1991, pp. 39–44.
45. Parenti, p. 27.
46. Benjamin Netanyahu, ed. TERRORISM: HOW THE WEST CAN WIN (New York: Avon Books, 1986), p. 9.
47. *Born on the Fourth of July* (Universal City Studios, 1989).
48. *JFK* (Warner Brothers, 1991).
49. Robert Axelrod and Douglas Dion, "The Further Evolution of Cooperation," *Science* **242**: 1385–1390.
50. Frances Kendall and Leon Louw, LET THE PEOPLE GOVERN (Bisho, Ciskei: Amagi Publications, Ltd., 1989), p. 84.
51. Frederick Martin Stern, THE CITIZEN ARMY: KEY TO DEFENSE IN THE ATOMIC AGE (New York: St. Martin's Press, 1957), pp. 156–158.

CHAPTER 21

1. Randy T. Simmons and Urs P. Kreuter, "Herd Mentality: Banning Ivory

Sales Is No Way to Save the Elephant," *Policy Review*, Fall 1989, p. 46.

2. Ronald N. Johnson and Gary D. Libecap, "Contracting Problems and Regulation: The Case of the Fishery," *American Economic Review* **12**: 1007, 1982.

3. Richard J. Agnello and Lawrence P. Donnelley, "Prices and Property Rights in the Fisheries," *Southern Economic Journal* **42**: 253–262, 1979.

4. Roy W. Spencer and John R. Christy, "Precise Monitoring of Global Temperature Trends from Satellites,' *Science* **247**: 1558–1562, 1990.

5. S. Fred Singer, "The Science Behind Global Environmental Scares," *Consumers' Research*, October 1991, p. 17.

6. Thomas R. Karl and Philip D. Jones, "Urban Bias in Area–Averaged Surface Air Temperature Trends," *Bulletin of the American Meteorological Society* **70**: 265–270, 1989.

7. Singer, p. 20.

8. "Volcanoes," VAN NOSTRAND'S SCIENTIFIC ENCYCLOPEDIA, VOL. 2 D.M. Considine, ed., (New York: Van Nostrand Reinhold, 1989), p. 2973.

9. Jane Shaw and Richard L. Stroup, "Can Consumers Save the Environment?" *Consumers' Research*, September 1990, pp. 11–12.

10. Sherwood B. Idso, CARBON DIOXIDE AND GLOBAL CHANGE: EARTH IN TRANSITION (Tempe, Arizona: IBR Press, 1989), pp. 67–107.

11. Kent Jeffreys, "Why Worry About Global Warming?" (Dallas, Tex.: National Center for Policy Analysis, 1991), p. 1.

12. Ibid., pp. 4–6.

CHAPTER 22: HOW TO GET THERE FROM HERE

1. Michael Walker, "Cold Reality: How They Don't Do It in Canada," *Reason*, March 1992, p. 38.

2. Tracey Tyler, "Frustrated Heart Patients Head to Ohio For Surgery," *Toronto Star*, January 22, 1989.

3. Ibid, p. 39.

4. Harry Schwartz, "The Infirmity of British Medicine," in R. Emmett Tyrell, Jr., ed. THE FUTURE THAT DOESN'T WORK: SOCIAL DEMOCRACY'S FAILURES IN BRITAIN (New York: Doubleday, 1977), p. 29.

5. END STAGE RENAL FAILURE (London: Office of Health Economics, 1980), pp. 3, 6.

6. John C. Goodman and Gerald L. Musgrave, "Twenty Myths About National Health Insurance" (Dallas, Tex.: National Center for Policy Analysis, 1991), pp. 22–27.

7. Laissez Faire Books, 942 Howard, San Francisco, CA 94103, 800/326-0996, Fax 415/541-0597. Libertarian Press, Spring Mills, PA 16875, 814/422-8801. Liberty Audio and Film Service, 824 W. Broad St., Richmond, VA 23220, 804/788-7008. Liberty Tree Network, 350 Sansome St., San Francisco, CA 94104, 415/981-1326. Renaissance Book Service, 2716 Ocean Park Blvd., #1062, Santa Monica, CA 90405. Freedom's Forum Bookstore, 1800 Market St., San Francisco, CA 94102, 415/864-0952.

8. Leon Louw and Frances Kendall, THE SOLUTION (Bisho, Ciskei: Amagi Publications, Ltd., 1986).

9. Leon Louw and Frances Kendall, AFTER APARTHEID (San Francisco: Institute for Contemporary Studies, 1987).

10. Kendall and Louw, p. 73.

11. Advocates for Self-Government, 3955 Pleasantdale Rd., #106-A, Atlanta, GA 30340, 404/417-1304, 800/932-1776, Fax 404/417-1305.

12. International Society for Individual Liberty, 1800 Market St., San Francisco, CA, 415/864-0952, Fax 415/864-7506.

13. *Index on Liberty*, Jan Sommerfelt Petterson & International Society for Individual Liberty (see contact information above to obtain copies).

14. Libertarian Party (USA), 1528 Pennsylvania Ave., S.E., Washington, DC 20003, 202/543-1988, 800/682-1776, Fax 202/546-6094.

15. Republican Liberty Caucus, 1717 Apathchee Parkway, Ste. 434, Tallahassee, FA 32301, 904/878-4464, Fax 904/878-4464.

16. Competitive Enterprise Institute, 233 Pennsylvania Ave., S.E., Washington, DC 20003, 202/547-1010, Fax 202/547-7757.

17. Reason Foundation, 3415 S. Sepulveda Blvd., Ste. 400, Los Angeles, CA 90034, 310/391-2245, Fax 310/391-4395.

18. Political Economy Research Center, 502 S. 19th Ave., # 211, Bozeman, MT 59715, 406/587-9591, Fax 406/586-7555.

19. *Journal of Libertarian Studies*, P.O. Box 4091, Burlingame, CA 94011, 800/325-7257.

20. National Center for Policy Analysis, 12655 N. Central Expy., Ste. 720, Dallas, TX 75243, 214/386-NCPA, Fax 214/386-0924.

21. Pacific Research Institute for Public Policy Research, 177 Post St.,San Francisco, CA 94108, 415/989-0833, Fax 415/989-2411.

22. Heartland Institute, 634 S. Wabash Ave., 2nd Floor, Chicago, IL 60605, 312/427-3060, Fax 312/427-4642.

23. Manhattan Institute for Policy Research, 52 Vanderbilt Ave., New York, NY 10017, 212/599-7000, Fax 212/599-3494.

24. Liberty Fund, Inc., 8335 Allison Pointe Trail, Ste. 300, Indianapolis, IN 46250-1687, 317/842-0880, Fax 317/577-9067.

25. Institute for Humane Studies, 4210 Roberts Rd., Fairfax, VA 22032, 703/323-1055, Fax 703/425-1536.

26. Foundation for Economic Education, 30 S. Broadway, Invington-on-Hudson, NY 10533, 914/591-7230.

27. Cato Institute, 224 Second St., S.E., Washington, DC 20003, 202/546-0200, Fax 202/546-0728.

28. Makinac Center, P.O. Box 568, Midland, MI 48640, 517/631-0900, Fax 517/631-0964.

29. Hillsdale College, 33 E. College St., Hillsdale, MI 49242, 517/437-7341, Fax 517/437-0190.

30. Institute for Justice, 1001 Pennsylvania Ave., N.W., Ste. 200 South, Washington, DC 20004.

31. James Madison Institute for Public Policy Studies, P.O. Box 13894, Tallahassee, FL 32317, 904/386-3131.

32. 21st Century Congress, 723 Aganier, San Antonio, TX 78212. 512/732-5692.

33. Freedom Now Project, 1317 Lakewood Dr., Fort Collins, CO 80521, 303/484-8184.

SIDEBAR INDEX

SUBJECT INDEX

If you enjoyed HEALING OUR WORLD, share it with your friends. Better yet, give them their own copy!

Quantity	Price each
1	$14.95
2–4	11.96
5–100	8.97
over 100	7.97

Make money making the world a better place! Use discounted books as a fund-raising tool for your church, school, or club.

***************************** *******************************

Name_____

Address_____

_____

Number of books = _____

Price per book = _____

Total for books = _____

Michigan residents add 4% sales tax = _____

Shipping (10% of total) = _____

Grand total = _____

Mail to check or money order to:

SunStar Press, P.O. Box 342, Kalamazoo, MI 49005-0342.